FROM LOU & PAULA F.

EVERYDAY
LOGIC

Play these other fun puzzle books by *USA TODAY*:

EVERYDAY LOGIC

200 PUZZLES

from The Nation's No. 1 Newspaper

Andrews McMeel
Publishing, LLC

Kansas City • Sydney • London

USA TODAY Everyday Logic copyright © 2008 by USA TODAY.
All rights reserved. Printed in the United States of America. No part of this
book may be used or reproduced in any manner whatsoever without
written permission except in the case of reprints in the context of reviews.
For information, write Andrews McMeel Publishing, LLC,
an Andrews McMeel Universal company, 1130 Walnut Street,
Kansas City, Missouri 64106.

10 11 12 BID 10 9 8 7 6 5 4 3

ISBN-13: 978-0-7407-7356-3
ISBN-10: 0-7407-7356-9

All puzzles copyright of Puzzler Media Ltd.
All puzzles supplied under license from Puzzler Media Ltd.—www.puzzler.com

www.andrewsmcmeel.com

puzzles.usatoday.com

USA TODAY®, its logo, and associated graphics are federally registered trademarks.
All rights reserved. All USA TODAY text, graphics, and photographs are used pursuant
to a license and may not be reproduced, distributed, or otherwise used without the
express written consent of Gannett Co., Inc.

ATTENTION: SCHOOLS AND BUSINESSES
Andrews McMeel books are available at quantity discounts with
bulk purchase for educational, business, or sales promotional use.
For information, please write to: Special Sales Department,
Andrews McMeel Publishing, LLC, 1130 Walnut Street,
Kansas City, Missouri 64106.

Solving Tips

The next few pages have all the instructions you'll need to tackle all the puzzles in this book. They may look a little complicated but you'll soon get the hang of things.

Logic Problems

With each standard problem we provide a chart that takes into account every possibility to be considered in the solution. First, you carefully read the statement of the problem in the introduction, and then consider the clues. Next, you enter in the chart all the information immediately apparent from the clues, using an **X** to show a definite **no** and a ✓ to show a definite **yes**. You'll find that this narrows down the possibilities and might even reveal some new definite information. So now you reread the clues with these new facts in mind to discover further positive/negative relationships. Be sure to enter information in all the relevant places in the chart, and to transfer newly discovered information from one part of the chart to all the other relevant parts. The smaller grid at the end of each problem is simply a quick-reference chart for all your findings.

Now try your hand at working through the example below—you'll soon get the hang of it.

EXAMPLE

Three children live on the same street. From the two clues given below, can you discover each child's full name and age?

Clues

1. Miss Brown is three years older than Mary.
2. The child whose surname Is White is 9 years old.

Solution

Miss Brown (clue 1) cannot be Brian, so you can place an **X** in the Brian/Brown box. Clue 1 tells us that she is not Mary either, so you can put an **X** in the Mary/Brown box. Miss Brown is therefore Anne, the only possibility remaining. Now place a ✓ in that box in the chart, with corresponding **X**s against the other possible surnames for Anne.

If Anne Brown is three years older than Mary (clue 1), she must be 10 and Mary, 7. So place ✓s in the Anne/10, Brown/10, and Mary/7 boxes, and **X**s in all the empty boxes in each row and column containing these ✓s. The chart now reveals Brian's age as 9, so you can place a ✓ in the Brian/9 box. Clue 2 tells us that White is 9 years old too, so he must be Brian. Place a ✓ in the White/9 box and **X**s in the remaining empty boxes in that row and column, then place a ✓ in the Brian/White box and **X**s in all the remaining empty boxes in that row and column. You can see now that the remaining unfilled boxes in the chart must contain ✓s, since their rows and columns contain only **X**s, so they reveal Green as the surname of 7-year-old Mary.

Anne Brown, 10.
Brian White, 9.
Mary Green, 7.

	Brown	Green	White	7	9	10
Anne	✓	X	X	X	X	✓
Brian	X			X		X
Mary	X			✓	X	X
7	X					
9	X					
10	✓	X	X			

	Brown	Green	White	7	9	10
Anne	✓	X	X	X	X	✓
Brian	X	X	✓	X	✓	X
Mary	X		X	✓	X	X
7	X		X			
9	X	X	✓			
10	✓	X	X			

USA TODAY.

The solving system for the puzzles that don't have grids is very similar. Read through the clues and insert any positive information onto the diagram. Then read through the clues again and use a process of elimination to start positioning the remaining elements of the puzzle. You may find it easier to make a few notes about which elements of the puzzle you know are linked but that cannot yet be entered on the diagram. These can be positioned once the other examples of those elements are positioned. If you find it difficult to know where to begin, use the starting tip printed upside down at the foot of the page.

Battleships

Before you look at the numbers around the grid, there are a number of squares you can fill in from the starter pieces given. If an end piece of a ship is given then the square next to it, in the direction indicated by the end, must also be part of a ship. If a middle piece is given, then the pieces on either side must also be ship parts; in this instance, you need some more information before you can decide which way the ship runs. Also, any square that is adjacent to an end piece (apart from those squares in the direction of the rest of the ship), any square touching the corners of a middle piece, and all squares around destroyers (one-square ships) must be sea.

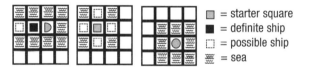

■ = starter square
■ = definite ship
□ = possible ship
≋ = sea

Now, look at the numbers around the grid and identify rows and columns in which the large aircraft carrier might be. Either from this or by looking at the next conse-quences of the remaining possibilities, you should be able to position this ship. Now fill in the sea squares around the carrier and move on to the smaller ships.

Domino Search

Starting this puzzle is just a matter of finding one domino (number pair) that is unique in the grid. It is often easiest to look for the double numbers first (0 0; 6 6). When you have discovered one or more of these unique possibilities, you will find that their position in the grid forces you to place one or more dominoes in order to fill in the shape of the grid left. Cross off all these dominoes in the check-grid for future reference. Now, look at the dominoes you have managed to fill in and check around the grid, especially near the edge of the grid or next to dominoes already positioned, where the possibilities are reduced, to find other examples of those number pairs. Since you have already positioned that domino, you know that the

second example you have found is not a pair and the domino must run in one of the other possible directions. Carry on in this vein, finding dominoes and then eliminating possibilities elsewhere in the grid until the puzzle is cracked.

Cell Block

Fill the grid by drawing blocks along the grid lines. Each block must contain the number of squares indicated by the digit inside it. Each block must contain only one digit. Blocks must be four-sided squares or rectangles, no "L" shapes, etc.

Codewords

This puzzle has no clues in the conventional sense. Instead, every different number printed in the main grid represents a different letter (with the same number always representing the same letter, of course). For example, if 7 turns out to be a "V," you can write in V wherever a square contains 7. We have completed a very small part of the puzzle to give you a start, but the rest is up to you.

Totalized

Totalized is meant to be solved in the head. Just follow the instructions from top to bottom, starting with the number given to reach an answer at the foot of the ladder. You have 25 seconds to complete the puzzle.

Wordwheel

Using only the letters in the Wordwheel, you have ten minutes to find as many words as possible, none of which may be plurals, foreign words, or proper nouns. Each word must be of three letters or more, all must contain the central letter, and letters can only be used once in every word. There is at least one nine-letter word in the wheel.

 USA TODAY.

Codewords

This puzzle has no clues in the conventional sense. Instead, every different number printed in the main grid represents a different letter (with the same number always representing the same letter, of course). For example, if 7 turns out to be a "V," you can write in V wherever a square contains 7. We have completed a very small part of the puzzle to give you a start, but the rest is up to you.

14		20	9				26		5		18
1	15	9	12	20	14		7	18	23	23	12	14
10		4		23		14		10		23		9
23	13	23	10	12	9	15	15	16		10	18	24
9		15		1		22						15
21	18	15	13	6	13 T	18 U	17 D	23		11	23	23
		23		23		1		12		9		
24	18	14		14	3	8	23	10	6	1	9	15
10						6		22		13		9
23	20	20		3	23	12	9	15	13	6	23	14
19		9		9		20		15		22		13
23	2	3	22	10	13		25	23	12	12	23	15
17		23		25				17		14		16

A B C Ø E F G H I J K L M N O P Q R S X Ø V W X Y Z

1	2	3	4	5	6	7	8	9	10	11	12	13 T
14	15	16	17 D	18 U	19	20	21	22	23	24	25	26

TOTALIZED

*The 25-second ultimate challenge from **Puzzler Brain Trainer***

Just follow the instructions from top to bottom, starting with the number given to reach an answer at the foot of the ladder.

EASY	MEDIUM	HARDER
8	**32**	**19**
MULTIPLY BY 5	DIVIDE BY 4	MULTIPLY BY 3
ADD 12	ADD 42	ADD $\frac{1}{3}$ OF IT
DIVIDE BY 4	50% OF IT	ADD 64
ADD 34	DIVIDE BY 5	DIVIDE BY 20
DOUBLE IT	MULTIPLY BY 7	TIMES ITSELF
TAKE AWAY 22	MULTIPLY BY 3	ADD $\frac{3}{7}$ OF IT
DIVIDE BY 12	ADD 3	DIVIDE BY 5
MULTIPLY BY 3	DIVIDE BY 9	MULTIPLY BY 11
ADD 11	TIMES ITSELF	TAKE AWAY 39
ANSWER	ANSWER	ANSWER

USA TODAY.

Cell Block

Fill the grid by drawing blocks along the grid lines. Each block must contain the number of squares indicated by the digit inside it. Each block must contain only one digit.

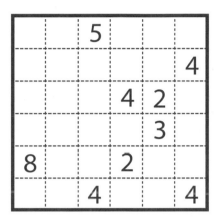

Wordwheel

Using only the letters in the Wordwheel, you have ten minutes to find as many words as possible, none of which may be plurals, foreign words, or proper nouns. Each word must be of three letters or more, all must contain the central letter, and letters can only be used once in every word. There is at least one nine-letter word in the wheel.

Extras

There's plenty of TV and film work around for "supporting actors." Below are details of jobs recently obtained by five professional "extras"—from the information given, can you work out the type of film each is working on, the famous star each is appearing with, and the number of days' work envisaged?

Clues

1. Sarah's appearing in a romantic comedy film—a "romcom"—which entails three days' more work than is available on the Jodie Dent picture.

2. Lynne has got four days' work, but not on a crime film.

3. Danny has got an extra role in the new Harry Fordson movie, but he's not booked for five days.

4. Kevin has secured an even number of days' work, one less than the extra on the Paddy Britt film.

5. There are six days' work available on the sci-fi film.

6. Kevin does not appear in the Donny Jepp film, which is a costume drama.

Extra	Type of film

	Costume drama	Crime	Romcom	Sci-fi	Thriller	Paddy Britt	Jodie Dent	Harry Fordson	Donny Jepp	Keeley Knight	4	5	6	7	10
Danny															
Kevin															
Lynne															
Sarah															
Vic															
4															
5															
6															
7															
10															
Paddy Britt															
Jodie Dent															
Harry Fordson															
Donny Jepp															
Keeley Knight															

Star	Days

Battleships

Do you remember the old game of battleships? These puzzles are based on that idea. Your task is to find the vessels in the diagram. Some parts of boats or sea squares have already been filled in, and a number next to a row or column refers to the number of occupied squares in that row or column. The boats may be positioned horizontally or vertically, but no two boats or parts of boats are in adjacent squares—horizontally, vertically, or diagonally.

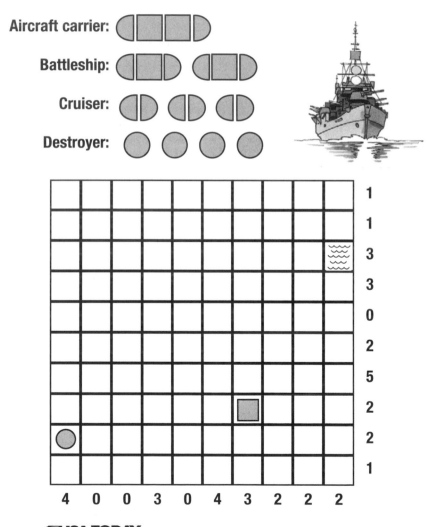

Aircraft carrier:

Battleship:

Cruiser:

Destroyer:

USA TODAY.

On Your Bike

On Sunday afternoon, four intrepid cyclists left the village on their bikes to enjoy a ride to locations in totally different directions. From the clues given below, can you name the places to the north, south, east, and west of the village, say who cycled there, and work out how long each ride took?

Clues

1. Mary cycled in a diametrically opposite direction from the rider who visited Frameleigh, whose journey took a shorter time.

2. Dorothy's trip took four minutes longer than the one to Chainford, which is the destination next counterclockwise from her own.

3. The ride to Peddleham took four minutes longer than the one that headed due north.

4. Spokesby is due east of our riders' home village; the ride there was shorter than the one undertaken by Noel.

Locations: Chainford; Frameleigh; Peddleham; Spokesby
Riders: Dorothy; Jack; Mary; Noel
Time taken: 20 mins; 24 mins; 28 mins; 32 mins

Location: _____
Rider: _____
Time: _____

Starting tip: Decide first who made the 20-minute journey.

The Lifestory Channel

The Lifestory Channel, a satellite TV station specializing in biographical material, is putting on a special evening of programs devoted to characters more or less well-known to logic problems solvers. From the clues below, can you work out the full name of the person who will be presenting the program at each listed time, and the name of its subject?

Clues

1. The program devoted to the life and military career of Uramis, one of "les autres Mousquetaires," will be presented by Cyril, and will be aired one hour earlier than the one being presented by Professor de Grey, who will be talking about his great-uncle Rupert.

2. Dr. Winston Bulford, the distinguished historian, will be appearing an hour before Mr. Milliken.

3. Neither Mr. Milliken nor Mr. Pinhorn will present the program at 8:00 p.m., and neither of them is Lucien.

4. Magnus, one of the channel's most popular presenters, isn't presenting the 6:00 p.m. program, and won't be talking about the Regency rake Beau Nydel.

5. At 10:00 p.m., viewers will be able to enjoy the true story of Sir Coward de Custarde, knight of King Arthur's Round Table.

Time	First name

 USA TODAY.

	Cyril	Desmond	Lucien	Magnus	Winston	Bulford	De Grey	Milliken	Pinhorn	Scrobby	Beau Nydel	Miss Raffles	Rupert de Grey	Sir Coward de Custarde	Uramis
6:00 p.m.															
8:00 p.m.															
9:00 p.m.															
10:00 p.m.															
11:00 p.m.															
Beau Nydel															
Miss Raffles															
Rupert de Grey															
Sir Coward de Custarde															
Uramis															
Bulford															
De Grey															
Milliken															
Pinhorn															
Scrobby															

Surname	Subject

Strangers in Town

Four couples visiting the old town of Netherlipp each took a different direction when they reached the signpost in the diagram, which was in the pedestrianized area of the old town. From the clues given below, can you say which attraction was mentioned on each of the arms numbered 1 to 4, and name the couple who headed in its direction?

Clues

1. Lewis and Maxine took the direction diametrically opposite to the botanical gardens.

2. Peter followed the arm next clockwise from the one consulted by Josie.

3. Arm 4 points the way to the museum.

4. Hannah and her partner followed the direction indicated by arm 1.

5. It was Jack and his wife who decided to visit the castle, which is in the direction next counterclockwise from the riverside walk.

Attractions: botanical gardens; castle; museum; riverside walk
Males: Adrian; Jack; Lewis; Peter
Females: Eileen; Hannah; Josie; Maxine

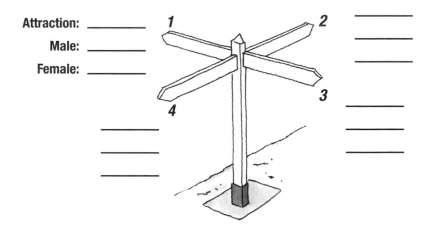

Attraction: _____
Male: _____
Female: _____

Starting tip: Identify first the attraction mentioned on arm 3.

Domino Search

A standard set of dominoes has been laid out, using numbers instead of dots for clarity. Using a sharp pencil and a keen brain, can you draw in the lines to show where each domino has been placed? You may find the check grid useful—crossing off each domino as you find it.

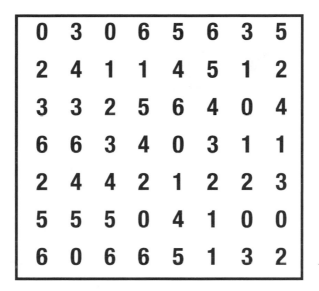

0	3	0	6	5	6	3	5
2	4	1	1	4	5	1	2
3	3	2	5	6	4	0	4
6	6	3	4	0	3	1	1
2	4	4	2	1	2	2	3
5	5	5	0	4	1	0	0
6	0	6	6	5	1	3	2

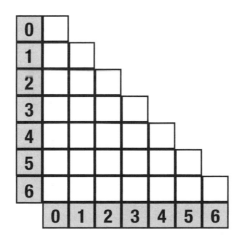

Codewords

This puzzle has no clues in the conventional sense. Instead, every different number printed in the main grid represents a different letter (with the same number always representing the same letter, of course). For example, if 7 turns out to be a "V," you can write in V wherever a square contains 7. We have completed a very small part of the puzzle to give you a start, but the rest is up to you.

6	23	4	12	23	22	2	13	■	23	17	2	11
24	■	24	■	15	■	18	■	19	■	1	■	1
14	23	11	9	13	■	20	2	15	6	8	1	15
2	■	26	■	24	■	24	■	1	■	9	■	15
10	24	1	18	■	22	10	23	8	8 **F**	25 **I**	9 **T**	25
■	■	2	■	4	■	9	■	8	■	■	■	8
9	20	10	25	15	15	■	21	2	10	13	2	7
23	■	■	23	■	5	■	10	■	9	■	■	■
4	20	24	25	10	19	24	7	■	3	25	6	13
9	■	14	■	25	■	24	■	23	■	17	■	15
8	15	25	10	9	2	16	■	13	23	1	11	23
1	■	11	■	7	■	24	■	12	■	15	■	11
15	24	22	13	■	19	24	24	13	9	25	11	22

A B C D E ~~F~~ G H ~~I~~ J K L M N O P Q R S ~~T~~ U V W X Y Z

1	2	3	4	5	6	7	8 **F**	9 **T**	10	11	12	13
14	15	16	17	18	19	20	21	22	23	24	25 **I**	26

TOTALIZED

The 25-second ultimate challenge from **Puzzler Brain Trainer**

Just follow the instructions from top to bottom, starting with the number given to reach an answer at the foot of the ladder.

EASY	MEDIUM	HARDER
13	**17**	**19**
ADD 41	MULTIPLY BY 3	TIMES ITSELF
DIVIDE BY 6	TAKE AWAY 27	TAKE AWAY 74
MULTIPLY BY 3	MULTIPLY BY 6	DIVIDE BY 7
TAKE AWAY 12	DIVIDE BY 12	TREBLE IT
MULTIPLY BY 4	MULTIPLY BY 8	ADD $\frac{2}{3}$ OF IT
TAKE AWAY 12	ADD 14	ADD $\frac{3}{5}$ OF IT
DIVIDE BY 8	DIVIDE BY 10	DIVIDE BY 4
MULTIPLY BY 4	TIMES ITSELF	ADD 83
ADD 19	TAKE AWAY 54	$\frac{3}{5}$ OF IT
ANSWER	**ANSWER**	**ANSWER**

Cell Block

Fill the grid by drawing blocks along the grid lines. Each block must contain the number of squares indicated by the digit inside it. Each block must contain only one digit.

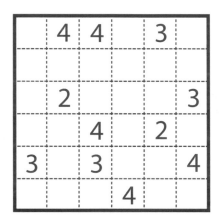

Wordwheel

Using only the letters in the Wordwheel, you have ten minutes to find as many words as possible, none of which may be plurals, foreign words, or proper nouns. Each word must be of three letters or more, all must contain the central letter, and letters can only be used once in every word. There is at least one nine-letter word in the wheel.

Battleships

Do you remember the old game of battleships? These puzzles are based on that idea. Your task is to find the vessels in the diagram. Some parts of boats or sea squares have already been filled in, and a number next to a row or column refers to the number of occupied squares in that row or column. The boats may be positioned horizontally or vertically, but no two boats or parts of boats are in adjacent squares—horizontally, vertically, or diagonally.

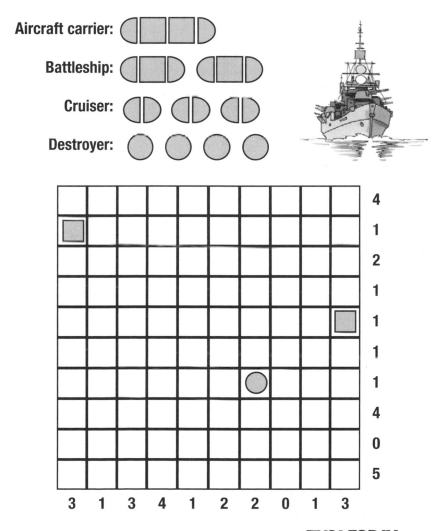

Aircraft carrier:

Battleship:

Cruiser:

Destroyer:

Row clues (top to bottom): 4, 1, 2, 1, 1, 1, 1, 4, 0, 5

Column clues (left to right): 3, 1, 3, 4, 1, 2, 2, 0, 1, 3

Cats' Chorus

Every night we have to suffer the wailing and caterwauling of the neighborhood cats. Below are details of the five worst offenders—from the information given, can you discover the name and type of each cat, the house number each belongs to (we all live on the even-numbered side of the road), and where each takes up station to begin its nightly chorus?

Clues

1. Daisy is from #8; Sooty is a black cat.

2. Bubble's not a tabby, and her house number is less than that of Cleo, who wails from outside the bedroom window.

3. The brindle cat is neither from #6, nor does it wail outside the back door.

4. The cat from #4 serenades us from the shed roof, but it isn't the brindle or the tabby.

5. The calico cat's house number is the next but one higher than that of the cat that wails from the garage roof.

6. The long-haired cat lives at #12.

Cat	Type

	Black	Brindle	Long-haired	Tabby	Calico	4	6	8	10	12	Garage roof	Garden wall	Outside back door	Outside window	Shed roof
Bubble															
Cleo															
Daisy															
Prince															
Sooty															
Garage roof															
Garden wall															
Outside back door															
Outside window															
Shed roof															
4															
6															
8															
10															
12															

House #	Location

Breakdown
Breakdown

Clearway Breakdown Service is continually monitoring its performance to ensure that it remains competitive. Below are details of five recent breakdowns—from the information given, can you work out which repairs were reported by the five members, the time it took the repairman to reach each car, and the time it took to fix the problem?

Clues

1. Mr. Hedley phoned Clearway about a dead battery problem; it took 5 minutes less to fix than Mrs. Langford's fault.

2. The broken clutch cable took twice as long to fix as Mrs. Langford's repair, and the repairman took 37 minutes to reach the car concerned, which was not that of Mr. Mills.

3. It took the repairman more than 30 minutes to reach the car that was overheating; it took 27 minutes to reach the car that took 10 minutes to fix.

4. The repairman who reached the breakdown in 22 minutes took longer to repair it than his colleague who took the longest time to get to the member concerned.

5. Mr. Hawkins had to wait 43 minutes by the roadside.

6. The misfire took longer to cure than the fuel blockage.

Member	Repair

	Broken clutch cable	Dead battery	Fuel blockage	Misfire	Overheating	Time to arrive 22 mins	27 mins	35 mins	37 mins	43 mins	Time to fix 5 mins	10 mins	15 mins	20 mins	25 mins
Mr. Hawkins															
Mr. Hedley															
Mrs. Langford															
Mr. Mills															
Mr. Robson															
Time to fix 5 mins															
10 mins															
15 mins															
20 mins															
25 mins															
Time to arrive 22 mins															
27 mins															
35 mins															
37 mins															
43 mins															

Mins to arrive	Mins to fix repair

Night on the Plains

The picture on the following page shows a small westbound wagon train circled up for the night somewhere on the Great Plains in the late 1850s; the circling is a prudent but, as it happens, unnecessary precaution and everybody is enjoying the opportunity to get out of the uncomfortable, overloaded wagons—each of which is carrying not just people and provisions but also household furniture and the tools of the father's trade—and relax. From the clues given, can you work out the name of the family traveling in each wagon, the number in the family, and the father's trade?

Clues

1. No family in any wagon has one more member than the families in the two adjacent wagons; the total number of persons in each pair of wagons opposite each other across the circle is 15.

2. The Ogdens' wagon is opposite the one in which the gunsmith and his family are traveling and next clockwise to the one carrying 6 people.

3. The blacksmith, his family, and his tools are going West in the wagon next clockwise from the Logans' and next counterclockwise from the farmer's; the blacksmith's wagon is carrying more people than either of the others.

4. Joshua Draper, who is a smith by trade, has one fewer family member traveling in his wagon than there are in the opposite wagon; the carpenter's wagon has two more passengers than the Willards', which is opposite the one belonging to the tinsmith and his family.

5. The Hatch family's wagon is next clockwise from the one that is carrying a married couple, their four children, and the wife's two unmarried sisters, and opposite the one with 9 people on board; the saddler and his family have the wagon immediately clockwise of the tinsmith's, which has an odd number of passengers, and immediately counterclockwise of the wagon with the fewest people on board.

6. Dan Monroe, who is not a smith of any kind, has one more person traveling in his wagon than are traveling in wagon C; wagon A has two more passengers than wagon F.

Family names: Draper; Hatch; Logan; Monroe; Ogden; Willard
Passengers: 5; 6; 7; 8; 9; 10
Trades: blacksmith; carpenter; farmer; gunsmith; saddler; tinsmith

Family: _____
Passengers: _____
Trade: _____

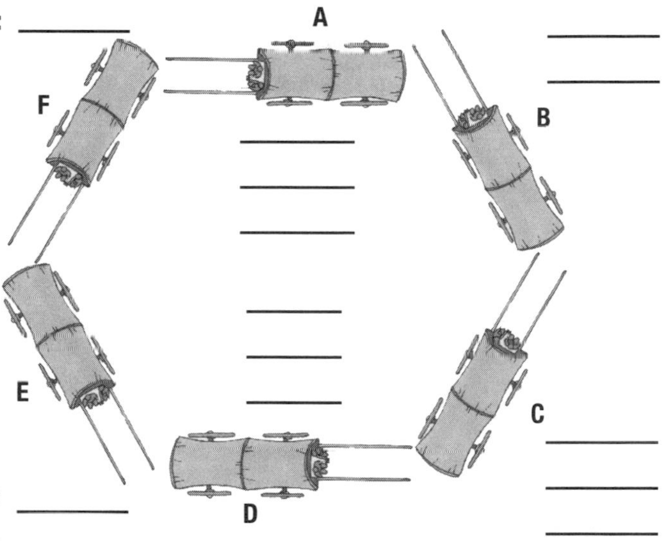

_____
_____
_____

A

F

B

_____
_____
_____

_____
_____
_____

E

C

Family: _____
Passengers: _____
Trade: _____

D

_____
_____
_____

Starting tip: Work out the numbers of passengers with the Hatches and the Drapers.

Brought to Book

The recent soccer match between Town and United was an ill-tempered affair, and the ref had to show five yellow cards. From the following information, can you work out the numbers and names of the five players booked, the rule infringement in each case, and the minute when each was shown the yellow card?

Clues

1. In the 10th minute, #9 was booked, followed in the 22nd minute by Davidson, who had lower-numbered shirt than #12, who was booked for verbal dissent.

2. In the second half, a player was booked in the 73rd minute for not retreating the full 10 yards before a free kick.

3. Neither #4 nor the one booked for faking injury had a surname beginning with D, but both were booked earlier than Da Costa.

4. Da Costa's shirt was the next lowest number before Linnell's.

5. The holding of the opponent infringement happened later than Perrin's booking.

6. Elstow was booked for a hard foul.

Number	Player

USA TODAY.

	Da Costa	Davidson	Elstow	Linnell	Perrin	Faking injury	Hard foul	Holding opponent	Not retreating	Verbal dissent	10	22	41	58	73
4															
7															
9															
12															
15															
10															
22															
41															
58															
73															
Faking injury															
Hard foul															
Holding opponent															
Not retreating															
Verbal dissent															

Infringement	Minute

Dinner with Friends

One of the great pleasures in life is sharing dinner with good friends, a pleasure that is multiplied when the food is particularly good and the meal is a celebration of some notable occasion; so, when Arnold Brighton received news that, after twenty years of trying, he had sold his first book, he invited four of his closest friends to the Case at Donkington, his favorite restaurant. From the clues given, can you work out which starter, main course, and dessert each of them enjoyed?

Clues

1. Martin picked the hot chicken and bacon salad for his starter, while Graham selected the raspberry torte as his dessert.

2. Rebecca didn't order muckalica (a Serbian pork dish) or the fresh fruit salad; the fresh fruit salad was not the dessert selected by the person who started the meal with grilled goat's cheese.

3. Arnold's main course was lamb with herbs; he didn't start with melon salad.

4. One member of the party started the meal with salmon and mozzarella terrine and had apple pie for dessert, but didn't choose either lamb with herbs or sole in orange sauce as a main course.

5. One of Arnold's guests had chimichangas, a Mexican dish made with chicken and almonds, followed by blackcurrant cheesecake.

6. The person who started with spinach and onion soup followed it with veal piccata.

Diner	Starter

USA TODAY.

	Chicken/bacon salad	Goat's cheese	Melon salad	Salmon terrine	Soup	Chimichangas	Lamb with herbs	Muckalica	Sole in orange	Veal piccata	Apple pie	Cheesecake	Fruit salad	Raspberry torte	Strawberry shortcake
Arnold															
Graham															
Martin															
Rebecca															
Tracey															
Apple pie															
Cheesecake															
Fruit salad															
Raspberry torte															
Strawberry shortcake															
Chimichangas															
Lamb with herbs															
Muckalica															
Sole in orange															
Veal piccata															

Main course	Dessert

March Hare's Tea Party

In a parallel universe to the one in *Alice in Wonderland*, Alice found herself attending another tea party, this time hosted by the March Hare, whose birthday it was. The host and his three guests were each invited to entertain the others during the course of the party. From the clues given below, can you say who sat in each of the seats numbered 1 to 4, and work out how each performed, and in what order? Note: Person is used for all four guests to avoid confusion.

Clues

1. It was, of course, the dormouse who snored out a song in his sleep for the entertainment of his fellow guests; this was some time after someone borrowed the Mad Hatter's hat as a prop for a conjuring act.

2. The person in seat 4 was the second to perform a party piece.

3. Alice was sitting next counterclockwise from the guest who danced a jig, who was an earlier performer.

4. The recitation was the third item to be performed at the party.

5. The host entertained next after the person in seat 3.

Guests: Alice; Dormouse; Mad Hatter; March Hare
Party pieces: danced; magic tricks; recited; snored song
Order: first; second; third; fourth

Guest: _____
Party piece: _____
Order: _____

Starting tip: Start by describing the fourth item of entertainment.

Feet of Clay

Podiatrist Lucy Clay is normally based at Parkville's Walnuttree Hospital, but for three days of next week she's "on the road"—traveling to outlying villages to hold clinics for patients who can't get into town. From the clues given, can you work out where Lucy will be holding her clinic on each of the listed days, which village it's in, and how many patients she's booked to see there?

Clues

1. Lucy will be at the Church Hall in Northtown earlier in the week than her visit to the village where she is expecting to treat 8 patients.

2. The Village Hall where Lucy will be working on Wednesday isn't in Plighwood.

3. Lucy is booked to see 7 patients on Friday.

	Church Hall	Village Hall	Parish Rooms	Goosebury	Plighwood	Northtown	6 patients	7 patients	8 patients
Monday									
Wednesday									
Friday									
6 patients									
7 patients									
8 patients									
Goosebury									
Plighwood									
Northtown									

Day	Venue	Village	Patients

Codewords

This puzzle has no clues in the conventional sense. Instead, every different number printed in the main grid represents a different letter (with the same number always representing the same letter, of course). For example, if 7 turns out to be a "V," you can write in V wherever a square contains 7. We have completed a very small part of the puzzle to give you a start, but the rest is up to you.

21		2		10		14		9		7		2
17	21	24	14	22	26	5	11	21		18	22	24
26		7		25		8		13		18 F		7
5	4	17	25	22	15	9		17	6	22 I	15	16
7						7				12 X		17
24	5	9		18	3	24	21	15	17	22	23	
16		3		8				3		15		17
	21	15	1	5	22	24	21	11		9	15	5
3		11				21						2
18	24	3	19	21		23	7	20	3	8	21	17
18		8		7		22		3		22		22
21	24	7		24	21	26	24	22	21	14	21	17
24		17		15		21		15		21		26

A B C D E F̷ G H X̷ J K L M N O P Q R S T U V W X̷ Y Z

1	2	3	4	5	6	7	8	9	10	11	12 X	13
14	15	16	17	18 F	19	20	21	22 I	23	24	25	26

TOTALIZED

*The 25-second ultimate challenge from **Puzzler Brain Trainer***

Just follow the instructions from top to bottom, starting with the number given to reach an answer at the foot of the ladder.

EASY	MEDIUM	HARDER
14	**28**	**6**
DOUBLE IT	75% OF IT	CUBE IT
ADD 12	ADD 100	TAKE AWAY 57
DIVIDE BY 10	DIVIDE BY 11	DIVIDE BY 3
MULTIPLY BY 4	MULTIPLY BY 8	MULTIPLY BY 4
ADD 17	ADD $\frac{1}{2}$ OF IT	ADD 50%OF IT
DIVIDE BY 3	TAKE AWAY 32	TAKE AWAY 6
MULTIPLY BY 6	DIVIDE BY 5	DIVIDE BY 6
TAKE AWAY 29	MULTIPLY BY 7	ADD 75% OF IT
DOUBLE IT	TAKE AWAY 67	MULTIPLY BY 9
ANSWER	**ANSWER**	**ANSWER**

Cell Block

Fill the grid by drawing blocks along the grid lines. Each block must contain the number of squares indicated by the digit inside it. Each block must contain only one digit.

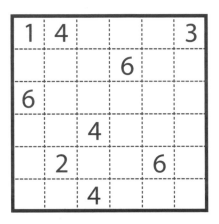

Wordwheel

Using only the letters in the Wordwheel, you have ten minutes to find as many words as possible, none of which may be plurals, foreign words, or proper nouns. Each word must be of three letters or more, all must contain the central letter, and letters can only be used once in every word. There is at least one nine-letter word in the wheel.

Pet Shop Boys

Four boys visited their local pet shop to buy items for their respective pets. From the clues given below, can you name each of the youngsters numbered 1 to 4, and work out what each came to buy, and in which order he was served?

Clues

1. The boy who bought a wheel to put in his hamster's cage is farther left in our diagram than Daniel, who was served sometime before the boy in position 4.

2. Marcus was the second of the four to be served by the owner of the pet shop.

3. Oliver, who had come into the pet shop for a packet of fish food, was served earlier than both his immediate neighbors in the diagram.

4. The dog collar and leash were bought by the young customer numbered 2.

Names: Craig; Daniel; Marcus; Oliver
Items bought: dog collar and leash; fish food; hamster wheel; toy for bird
Order: first; second; third; fourth

Name:	_____	_____	_____	_____
Item:	_____	_____	_____	_____
Order:	_____	_____	_____	_____

Starting tip: Begin by placing the boy who bought the hamster wheel.

Hand-Reared

Four of the young ladies who work at Eastwood Zoo have been given special assignments in connection with young creatures recently born there—they've been told to hand-rear them. From the clues below, can you work out the full name of each of the young ladies, and the name and breed of the creature she's hand-rearing?

Clues

1. Denise finds herself faced with the rather challenging task of hand-rearing the African Giant Vulture.

2. Neither Yvonne nor the zookeeper assigned to raise a jaguar that she has called Prince is surnamed Fleming.

3. Ms. Ross is hand-rearing the young creature she has named Sasha.

4. Patsy, who's raising Toto, isn't Ms. Kirk, who's looking after the baby chimpanzee.

> **Note:** If, for example, we say "The shopkeeper is **neither** Mark **nor** Spencer," it means that Mark is not the shopkeeper **and** Spencer is not the shopkeeper and that Mark is not Spencer.

First name	Surname

	Fleming	Kirk	Ross	Thomas	Gemma	Prince	Sasha	Toto	Alligator	Chimpanzee	Jaguar	Vulture
Denise												
Karen												
Patsy												
Yvonne												
Alligator												
Chimpanzee												
Jaguar												
Vulture												
Gemma												
Prince												
Sasha												
Toto												

Creature	Type

Domino Search

A standard set of dominoes has been laid out, using numbers instead of dots for clarity. Using a sharp pencil and a keen brain, can you draw in the lines to show where each domino has been placed? You may find the check grid useful—crossing off each domino as you find it.

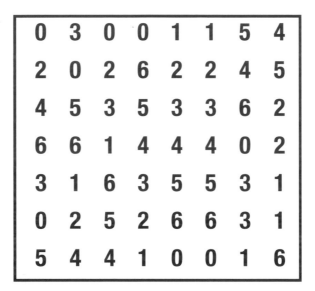

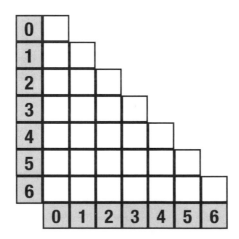

Battleships

Do you remember the old game of battleships? These puzzles are based on that idea. Your task is to find the vessels in the diagram. Some parts of boats or sea squares have already been filled in, and a number next to a row or column refers to the number of occupied squares in that row or column. The boats may be positioned horizontally or vertically, but no two boats or parts of boats are in adjacent squares—horizontally, vertically, or diagonally.

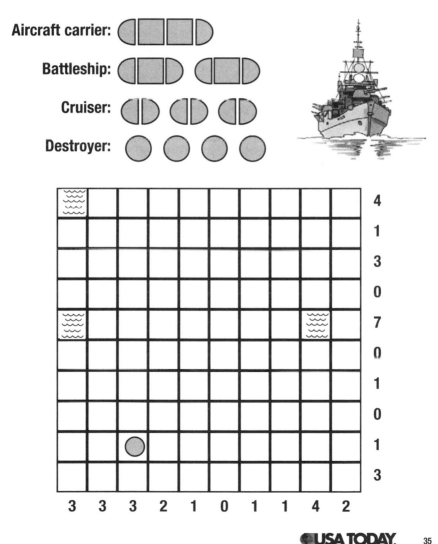

Aircraft carrier:

Battleship:

Cruiser:

Destroyer:

≈										4
										1
										3
										0
≈								≈		7
										0
										1
										0
		◯								1
										3
3	3	3	2	1	0	1	1	4	2	

Further Cases

AlbionTV has commissioned a series of original TV dramas based on Sherlock Holmes and the other characters created by Sir Arthur Conan Doyle, each of which will feature a real-life character. From the clues below, can you work out the title of each episode of the series, the name of the writer, and the identity of the real-life character who appears in it?

Clues

1. The episode in which Oscar Wilde is an important witness in the murder of a famous actress will be screened immediately after *The Adventure of the Stolen Sword* and immediately before the episode written by Jonathan Small.

2. *The Adventure of the Broken Man* by Alec MacDonald will be broadcast immediately after the episode in which the initial suspects in the case include a certain young soldier named Winston Churchill, of whom Holmes gets to remark, "Mark my words, Watson—the world will hear more of that young man."

3. The first episode of the series, which features Sir Robert Baden-Powell (later Lord Baden-Powell) as the man who engages Holmes to prove the innocence of a friend accused of a ghastly crime, is not called *The Adventure of the Red Queen*.

4. One of the characters in *The Adventure of the Beggar's Book* is Cecil Rhodes; this episode was scripted by a male writer.

5. Laura Lyons wrote episode 3.

6. Robert St. Simon wrote the episode that features the real-life—though still anonymous—serial killer known as Jack the Ripper.

Episode	Title

	Beggar's Book	Broken Man	Dying Lion	Red Queen	Stolen Sword	Alec MacDonald	Jonathan Small	Laura Lyons	Nancy Devoy	Robert St. Simon	Cecil Rhodes	Jack the Ripper	Oscar Wilde	Robert Baden-Powell	Winston Churchill
1															
2															
3															
4															
5															
Cecil Rhodes															
Jack the Ripper															
Oscar Wilde															
Robert Baden-Powell															
Winston Churchill															
Alec MacDonald															
Jonathan Small															
Laura Lyons															
Nancy Devoy															
Robert St. Simon															

Writer	Character

USA TODAY. 37

The Old School

The picture on the following page, the property of my neighbor Mrs. French, shows the entrances (separate ones were provided for boys and girls in those days!) to St. Gregory's School, Storbury, just after the First World War, when Mrs. French's granny was a pupil there. From the clues given, can you work out the full name of each of the pupils shown?

Clues

1. The boy forenamed Archie and the girl surnamed Clare occupy the same numbered position in their respective groups.

2. The youngsters surnamed Keble and Wadham are of different sexes, and each occupies a different numbered position at one end of their respective group.

3. Girl number 1, who is not Mary, is the daughter of Paul Pembroke, a local policeman.

4. Simon is immediately right of Len, and his surname appears somewhere before Len's in the alphabetical list.

5. Elsie's position is indicated by a number two higher than that which marks the boy called Merton.

6. There are three persons, including the teacher, separating Jack Darwin and Hattie.

7. The surname of girl number 2 appears in the alphabetical list immediately after that of boy number 4.

First names: Amy; Archie; Elsie; Hattie; Jack; Len; Mary; Simon
Surnames: Clare; Darwin; Hall; Keble; Linacre; Merton; Pembroke; Wadham

First name: _____ _____ _____ _____

Surname: _____ _____ _____ _____

_____ _____ _____ _____

_____ _____ _____ _____

Starting tip: Begin by working out the name of boy number 1.

B-Movie Heroes

A recent issue of a cinema nostalgia magazine carried a feature on five actors who, back in the 1940s, each starred in a series of "B-movies" (films designed to be shown as second features) playing a specific hero. From the clues below, can you work out each actor's name, the name and description of his series character, and the number of films in the series?

Clues

1. Tony Vernon appeared in a shorter movie series than did the man who made his name playing soldier of fortune Gil Dane.

2. Mike Norris's character was a Texas Ranger operating in the modern day (well, 1940s, anyway) Wild West.

3. The crime-fighting doctor, who was not called Rob Farmer, featured in fewer movies than the tough private eye.

4. Doyle Embury appeared in the shortest series of movies, playing his hero just 10 times.

5. Alan Belson's series was made up of the number of films that appears in the numerical list immediately below the length of the series featuring Mac McGee.

6. John Kramer played Nick Delaney in a series that did not comprise exactly 17 or 19 films.

7. The character Jay Dyson featured in a series of 14 movies.

Actor	Name

	Gil Dane	Jay Dyson	Mac McGee	Nick Delaney	Rob Farmer	Doctor	Federal agent	Private eye	Texas Ranger	Soldier of fortune	10 films	14 films	17 films	19 films	22 films
Alan Belson															
Doyle Embury															
John Kramer															
Mike Norris															
Tony Vernon															
10 films															
14 films															
17 films															
19 films															
22 films															
Doctor															
Federal agent															
Private eye															
Texas Ranger															
Soldier of fortune															

Description	Films

It Must Be True...

A notable personality given to traveling incognito and living a high life accompanied by undesirable (in a social sense) female companions was recently reported in the gossip columns of five different newspapers to have been in five different locations at almost the same time of the same day in various parts of Europe. From the clues given below, can you say exactly where and at what time he was reported by each columnist as having been spotted by his or her name-dropping informants?

Clues

1. The sighting in the sauna in Helsinki immediately preceded time-wise the one reported in Hugh Codham's column.

2. Rome was where the ubiquitous celebrity was reported to be by Tanya Tittle in an earlier sighting than the one in the nightclub, which was also recorded by a female columnist.

3. Eleven o'clock was the time of the alleged sighting in Paris, which did not take place in a hotel.

4. The timing in Tina Tattle's report was earlier than that of the London sighting, but later than the one in Munich.

5. Whelan Ventitt's column referred to an encounter at 9:30 p.m.

6. One report told of a meeting in an exclusive restaurant at 10 o'clock.

7. The rave was the location specified in Lotta Drivell's notebook.

Columnist	City

	Helsinki	London	Munich	Paris	Rome	Hotel	Nightclub	Rave	Restaurant	Sauna	9:30	10:00	10:30	11:00	11:30
Hugh Codham															
Lotta Drivell															
Tanya Tittle															
Tina Tattle															
Whelan Ventitt															
9:30															
10:00															
10:30															
11:00															
11:30															
Hotel															
Nightclub															
Rave															
Restaurant															
Sauna															

Location	Time

Codewords

This puzzle has no clues in the conventional sense. Instead, every different number printed in the main grid represents a different letter (with the same number always representing the same letter, of course). For example, if 7 turns out to be a "V," you can write in V wherever a square contains 7. We have completed a very small part of the puzzle to give you a start, but the rest is up to you.

	10		15		10 **I**		21		22		3	
1	17	14	23	20	11 **S**		19	2	26	12	1	3
	6		2		7 **L**		13		23		11	
1	20	1	11		1	15	2		18	21	25	11
			11		11		10				10	
16	24	1	21	8		25	26	23	25	23	11	1
	21		6		15		1		21		1	
2	17	8	21	4	1	3		5	26	2	11	24
	3				17		11		21			
9	23	23	11		8	23	25		11	21	12	1
	2		2		24		21		10		21	
11	8	1	26	1	23		16	21	8	1	26	20
	11		1		7		17		1		20	

A B C D E F G H X J K X M N O P Q R X T U V W X Y Z

1	2	3	4	5	6	7 **L**	8	9	10 **I**	11 **S**	12	13
14	15	16	17	18	19	20	21	22	23	24	25	26

TOTALIZED

The 25-second ultimate challenge from **Puzzler Brain Trainer**

Just follow the instructions from top to bottom, starting with
the number given to reach an answer at the foot of the ladder.

EASY	MEDIUM	HARDER
17	**21**	**96**
ADD 28	MULTIPLY BY 5	66 ⅔% OF IT
TAKE AWAY 9	TAKE AWAY 29	DIVIDE BY 16
DIVIDE BY 3	DIVIDE BY 4	ADD 500% TO IT
MULTIPLY BY 5	ADD 53	MULTIPLY BY 7
TAKE AWAY 31	75% OF IT	TAKE AWAY 87
ADD 13	MULTIPLY BY 4	DIVIDE BY 3
DIVIDE BY 6	DIVIDE BY 8	ADD 48
MULTIPLY BY 8	DOUBLE IT	⅖ OF IT
TAKE AWAY 14	DIVIDE BY 18	TIMES ITSELF
ANSWER	**ANSWER**	**ANSWER**

Cell Block

Fill the grid by drawing blocks along the grid lines. Each block must contain the number of squares indicated by the digit inside it. Each block must contain only one digit.

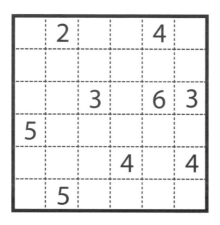

Wordwheel

Using only the letters in the Wordwheel, you have ten minutes to find as many words as possible, none of which may be plurals, foreign words, or proper nouns. Each word must be of three letters or more, all must contain the central letter, and letters can only be used once in every word. There is at least one nine-letter word in the wheel.

Battleships

Do you remember the old game of battleships? These puzzles are based on that idea. Your task is to find the vessels in the diagram. Some parts of boats or sea squares have already been filled in, and a number next to a row or column refers to the number of occupied squares in that row or column. The boats may be positioned horizontally or vertically, but no two boats or parts of boats are in adjacent squares—horizontally, vertically, or diagonally.

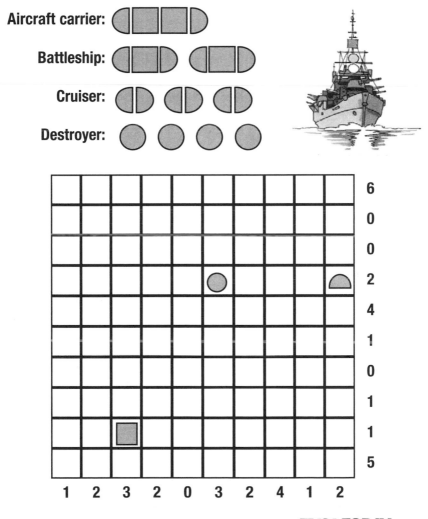

Aircraft carrier:

Battleship:

Cruiser:

Destroyer:

										6
										0
										0
					◐				◖	2
										4
										1
										0
										1
		■								1
										5

| 1 | 2 | 3 | 2 | 0 | 3 | 2 | 4 | 1 | 2 |

Conspiracy Theories

There are loads of conspiracy theories around these days, and I really enjoy reading about them; I don't believe them, but I enjoy reading about them. A friend who edits an odd little magazine recently let me read through five submitted articles about different conspiracies (none of which were published). From the clues, can you fully identify the author of each piece, what pen name he used, and what he was writing about?

Clues

1. Neither Mr. Meagles nor the man who was convinced that UFOs visit Earth as part of a secret pact with the Knights Templar used the pen name Mercurius.

2. Colossus wrote about a bunch of aliens who were conspiring with the Druids to kidnap humans in the Bermuda Triangle; Spyglass was the nom de plume of a schoolteacher named Blimber.

3. Neither Lancelot, alias Warlock, nor Oswald was responsible for claiming that the sinking of the *Titanic* never took place but was a conspiracy between the British Royal Family and the people who live in the center of the earth to get rid of mutants who threatened to expose their secrets.

4. Egbert Sleary was not Mercurius.

5. Neither Oswald nor Soothsayer was either Chickweed or the idiot—er, author who wrote about the UFO conspiracy.

6. Ambrose propounded the interesting theory that the recent apparent increase in diabetes was a British conspiracy to administer mind-controlling drugs to prepare us to rejoin as a colony of the British Empire; he and Zachary both had seven-letter surnames.

First name	Surname

	Blimber	Chickweed	Jeddler	Meagles	Sleary	Colossus	Mercurius	Soothsayer	Spyglass	Warlock	Diabetes	Bermuda Triangle	Kennedy assassination	Titanic sinking	UFOs
Ambrose															
Egbert															
Lancelot															
Oswald															
Zachary															
Diabetes															
Bermuda Triangle															
Kennedy assassination															
Titanic sinking															
UFOs															
Colossus															
Mercurius															
Soothsayer															
Spyglass															
Warlock															

Pen name	Conspiracy

Out of Space

The StarForce of the Confederation of Planets is a remarkably successful organization, but during the 24th century a number of starship types were introduced that were found unsuitable if not downright dangerous and scrapped within a couple of years. From the clues below, can you work out which class of ship was introduced in each of the listed years, what it was intended to do, and why it was scrapped?

Clues

1. It was in the year 2400 that the StarForce adopted the ship type that was quickly found to be far too complex, requiring constant servicing and repair.

2. The patrol ship was found to be prone to break-up when operating at speeds faster than that of light, with four lost in the one year they were in service.

3. The ship type scrapped because it was underpowered, which was not the Tiger class, was introduced earlier than the one that turned out to be unstable at low speed.

4. In the year 2340, the StarForce adopted a new design of survey ship intended to explore those areas of space where no one had gone before.

5. The escort ship was introduced fifteen years before the Prahun class—a Prahun (pronounced "prune") being a large predatory flying reptile from the planet Trehenna.

6. The Emerald class light transport was introduced fifteen years before the starship that was taken out of service because of its short range.

7. In 2355, the StarForce adopted the Kilorik class, named for a Rhylsian fruit tree—very boring, like everything else about Rhylsia.

Year	Class

	Emerald	Firebird	Kilorik	Prahun	Tiger	Escort	Light transport	Patrol ship	Survey ship	Transport	Broke up at speed	Short range	Too complex	Underpowered	Unstable
2340															
2355															
2370															
2385															
2400															
Broke up at speed															
Short range															
Too complex															
Underpowered															
Unstable															
Escort															
Light transport															
Patrol ship															
Survey ship															
Transport															

Purpose	Reason

Chopper Cabs

Chopper Cabs is a helicopter taxi service operating from the center of Manhattan, flying celebrities, business tycoons, and other people with lots of money to destinations throughout the island and the closer parts of the Northeast. The picture shows four helicopters taking off at about 9:45 a.m. today; from the clues below, can you work out the name of each one's pilot, the number of passengers it's carrying, and its destination?

Clues

1. The helicopter flying to the Hamptons is immediately west of the one that has only 1 passenger.

2. Jenny Kite is piloting the chopper next east from the one heading for Hyannis Port; the pilot of the latter has fewer passengers—but not just one less—in his helicopter than Jenny has in hers.

3. Roy Swan's helicopter has more passengers—but not just one more—than the helicopter next west from it.

4. The chopper carrying 3 passengers is more than one place east of the one piloted by Vince Wren; neither of them is heading for Martha's Vineyard.

5. The two helicopters with male pilots are not in adjacent positions; one of them has one more passenger than the other.

Pilots: Jenny Kite; Roy Swan; Sue Teal; Vince Wren
Numbers of passengers: 1; 2; 3; 4
Destinations: Hyannis Port; the Hamptons; Martha's Vineyard; Woodstock

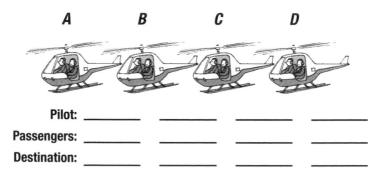

	A	**B**	**C**	**D**
Pilot:				
Passengers:				
Destination:				

Starting tip: Work out how many passengers are with Roy Swan.

Days Out

With the kids on vacation from school, hack writer Bob Wheel managed to free up enough time from his busy schedule to take them to three attractions last week. From the clues given, can you work out what the Wheel family visited on each of the listed days, where it's located, and how they traveled?

Clues

1. The Wheels traveled to Kansas City two days before they made the car journey.

2. They traveled to the Natural History Museum by train.

3. The Louisberg Cider Mill is in Parkville.

4. On Wednesday they went on a bus excursion organized by a local company.

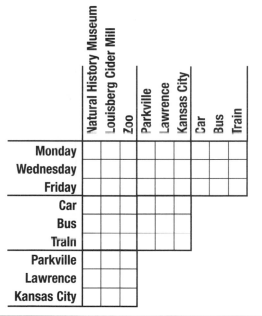

	Natural History Museum	Louisberg Cider Mill	Zoo	Parkville	Lawrence	Kansas City	Car	Bus	Train
Monday									
Wednesday									
Friday									
Car									
Bus									
Train									
Parkville									
Lawrence									
Kansas City									

Day	Attraction	Location	Transport

Vacation Reading

We're off on vacation next week, and my wife has equipped herself with three of the historical romances she loves to read on the beach. From the clues below, can you work out the title of each one, its author, the period in which it is set, and the number of pages it has?

Clues

1. *False and True Love* has only 200 pages.

2. *Not for Love* is by Melissa Reveling, one of my wife's favorite writers.

3. The book set in the Civil War is fifty pages longer than the one written by Honoria Blount, which isn't *King of Love*.

4. Anna Estensen's book is set in Elizabethan England, and involves the romance between a doctor's daughter and a ship's captain.

	Anna Estensen	Honoria Blount	Melissa Reveling	Civil War	Elizabethan	Regency	200 pages	250 pages	300 pages
False and True Love									
King of Love									
Not for Love									
200 pages									
250 pages									
300 pages									
Civil War									
Elizabethan									
Regency									

Title	Writer	Period	Length

Getting an Eiffel

One morning, four married couples were among the hundreds of tourists who decided to visit the Eiffel Tower in Paris. At the moment shown in our diagram, one pair were on the ground, about to start their ascent, another duo were already at the summit, enjoying the panoramic view, and the other couples were at a different one of the intermediate platforms. From the clues given below, can you fully identify the pair at each stage?

Clues

1. Martin is at a higher level than the Cleggs, but Helena is below them, while Thomas is not still at ground level.

2. Victoria is at the next level below Mr. and Mrs. Wylie.

3. Oliver and Leonie are at the next level above the Gibsons.

4. The couple who have stopped at the first stage for a view of the relatively immediate scene are the Bakers.

Husbands: Andrew; Martin; Oliver; Thomas
Wives: Daphne; Helena; Leonie; Victoria
Surnames: Baker; Clegg; Gibson; Wylie

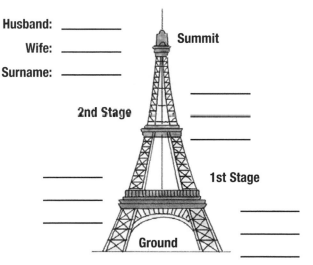

Husband: _____
Wife: _____
Surname: _____

Summit

2nd Stage

1st Stage

Ground

Starting tip: Start by placing the Gibsons.

Coffee Break

The picture below shows four nurses from Storbury's St. Leonard's Hospital, lining up to get a cup of coffee out of the hot drinks machine in the staff cafeteria. From the clues below, can you work out each woman's full name, and to which ward or department she is assigned?

Clues

1. Nurse Otley is currently working on Kennerly Ward, which handles female patients recovering from surgery.

2. Sally, who nurses male cardiac patients on Penryn Ward, is standing next but one to Nurse Parsons.

3. Figure C is Nurse Baxter.

4. Diane Milligan is somewhere ahead of Helen in the line.

5. Nancy isn't the nurse/practitioner who is currently assigned to Accident & Emergency (A&E).

First names:
Diane; Helen;
Nancy; Sally
Surnames:
Baxter; Milligan;
Otley; Parsons
**Wards/
Departments:**
A&E; Kennerly;
Penryn; Sackville

First name: _____ _____ _____ _____

Surname: _____ _____ _____ _____

Ward/Dept: _____ _____ _____ _____

Starting tip: Work out Sally's surname.

Battleships

Do you remember the old game of battleships? These puzzles are based on that idea. Your task is to find the vessels in the diagram. Some parts of boats or sea squares have already been filled in, and a number next to a row or column refers to the number of occupied squares in that row or column. The boats may be positioned horizontally or vertically, but no two boats or parts of boats are in adjacent squares—horizontally, vertically, or diagonally.

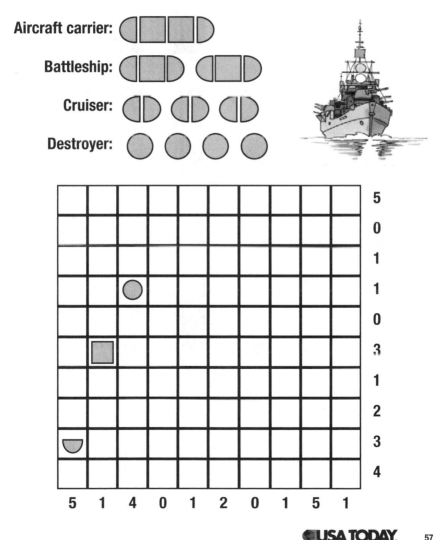

Aircraft carrier:

Battleship:

Cruiser:

Destroyer:

										5
										0
										1
		○								1
										0
	▢									3
										1
										2
										3
										4

5 1 4 0 1 2 0 1 5 1

Codewords

This puzzle has no clues in the conventional sense. Instead, every different number printed in the main grid represents a different letter (with the same number always representing the same letter, of course). For example, if 7 turns out to be a "V," you can write in V wherever a square contains 7. We have completed a very small part of the puzzle to give you a start, but the rest is up to you.

20	2	10	7	8	16	24		21	8	18	24	7
25		8		1		12		19		2		21
2	9	24	19	2		2	15	26	2	9	8	2
9				3		10		20				18
1	2	18	18	24	9	7		21	25	2	21	8
		23				24		12		12		19
7	15	26	2	9	24		4	24	13	8	19	3
15		18		2		7				22		
26	10 P	7 S	24 E	18		11	2	6	18	8	19	3
2				18		2		2				9
7	25	2	12	12	23	18		9	26	1	22	2
25		20		24		25		20		2		19
5	8	24	12	14		24	17	24	20	18	24	14

A B C D E̸ F G H I J K L M N O P̸ Q R S̸ T U V W X Y Z

1	2	3	4	5	6	7 S	8	9	10 P	11	12	13
14	15	16	17	18	19	20	21	22	23	24 E	25	26

TOTALIZED

The 25-second ultimate challenge from **Puzzler Brain Trainer**

Just follow the instructions from top to bottom, starting with the number given to reach an answer at the foot of the ladder.

EASY	MEDIUM	HARDER
9	**48**	**13**
MULTIPLY BY 5	DIVIDE BY 12	TIMES ITSELF
ADD 11	TIMES ITSELF	ADD 76
DIVIDE BY 8	MULTIPLY BY 11	DIVIDE BY 5
ADD 24	DIVIDE BY 4	MULTIPLY BY 7
MULTIPLY BY 3	ADD 27	TAKE AWAY 196
TAKE AWAY 51	MULTIPLY BY 3	DIVIDE BY 3
DIVIDE BY 3	ADD 39	ADD 23
ADD 18	TAKE AWAY 72	$^5/_8$ OF IT
DOUBLE IT	DIVIDE BY 9	ADD $^3/_5$ OF IT
ANSWER	**ANSWER**	**ANSWER**

Cell Block

Fill the grid by drawing blocks along the grid lines. Each block must contain the number of squares indicated by the digit inside it. Each block must contain only one digit.

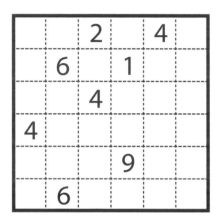

Wordwheel

Using only the letters in the Wordwheel, you have ten minutes to find as many words as possible, none of which may be plurals, foreign words, or proper nouns. Each word must be of three letters or more, all must contain the central letter, and letters can only be used once in every word. There is at least one nine-letter word in the wheel.

Domino Search

A standard set of dominoes has been laid out, using numbers instead of dots for clarity. Using a sharp pencil and a keen brain, can you draw in the lines to show where each domino has been placed? You may find the check grid useful—crossing off each domino as you find it.

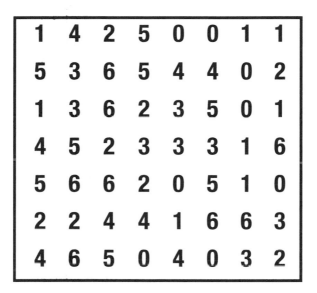

1	4	2	5	0	0	1	1
5	3	6	5	4	4	0	2
1	3	6	2	3	5	0	1
4	5	2	3	3	3	1	6
5	6	6	2	0	5	1	0
2	2	4	4	1	6	6	3
4	6	5	0	4	0	3	2

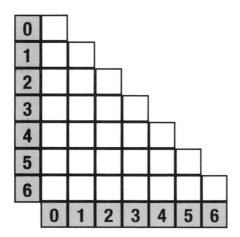

2020 Visions

The new science fiction book *2020 Visions* is a collection of five novelettes on the common theme of life on Earth in the year 2020, and for some reason none of them are very optimistic. From the clues below, can you work out the name of each of the authors who has contributed to the book, the title of his or her story and the problem that the story envisages confronting the world in the year 2020?

Clues

1. Mr. Rocklynne is neither Donald nor the author of *Endgame*.

2. Abigail's story depicts Earth in 2020 as racked by worldwide famine, with wars being fought for the possession of the shrinking areas of fertile farmland, while Smith's has it falling victim to an unstoppable invasion by a very strange race of aliens.

3. Joanne, who wrote *The Horsemen*, isn't Leinster.

4. *Dog Days*, which is not Rocklynne's story, features an Earth dying from the toxic and irreversible pollution of its air and water.

5. It was Wells (no relation to the great H. G.) who wrote *Judgment*.

6. Michael Burrough's story isn't the one in which Earth's population is virtually wiped out by a man-made plague; neither of these stories is called *Red Sky*.

First name	Surname

	Burroughs	Leinster	Rocklynne	Smith	Wells	Dog Days	Endgame	Judgment	Red Sky	The Horsemen	Alien invasion	Famine	Nuclear war	Plague	Toxic pollution
Abigail															
Donald															
Joanne															
Michael															
Stephen															
Alien invasion															
Famine															
Nuclear war															
Plague															
Toxic pollution															
Dog Days															
Endgame															
Judgment															
Red Sky															
The Horsemen															

Note: If, for example, we say "The shopkeeper is **neither** Mark **nor** Spencer," it means that Mark is not the shopkeeper **and** Spencer is not the shopkeeper and that Mark is not Spencer.

Title	Problem

Special Requirements

In the 25th century, the interplanetary liners of TriGalaxy Spaceways get to carry all kinds of passengers, some of whom have very unusual requirements and can't make use of the normal accommodation, so cabins 1 to 5 on each of TriGalaxy's vessels are fitted up for quick and easy adaption. The details below relate to one flight of the liner from Terra to Carremon, a world in orbit around the star Merseia Dexter; from the clues given, can you work out the name of the passenger in each of the special cabins, their planetary origin, and their particular requirement?

Clues

1. The cabin that has been provided with a methane atmosphere has a higher number than the one assigned to the Pimtrian passenger, and is numbered immediately below the cabin in which Bodi-Nadi will be traveling.

2. The Gunitrian's cabin has to be totally dark, because even the lowest light levels would cause him/her (Gunitrians switch genders cyclically) unbearable pain.

3. Sinuwei has been assigned the cabin numbered immediately above the one adapted to provide its occupant with the subzero (Celsius) temperature it requires.

4. The cabin adapted to provide low gravity is not Y'Alidan's, which isn't cabin 1.

5. Cabin 3's atmosphere is being filtered to remove all water vapor, which could poison the passenger who is to travel in it.

6. The Dravian traveler's cabin is numbered lower than the Jirrizic's but higher than the Ordolase's.

7. Lurimeg will be accommodated in cabin 5.

Cabin	Passenger

	Bodi-Nadi	Hravpak	Lurimeg	Sinuwei	Y'Alidan	Dravian	Gunitrian	Jirrizic	Ordolase	Pimtrian	Low gravity	Methane atmos	No water vapor	Subzero temp	Total darkness
1															
2															
3															
4															
5															
Low gravity															
Methane atmos															
No water vapor															
Subzero temp															
Total darkness															
Dravian															
Gunitrian															
Jirrizic															
Ordolase															
Pimtrian															

Planet	Requirement

Wilde Types

As usual the five Wilde brothers have booked a range of adventure vacations this year. From the following information, can you discover for what part of the world each is bound, what they will be doing there, and for how many weeks?

Clues

1. The five brothers' names are in alphabetical order in reverse order of their births, and neither the youngest, Alexander, nor the climber are off to Europe, but both will be away for fewer weeks than the brother vacationing in Pyrenees.

2. The brother bound for the Pyrenees was born immediately after the one flying to Brazil.

3. Ranulph is going pony-trekking, and is older than his brother who is spending two weeks in Austria.

4. The hiker's vacation will be longer than the one spent in Mexico.

5. One of the brothers will spend five weeks cycling, while Hector will be away for just one week.

6. One of the brothers is going diving in the Seychelles.

Brother	Country

	Austria	Brazil	Mexico	Pyrenees	Seychelles	Climbing	Cycling	Diving	Hiking	Pony-trekking	1 week	2 weeks	3 weeks	4 weeks	5 weeks
Alexander															
Ferdinand															
Hector															
Ranulph															
Sebastian															
1 week															
2 weeks															
3 weeks															
4 weeks															
5 weeks															
Climbing															
Cycling															
Diving															
Hiking															
Pony-trekking															

Activity	Weeks

Bust Up

In each of the ground-floor rooms of his house, a musician has a bust of one of his four favorite composers. From the clues given below, can you describe each of rooms 1 to 4, name the composer whose bust adorns it, and say where exactly it sits?

Clues

1. The library, where the bust is on a bookshelf, and the room containing a bust of Beethoven have consecutive numbers on the plan.

2. The music room is indicated by a lower number than the one with a bust on the sideboard, neither being room 2.

3. The bust of Bach is in a higher-numbered room than both the lounge and the room where a bust can be admired on the mantelpiece, which is not number 1.

4. Mozart sits proudly on an occasional table, but not in the dining area, which is indicated by a higher number, but is not room 4.

Descriptions: dining area; library; lounge; music room
Composers: Bach; Beethoven; Chopin; Mozart
Locations: bookshelf; mantelpiece; occasional table; sideboard

Room: _____ *1*   *2*
Bust: _____
Location: _____

3   *4*   Kitchen

Front door   W.C.

Starting tip: First describe room 4.

Battleships

Do you remember the old game of battleships? These puzzles are based on that idea. Your task is to find the vessels in the diagram. Some parts of boats or sea squares have already been filled in, and a number next to a row or column refers to the number of occupied squares in that row or column. The boats may be positioned horizontally or vertically, but no two boats or parts of boats are in adjacent squares—horizontally, vertically, or diagonally.

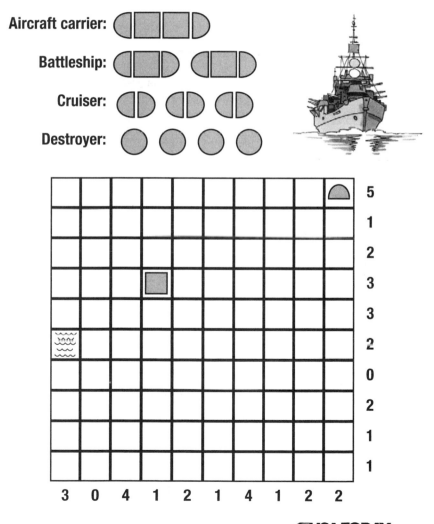

Aircraft carrier:

Battleship:

Cruiser:

Destroyer:

Giving Up

Five friends have so far been successful in giving up smoking, having each been heavy smokers for many years. From the information given below, can you work out how many cigarettes a day each used to smoke, the number of weeks each has been smoke-free, and the kind of help each used?

Clues

1. It's still less than six weeks since Dai Coffin had his last cigarette; he didn't use nicotine gum to help him.

2. One of the five got themselves sponsored to give up their 20-a-day habit, and has so far not smoked for an even number of weeks.

3. Jackie Tinn used to smoke 40 a day, but she isn't the one who has been cigarette-free for five weeks; Eileen Hale hasn't smoked for four weeks, while one of the men hasn't had a cigarette for seven weeks.

4. Virginia Hook used hypnotism to help her kick the habit.

5. Willpower alone didn't help stop the 15-a-day habit, but nicotine patches have helped one of the five give up for two weeks.

6. The 10-a-day smoker hasn't touched one for eight weeks.

Former smoker	No. smoked

	10	15	20	30	40	2 weeks	4 weeks	5 weeks	7 weeks	8 weeks	Hypnotism	Nicotine gum	Nicotine patches	Sponsorship	Willpower
Bernard Ash															
Dai Coffin															
Eileen Hale															
Jackie Tinn															
Virginia Hook															
Hypnotism															
Nicotine gum															
Nicotine patches															
Sponsorship															
Willpower															
2 weeks															
4 weeks															
5 weeks															
7 weeks															
8 weeks															

Weeks	Help used

Clubbing Coppers

Some of the nightclubs in Brownville are run by honest men, just out to make a fair profit—but some of them are run by outright crooks, who use them for purposes unconnected with their legitimate business. Five of the latter sort are going to be raided by the police tonight; from the clues below, can you work out the name and address of each of these clubs, the name of the police officer leading the raid on it, and what the police will be looking for?

Clues

1. The Aztec Club, which is not on Lincoln Street, will be raided by one of the teams led by a sergeant, while the club on Walpole Lane will be searched for stolen goods; Inspector Harvey isn't taking his squad to either Lincoln Street or Walpole Lane.

2. The club where the police expect to find forged credit cards and the equipment for turning them out, the Equator Club, the club to be raided by Inspector Mullen and his men, and the club on Lincoln Street are four different establishments; Inspector Mullen isn't going to raid Foxx's.

3. The club called Mr. Hyde (after Dr. Jekyll's dark side), which is on Forsyth Street, is not the one where the police expect to find the cash stolen in a bank robbery yesterday morning.

4. Sergeant Pomeroy and his men are from the Drugs Squad, and that's what they'll be looking for.

5. Sergeant Lyndon and his men will be raiding the club on Erskine Street.

6. Inspector Carter will be leading the raid on the Chicago Club.

Club	Address

	Buckland Street	Erskine Street	Forsyth Street	Lincoln Street	Walpole Lane	Insp. Carter	Insp. Harvey	Sgt. Lyndon	Insp. Mullen	Sgt. Pomeroy	Drugs	Forged cards	Guns	Stolen cash	Stolen goods
Aztec															
Chicago															
Equator															
Foxx's															
Mr. Hyde															
Drugs															
Forged cards															
Guns															
Stolen cash															
Stolen goods															
Insp. Carter															
Insp. Harvey															
Sgt. Lyndon															
Insp. Mullen															
Sgt. Pomeroy															

CHICAGO NIGHT CLUB

MEMBERS ONLY

Police Officer	Looking for

Codewords

This puzzle has no clues in the conventional sense. Instead, every different number printed in the main grid represents a different letter (with the same number always representing the same letter, of course). For example, if 7 turns out to be a "V," you can write in V wherever a square contains 7. We have completed a very small part of the puzzle to give you a start, but the rest is up to you.

22		5		9		26		15		2		9
10	22	12	12	26	19	19	22	25		25	22	12
				L	N							
25		19		10		22		8		15		25
14	13	25	3	22	19	14		9	19	24	8	23
26						10				12		9
13	24	1		4	13	25	19	9	18	22	16	
23		26		26				25		19		26
	22	19	2	26	19	9	26	11		14	25	14
9		26				2						24
20	26	18	4	23		13	26	7	5	26	9	4
25		22		25		25		5		19		22
21	22	4		13	26	17	13	22	26	6	26	9
26		9		11		9		3		23		4

A B C D E̸ F G H I J K L̸ M N̸ O P Q R S T U V W X Y Z

1	2	3	4	5	6	7	8	9	10	11	12	13
											L	
14	15	16	17	18	19	20	21	22	23	24	25	26
					N							E

TOTALIZED

*The 25-second ultimate challenge from **Puzzler Brain Trainer***

Just follow the instructions from top to bottom, starting with
the number given to reach an answer at the foot of the ladder.

EASY	MEDIUM	HARDER
14	**32**	**17**
ADD 28	DIVIDE BY 4	MULTIPLY BY 11
DIVIDE BY 6	TIMES ITSELF	TAKE AWAY 75
MULTIPLY BY 8	TAKE AWAY 17	DIVIDE BY 7
TAKE AWAY 21	DOUBLE IT	TIMES ITSELF
DIVIDE BY 7	TAKE AWAY 37	ADD 89
DOUBLE IT	ADD $\frac{1}{3}$ OF IT	DIVIDE BY 15
ADD 14	TAKE AWAY 18	ADD 61
DOUBLE IT	MULTIPLY BY 4	ADD 75% OF IT
TAKE AWAY 17	DIVIDE BY 8	DIVIDE BY 7
ANSWER	**ANSWER**	**ANSWER**

Cell Block

Fill the grid by drawing blocks along the grid lines. Each block must contain the number of squares indicated by the digit inside it. Each block must contain only one digit.

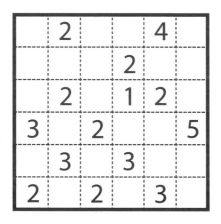

Wordwheel

Using only the letters in the Wordwheel, you have ten minutes to find as many words as possible, none of which may be plurals, foreign words, or proper nouns. Each word must be of three letters or more, all must contain the central letter, and letters can only be used once in every word. There is at least one nine-letter word in the wheel.

USA TODAY.

Fully Furnished

Outside houses number 3, 5, 11, and 15 on a local road is a different item from the street. From the clues given below, can you fully identify the home owner at each address, and describe the item in front of his or her home?

Clues

1. The fire hydrant is outside a higher-numbered house than that of Anna, whose surname is not Norton.

2. The house near the bus stop and the one owned by the person named Byers are in an adjacent pair of duplexes, the latter bearing the higher number.

3. The street light is in front of house number 5, which is not where Nathan Pickles lives.

4. Terry's house, which does not have the manhole cover in the road outside, is number 11, while the resident named Allen lives at number 15.

First names: Anna; Myra; Nathan; Terry
Surnames: Allen; Byers; Norton; Pickles
Items: bus stop; fire hydrant; manhole cover; street light

| 1 | 3 | 5 | 7 | 9 | 11 | 13 | 15 |

First name:	_____	_____	_____	_____
Surname:	_____	_____	_____	_____
Item:	_____	_____	_____	_____

Starting tip: First identify the item outside Terry's house.

Park and Ride

Our diagram shows four adjoining spaces in a park-and-ride car park at the outer edge of town. From the clues given below, can you work out the make of each of cars 1 to 4, name their respective drivers, and say how many people from each car boarded the bus into town?

Clues

1. Carole's car is in an adjoining space to the Rover, from which two bus passengers alighted.

2. The Hyundai, which is parked in space number 2, is not the vehicle occupied only by its driver.

3. Three people were in the car using space number 4, which is not the Saab.

4. Janine parked her car in space 3.

5. Steve's car had one fewer person aboard than the Jaguar.

Cars: Hyundai; Jaguar; Rover; Saab
Drivers: Carole; Janine; Luke; Steve
Number aboard: 1; 2; 3; 4

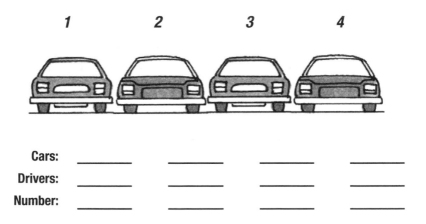

	1	2	3	4
Cars:				
Drivers:				
Number:				

Starting tip: Work out first how many people were in the Hyundai.

USA TODAY.

To the Clinic

Three of the senior citizens who meet at the Appleyard Grove Day Center, chatting over lunch, discovered that each has a hospital appointment next week. From the clues below, can you work out each one's full name, which clinic they're attending, and the day of their appointment?

Clues

1. The senior surnamed Kildare has an appointment later in the week than the one who will be attending the Arthritis Clinic.

2. Edna's appointment is for the Diabetes Clinic.

3. Ivy Jekyll is a regular attender at the Center.

4. The woman surnamed Dolittle has an appointment next Friday.

	Dolittle	Jekyll	Kildare	Arthritis	Cardiac	Diabetes	Monday	Wednesday	Friday
Arnold									
Edna									
Ivy									
Monday									
Wednesday									
Friday									
Arthritis									
Cardiac									
Diabetes									

First name	Surname	Clinic	Day

Call Me Lucky

Felix "Lucky" Charme was born in 1900, and is now 106 years old, still hale and hearty despite a long and adventurous life that, apart from fighting in two World Wars (he lied about his age and joined the navy at the age of 14), has seen him survive five other fairly major life-threatening incidents. From the clues below, can you work out which disaster occurred on what continent, and the month and year in which it took place?

Clues

1. The most recent disaster took place in January of 1966, but not in Africa or North America; the African incident didn't take place in the month of March or the year 1949.

2. The volcanic eruption, which disrupted an archaeological expedition in which "Lucky" was participating, wasn't in North America, and took place in an earlier month of the year than the crash of the experimental airship that "Lucky" was crewing with the designer.

3. It was in 1953 that the airship crashed; the pirate attack took place, amazingly, in Europe—or, at least, the territorial waters of a European country—while "Lucky" was acting as captain of a chartered yacht.

4. The incident in South America took place four months later in its respective year than the disaster of 1924.

5. It was in the month of May that "Lucky" survived the wreck of the tramp steamer *Sea Witch*, on which he was acting as first mate.

6. It was one September that "Lucky" fortunately survived a dangerous incident in Asia.

Incident	Continent

 ■USA TODAY.

	Africa	Asia	Europe	North America	South America	January	March	May	July	September	1924	1937	1949	1953	1966
Airship crash															
Landslide															
Pirate attack															
Shipwreck															
Volcanic eruption															
1924															
1937															
1949															
1953															
1966															
January															
March															
May															
July															
September															

Month	Year

Grumbly Old Codgers

The TV series *Grumbly Old Codgers* has struck a chord with many late-middle-aged men, and features several male celebrities of a certain age holding forth on their pet hates in modern life. Below are details of five of the participants—from the information given, can you discover in what field each is well known, their ages, and what it is that infuriates each of them?

Clues

1. Ivor Growse is a well-known comedian, but it isn't body piercing that he rants about.

2. The singer is enraged by speed cameras, but neither he nor the actor is 53; computers are not the number one grumble of either Malcolm Tent, the 49-year-old, or the actor; these are three different people.

3. Saul Dyer is not the 49-year-old; Billy Aker is 52.

4. Terry Bull is not an actor, and he's over 55.

5. The 58-year-old can't abide the fast food culture.

6. The DJ is 56.

Celebrity	Field

	Actor	Comedian	DJ	Novelist	Singer	49	52	53	56	58	Body piercing	Computers	Fast food	Reality TV	Speed cameras
Billy Aker															
Terry Bull															
Saul Dyer															
Ivor Growse															
Malcolm Tent															
Body piercing															
Computers															
Fast food															
Reality TV															
Speed cameras															
49															
52															
53															
56															
58															

Age	Grumble

Battleships

Do you remember the old game of battleships? These puzzles are based on that idea. Your task is to find the vessels in the diagram. Some parts of boats or sea squares have already been filled in, and a number next to a row or column refers to the number of occupied squares in that row or column. The boats may be positioned horizontally or vertically, but no two boats or parts of boats are in adjacent squares—horizontally, vertically, or diagonally.

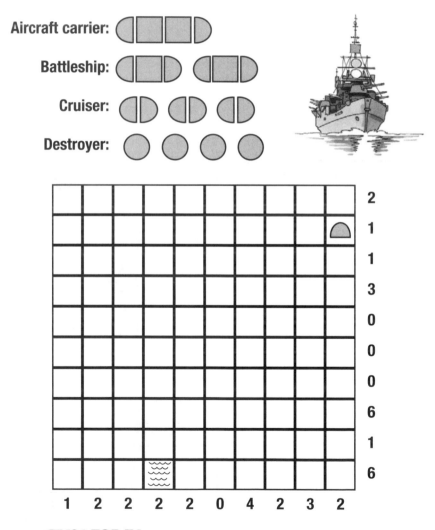

Aircraft carrier:

Battleship:

Cruiser:

Destroyer:

Stepping Down

Four people are lucky enough to own houses on the cliff tops at a seaside location. Each house has a private stairway to the sands below, consisting of a different number of steps. From the clues given below, can you name each house and its owner, and work out how many steps the latter must negotiate to get down to the beach?

Clues

1. The house rather unnecessarily called Clifftops is farther west along the cliffs than the one owned by Richard, which has fewer steps.

2. The house with 39 steps down to the beach is owned by Angela; it is the immediate easterly neighbor of the one with 43 steps.

3. Jeremy's house, which is named Shangri-La, is not next door but one to Windyridge.

4. Westward Ho! boasts the largest number of steps,48; it is not number 1 in our diagram.

Houses: Clifftops; Shangri-La; Westward Ho!; Windyridge
Owners: Angela; Glenda; Jeremy; Richard
Steps: 37; 39; 43; 48

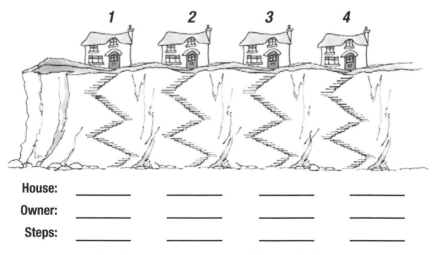

House: _____ _____ _____ _____
Owner: _____ _____ _____ _____
Steps: _____ _____ _____ _____

Starting tip: Begin by naming Richard's house.

Cowboy Heroes

My brother Paul is a great fan of the "pulp" Western magazines from the 1930s and 1940s, and has copies of covers from four of them—showing his favorite heroes, who all featured in long series of stories—hanging on his study wall. From the clues below, can you fill in on the plan the full name of each hero shown, his occupation, the name of his horse, and the state in which he operated?

Clues

1. Lucky doesn't feature in picture A, and Johnny didn't operate in Texas.

2. McCoy operated exclusively in California, although—according to his background as given in the stories—he had been born in Virginia back before the Civil War, in which he had fought for the Confederacy.

3. The professional gambler—who, although he knew all the tricks of the trade, always played an honest game—rode the big black horse called Prince.

4. Dusty's horse was called Buck (which is what he did if anyone but his master tried to ride him), and the gunfighter—who would only hire out to someone who he believed was in the right—was surnamed Steele; neither of these men appears in picture C.

5. The man in picture D is the one forenamed Ambrose but always known by his nickname of Bowie.

6. The U.S. Marshal worked in Arizona; his picture is somewhere to the right of the one showing Wyler seated on his huge roan stallion Randy.

First names/Nicknames: Bowie; Dusty; Johnny; Lucky
Surnames: Flynn; McCoy; Steele; Wyler
Occupations: gambler; gunfighter; U.S. Marshal; wandering cowboy
Horse: Buck; Prince; Randy; Warrior
States: Arizona; California; Montana; Texas

First name:	_____	_____
Surname:	_____	_____
Occupation:	_____	_____
Horse:	_____	_____
State:	_____	_____
	_____	_____
	_____	_____
	_____	_____
	_____	_____
	_____	_____

Starting tip: Work out the surname of the U.S. Marshal.

Hollywood Hopefuls

In the heyday of Hollywood, five aspiring actresses headed west to seek their fortunes on the silver screen under romantic-sounding stage names. From the information given below, can you discover in which year each arrived in Los Angeles, her home state and real name, and the name under which she found fame and fortune?

Clues

1. The girl who would become actress Sabrina Banks was born in Illinois, while Eunice Wigg hailed from New York.

2. The country girl from Ohio arrived in Hollywood in 1929, but didn't find fame as Meryl Day.

3. Audrey Mullett arrived in "Tinseltown" the year before the girl from Louisiana, while the aspiring actress from Missouri arrived two years earlier than Simone Lamont was discovered.

4. The girl who would become Imogen Valentine arrived in 1930.

5. Hyacinth Mudge traveled west in 1932.

6. Grace Waghorn only needed to change her surname slightly.

Year	Home state

	Illinois	Louisiana	New York	Missouri	Ohio	Janice Allibone	Hyacinth Mudge	Audrey Mullett	Grace Waghorn	Eunice Wigg	Sabrina Banks	Meryl Day	Grace Horne	Simone Lamont	Imogen Valentine
1929															
1930															
1932															
1933															
1934															
Sabrina Banks															
Meryl Day															
Grace Horne															
Simone Lamont															
Imogen Valentine															
Janice Allibone															
Hyacinth Mudge															
Audrey Mullett															
Grace Waghorn															
Eunice Wigg															

Real name	Screen name

Codewords

This puzzle has no clues in the conventional sense. Instead, every different number printed in the main grid represents a different letter (with the same number always representing the same letter, of course). For example, if 7 turns out to be a "V," you can write in V wherever a square contains 7. We have completed a very small part of the puzzle to give you a start, but the rest is up to you.

	18	4	22	9	25	23	12		5	24	24	18
18		6		16		19			5		23	
11 C	6	22	2	10		15	19	23	23	14	16	12
16 O		9		5		19		22			22	
26 W	22	15	5		19	9	17	1	5	18	10	18
23		18		25		25		6		22		
	22	10	23	22	18		7	5	6	24	18	
		5		10		19		23		16		16
18	1	6	25	5	16	9	18		18	10	1	3
	9			22		21		16		5		3
20	19	13	10	1	6	5		25	22	1	8	5
	2		19			9		6		6		6
23	12	6	5		22	10	7	5	19	18	10	

A B C̸ D E F G H I J K L M N Ø̸ P Q R S T U V W̸ X Y Z

1	2	3	4	5	6	7	8	9	10	11 C	12	13
14	15	16 O	17	18	19	20	21	22	23	24	25	26 W

TOTALIZED

The 25-second ultimate challenge from **Puzzler Brain Trainer**

Just follow the instructions from top to bottom, starting with the number given to reach an answer at the foot of the ladder.

EASY	MEDIUM	HARDER
6	**15**	**13**
MULTIPLY BY 5	MULTIPLY BY 4	TIMES ITSELF
ADD 45	DIVIDE BY 12	TAKE AWAY 27
DIVIDE BY 3	TIMES ITSELF	ADD 50% OF IT
ADD 13	MULTIPLY BY 5	ADD 123
DIVIDE BY 2	TAKE AWAY 57	DIVIDE BY 12
MULTIPLY BY 6	LESS $\frac{1}{4}$ OF IT	ADD $\frac{3}{7}$ OF IT
TAKE AWAY 34	MULTIPLY BY 3	TIMES ITSELF
DOUBLE IT	TAKE AWAY 81	DIVIDE BY 8
TAKE AWAY 41	DIVIDE BY 9	LESS $\frac{5}{8}$ OF IT
ANSWER	**ANSWER**	**ANSWER**

Cell Block

Fill the grid by drawing blocks along the grid lines. Each block must contain the number of squares indicated by the digit inside it. Each block must contain only one digit.

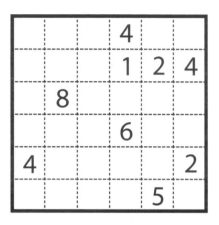

Wordwheel

Using only the letters in the Wordwheel, you have ten minutes to find as many words as possible, none of which may be plurals, foreign words, or proper nouns. Each word must be of three letters or more, all must contain the central letter, and letters can only be used once in every word. There is at least one nine-letter word in the wheel.

Domino Search

A standard set of dominoes has been laid out, using numbers instead of dots for clarity. Using a sharp pencil and a keen brain, can you draw in the lines to show where each domino has been placed? You may find the check grid useful—crossing off each domino as you find it.

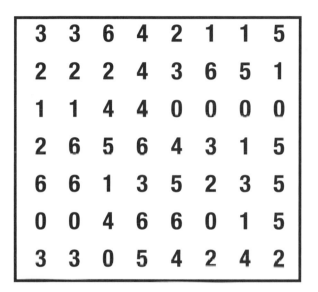

3	3	6	4	2	1	1	5
2	2	2	4	3	6	5	1
1	1	4	4	0	0	0	0
2	6	5	6	4	3	1	5
6	6	1	3	5	2	3	5
0	0	4	6	6	0	1	5
3	3	0	5	4	2	4	2

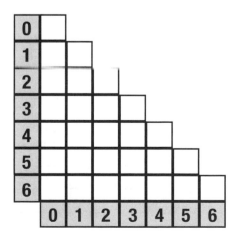

Dump It!

There's a car at each of the five dumpsters at the recycling center, and their drivers are dropping off various items or bundles into the appropriate container. From the following information, can you discover which dumpster each driver is parked by, the number of items or bundles he or she is throwing in, and the make of car in each case?

Clues

1. The Chevrolet car is parked at the metals dumpster, carrying fewer articles than Mr. Sachs has in his car.

2. Six bags of garden waste are being emptied into the green waste dumpster, but not from the Toyota; the Toyota is carrying fewer items or bundles than are being deposited in the household dumpster.

3. There are 5 items or bundles in the back of the Fiat, which is not Mr. Binnett's car, while Mrs. Heap drives a Ford.

4. The 8 items are not heading for the wood dumpster.

5. Mr. Thrower is disposing of 10 items or bundles.

6. Mrs. Riddings is parked at the paper dumpster.

Dumpster	Driver

	Mr. Binnett	Mrs. Heap	Mrs. Riddings	Mr. Sachs	Mr. Thrower	5	6	8	10	12	Fiat	Ford	Toyota	Chevrolet	Volvo
Green waste															
Household															
Metal															
Paper															
Wood															
Fiat															
Ford															
Toyota															
Chevrolet															
Volvo															
5															
6															
8															
10															
12															

Items/bundles	Car

Under Par

The picture below shows the four leading players in the Easton Open Golf Tournament, chatting as they wait to go out for the final round to decide who will take this year's $20,000 prize. From the clues below, can you fill in each man's name, the country he's from, and his score, expressed in strokes under par?

Clues

1. The American player, who is 4 under par at the moment, is standing immediately left of the Australian, Don "Magnum" Magnus.

2. Figure D is the veteran Canadian.

3. Figure A's score is lower (i.e., further under par) than Shane Hardie's.

4. Rick Simons is standing immediately right of the Englishman, who has made a lower score than Simons so far.

5. Glen Boyd is not the current leader, whose score is 7 under par; the former is somewhere left of the latter.

Golfers: Don Magnus; Glen Boyd; Rick Simons; Shane Hardie
Countries: Australia; Canada; England; United States
Scores: 4 under par; 5 under par; 6 under par; 7 under par

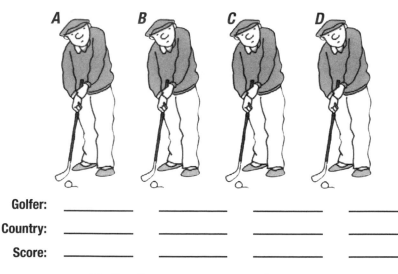

	A	B	C	D
Golfer:				
Country:				
Score:				

Starting tip: Decide which golfer is from the U.S.

USA TODAY.

Battleships

Do you remember the old game of battleships? These puzzles are based on that idea. Your task is to find the vessels in the diagram. Some parts of boats or sea squares have already been filled in, and a number next to a row or column refers to the number of occupied squares in that row or column. The boats may be positioned horizontally or vertically, but no two boats or parts of boats are in adjacent squares—horizontally, vertically, or diagonally.

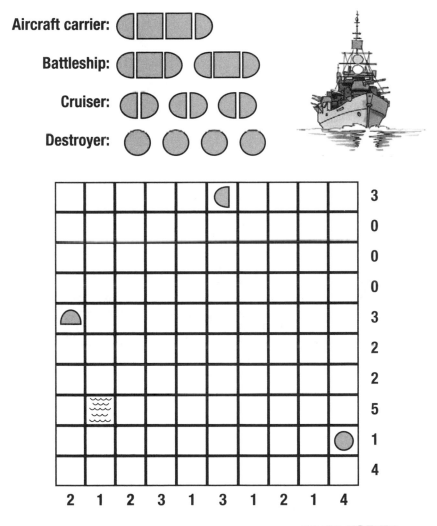

Aircraft carrier:

Battleship:

Cruiser:

Destroyer:

Elevated Art

Between the two World Wars, the top floor of each of the four houses in the Paris street depicted in our diagram was rented by a struggling artist who eked out a living by producing pictures of different types. From the clues given below, can you fully identify the artist at each address and describe his work?

Clues

1. Pierre's studio was at a higher number than Lacoste's, but a lower number than the one rented by the landscape artist.

2. Number 25 was home to Arsène.

3. The portrait painter lived next door to Yves.

4. Mercier painted abstract pictures; his next door neighbor was Grègoire, whose surname was not Robert.

5. The painter named Dupont did not rent a room at number 27.

First names: Arsène; Grègoire; Pierre; Yves
Surnames: Dupont; Lacoste; Mercier; Robert
Genres: abstract; landscape; portrait; still life

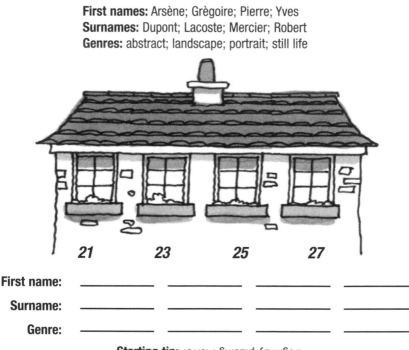

	21	23	25	27
First name:				
Surname:				
Genre:				

Starting tip: Begin by placing Pierre.

Sporting Stars

Three schoolgirls from Omaha have been chosen to represent their city in the National Schools Athletics Championship. From the clues below, can you work out each one's full name, the school she attends, and the event in which she'll be competing?

Clues

1. Diane Piggott's mother was also very good at sports as a schoolgirl.

2. Karen, who attends Hillside School, will not be taking part in the 400 meter hurdles.

3. The girl surnamed Cooper goes to Windsor Green School.

4. The high jumper is a pupil at St. Peter's School.

	Cooper	Piggott	Stewart	Hillside	St. Peter's	Windsor Green	400m hurdles	High jump	100m
Diane									
Karen									
Shelley									
400m hurdles									
High jump									
100m									
Hillside									
St. Peter's									
Windsor Green									

First name	Surname	School	Event

On the Red-eye

Among the passengers on the Associated Amalgamated Airways (AAA) late-night flight to New York (colloquially known as "the red-eye") were five, traveling onward from New York to other destinations in the U.S., who were not what they seemed. From the clues below, can you work out the name and job that each of these people (or, in some cases, "people") claimed, their final destination, and who or what they really were?

Clues

1. The alien is carefully disguised, but if you look very closely you can still make out the outline of the third eye in the middle of its forehead; it's an advance scout for the invading forces of the Micovan Horde, but is not heading for Memphis—so at least Graceland is safe for now.

2. The man heading for Pittsburgh is actually an industrial spy, out to steal the secrets of a newly developed piece of electronic equipment.

3. The traveler pretending to be a solicitor, who is actually Europe's top hired killer on the way to carry out a contract in the U.S., is not the man—well, at least he seems to be a man—traveling to Minneapolis using a passport in the name of Terry Wiles.

4. The passenger heading for St. Louis really is a TV critic—but not just a TV critic.

5. The traveler using the name Babs Curry is a qualified dentist, among other things; she—well, at least she seems to be a she—isn't on the way to Atlanta.

6. Gary Hearn's passport says he's a 35-year-old Englishman, but actually he's a 300-year old Transylvanian vampire–so you know why he's taking the night flight; Sean Tallis isn't the passenger described as an engineer.

Name	Occupation

  **USA TODAY.**

	Dentist	Engineer	Pilot	Solicitor	TV critic	Atlanta	Memphis	Minneapolis	Pittsburgh	St. Louis	Alien	Hired killer	Industrial spy	Jewel thief	Vampire
Babs Curry															
Gary Hearn															
Jessica Kay															
Sean Tallis															
Terry Wiles															
Alien															
Hired killer															
Industrial spy															
Jewel thief															
Vampire															
Atlanta															
Memphis															
Minneapolis															
Pittsburgh															
St. Louis															

AAA FLIGHT TO NEW YORK

Destination	Secret identity

Sporting Gossip

The *Daily Lantern*'s Sporting Gossip feature this morning contains stories about five sports stars (if, that is, you count darts as a sport); from the clues below, can you work out each man's full name, what his sport is, and what the *Lantern*'s story about him is?

Clues

1. It's the veteran darts champion who's alleged to be going on a diet in an attempt to get his weight down below 300 pounds; his surname contains an even number of letters.

2. Anthony is—at least, according to the *Lantern*'s reporter—retiring from international competition at the end of the year.

3. Dean—whose real first name is Percy, but for some reason is never used—isn't Strong.

4. Lloyd Duffy doesn't play tennis, and, as he isn't married, even the *Lantern* can't think he's getting divorced.

5. Toby, who isn't Frost, is a professional golfer.

6. Costigan, the football player, has a shorter first name than the tennis star.

7. It's Mr. Onslow who is said to be recovering in a private clinic from what's described as "a mystery illness"—and which the *Lantern* hints might be alcohol-related with the subtle headline "Onslow Drying Out Again."

First name	Surname

	Costigan	Duffy	Frost	Onslow	Strong	Boxing	Darts	Football	Golf	Tennis	Divorcing	Emigrating	Recovering	Retiring	Dieting
Anthony															
Dean															
Jeff															
Lloyd															
Toby															
Divorcing															
Emigrating															
Recovering															
Retiring															
Dieting															
Boxing															
Darts															
Football															
Golf															
Tennis															

Sport	Story

Codewords

This puzzle has no clues in the conventional sense. Instead, every different number printed in the main grid represents a different letter (with the same number always representing the same letter, of course). For example, if 7 turns out to be a "V," you can write in V wherever a square contains 7. We have completed a very small part of the puzzle to give you a start, but the rest is up to you.

7		8		12		6		20		16		15
2	20	10	15	2	17	22	15	8		20	14	22
2		9		19		22 N		9		6		6
23	9	23	9	22	10	2 O		12	20	18	1	8
9				8		3 Y			1			11
12	17	13		17	22	8	2	23	22	17	6	
		14		12				6		22		
	11	2	26	9	14	17	22	15		15	6	12
25		24				22		22				17
2	25	9	3	8		5	4	9	21	17	22	15
6		18		4		4		10		18		9
14	6	10		6	10	2	23	17	8	9	14	8
8		8		25		19		18		8		10

A B C D E F G H I J K L M N̸ Ø P Q R S T U V W X Y̸ Z

1	2 O	3 Y	4	5	6	7	8	9	10	11	12	13
14	15	16	17	18	19	20	21	22 N	23	24	25	26

TOTALIZED

*The 25-second ultimate challenge from **Puzzler Brain Trainer***

Just follow the instructions from top to bottom, starting with the number given to reach an answer at the foot of the ladder.

EASY	MEDIUM	HARDER
15	**12**	**79**
MULTIPLY BY 3	TIMES ITSELF	TAKE AWAY 37
ADD 21	DIVIDE BY 6	MULTIPLY BY 3
DIVIDE BY 3	ADD $\frac{1}{2}$ OF IT	DIVIDE BY 6
ADD 19	DOUBLE IT	ADD $\frac{2}{3}$ OF IT
DOUBLE IT	DIVIDE BY 8	MULTIPLY BY 9
TAKE AWAY 12	TIMES ITSELF	DIVIDE BY 5
DIVIDE BY 5	TAKE AWAY 49	ADD $\frac{5}{9}$ OF IT
DOUBLE IT	MULTIPLY BY 3	DIVIDE BY 7
DIVIDE BY 4	DIVIDE BY 6	TIMES ITSELF
ANSWER	**ANSWER**	**ANSWER**

Cell Block

Fill the grid by drawing blocks along the grid lines. Each block must contain the number of squares indicated by the digit inside it. Each block must contain only one digit.

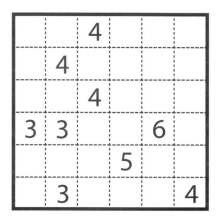

Wordwheel

Using only the letters in the Wordwheel, you have ten minutes to find as many words as possible, none of which may be plurals, foreign words, or proper nouns. Each word must be of three letters or more, all must contain the central letter, and letters can only be used once in every word. There is at least one nine-letter word in the wheel.

An Eye for a Picture

Arthur Nuvo—Art to his friends—knows a bit about paintings, and recently picked up three paintings worth $1,000 each for next to nothing. From the clues given, can you work out the title of each painting, the artist who painted it, how much Art bought it for, and where he bought it?

Clues

1. Art spotted *Autumn Scene* for sale on a stall in a street market.

2. The picture by Angus McRay, an important Scottish artist, cost Art just $15.

3. The picture Art found in a junk shop wasn't priced at $10; it wasn't the work of Enrico Giano, who did not paint *Hyacinths*.

4. One picture cost Art $5 at a garage sale; *Still Life* cost less than the painting by Luc Le Beau.

	Angus McRay	Enrico Giano	Luc Le Beau	$5	$10	$15	Garage sale	Junk shop	Market stall
Autumn Scene									
Hyacinths									
Still Life									
Garage sale									
Junk shop									
Market stall									
$5									
$10									
$15									

Painting	Artist	Price	Bought from

Terry Bull Taxis

Four drivers employed by Terry Bull Taxis were unavailable to be contacted at various times one day last week when Mandy Bull, Terry's wife, known to all the drivers as "Jaws," was working the switchboard. From the clues given below, can you identify the driver of the cabs parked in each of positions 1 to 4 in the town center plan, say what time Mandy tried to contact him, and work out what he was doing at the time?

Clues

1. The taxi parked while its driver placed a bet is farther east than Melvyn's, but farther west than the one Mandy attempted to contact at 9:50 a.m.

2. Vikram's cab and the one parked while its driver answered a call of nature are not both either on the main road or one of the side streets, the latter was not called at 11:10 a.m.

3. The driver who failed to respond to "Jaws" at 3:15 p.m. was paying an illicit visit to a lady friend at the time; his cab is not number 1.

4. The taxi whose driver was buying a packet of cigarettes is separated by only one in the diagram from Leroy's, called at 2:55 p.m.

5. Adam's cab is not shown in position 2.

Drivers: Adam; Leroy; Melvyn; Vikram
Times of calls: 9:50 a.m.; 11:10 a.m.; 2:55 p.m.; 3:15 p.m.
Reasons: buying cigarettes; call of nature; placing a bet; visiting a lady

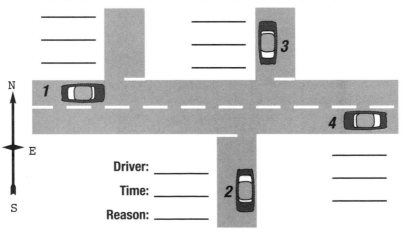

Starting tip: Work out the time at which cab number 1 was called.

Guilty!

The picture below shows the four members of a gang of bank robbers as they leave the court after being found guilty and sentenced to various terms of imprisonment. From the clues below, can you fill in each prisoner's name and the length of his sentence?

Clues

1. None of the prisoners has the surname usually associated with his forename in a criminal context.

2. Mr. Hood has received a 5-year sentence.

3. Jesse has been "sent down" for 8 years; the man sentenced to 6 years in jail is not figure A, who is not Dick.

4. Mr. Turpin has received a sentence one year shorter than figure D's.

5. The man who has been given 7 years is next to—but not handcuffed to!—his brother-in-law.

6. Robin is not figure C in the picture.

First names: Bill; Dick; Jesse; Robin
Surnames: Hood; James; Sikes; Turpin
Prison terms: 5 years; 6 years; 7 years; 8 years

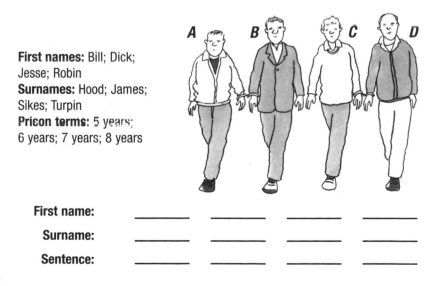

First name: _____ _____ _____ _____

Surname: _____ _____ _____ _____

Sentence: _____ _____ _____ _____

Starting tip: Work out Jesse's surname.

A Dearth of Conversation

Five workers at the multinational Penny Corporation's office complex in Parkville share the same table in the cafeteria every lunch time—but they hardly ever speak to each other, because they're too busy eating, drinking, and reading. From the clues given, can you work out what each member of the quintet ate, drank, and read at lunchtime today?

Clues

1. Barry Cole drank a glass of soda but did not eat egg sandwiches; Kevin Lynn had a (large size) turkey sandwich.

2. Nancy Owen's meal didn't include any bacon, and she wasn't the person reading a travel book about vacations in the Rocky Mountains; Gary Hines was reading the tabloid *Daily Lantern*—or, at least, looking at the pictures.

3. One member of the group read the local paper and drank milk, but did not eat anything containing egg.

4. One of the ladies had egg and bacon for lunch, as she'd missed her breakfast.

5. A cup of very sweet tea and two rounds of greasy bacon sandwiches was the lunch menu selected by one of those at the table; the coffee drinker didn't read the magazine *Daily Bulletin*.

6. The person eating the cheese-and-pickle sandwiches was engrossed in *Murder Must Advertise*, the classic Dorothy L. Sayers whodunnit.

Name	Drink

	Milk	Coffee	Soda	Mineral water	Tea	Bacon sandwiches	Cheese/pickle s'ches	Turkey sandwich	Egg and bacon	Egg sandwiches	Magazine	Local paper	Tabloid paper	Travel book	Whodunnit
Barry Cole															
Gary Hines															
Kevin Lynn															
Nancy Owen															
Sue Taylor															
Magazine															
Local paper															
Tabloid paper															
Travel book															
Whodunnit															
Bacon sandwiches															
Cheese/pickle s'ches															
Turkey sandwich															
Egg and bacon															
Egg sandwiches															

Meal	Reading matter

Dawn Raid

Early this morning police raided five addresses in town and arrested five members of a gang believed to have been involved in a recent major crime. From the following information, can you discover the time that each address was raided, the individual taken into custody, and his criminal specialty?

Clues

1. At 5:05 a.m. the forger's house was raided; neither he nor the man arrested 5 minutes later was Splinters Dave.

2. At 5:07 a.m. Crazy Chris's house was raided.

3. The Copse Road address was raided 10 minutes after the sneak thief was arrested.

4. Smiling Sid's house was raided after the safecracker was arrested on Crooke Street.

5. Getaway driver Wheels Wilf wasn't arrested at 5:20 a.m., and he doesn't live in Laws Close.

6. Ronnie the Rabbit lives on Larson Road.

Time	Address

	Copse Road	Crooke Street	Larson Road	Laws Close	Peel Lane	Crazy Chris	Ronnie the Rabbit	Smiling Sid	Splinters Dave	Wheels Wilf	Car thief	Forger	Getaway driver	Safecracker	Sneak thief
5:05 a.m.															
5:07 a.m.															
5:10 a.m.															
5:15 a.m.															
5:20 a.m.															
Car thief															
Forger															
Getaway driver															
Safecracker															
Sneak thief															
Crazy Chris															
Ronnie the Rabbit															
Smiling Sid															
Splinters Dave															
Wheels Wilf															

Criminal	Specialty

Battleships

Do you remember the old game of battleships? These puzzles are based on that idea. Your task is to find the vessels in the diagram. Some parts of boats or sea squares have already been filled in, and a number next to a row or column refers to the number of occupied squares in that row or column. The boats may be positioned horizontally or vertically, but no two boats or parts of boats are in adjacent squares—horizontally, vertically, or diagonally.

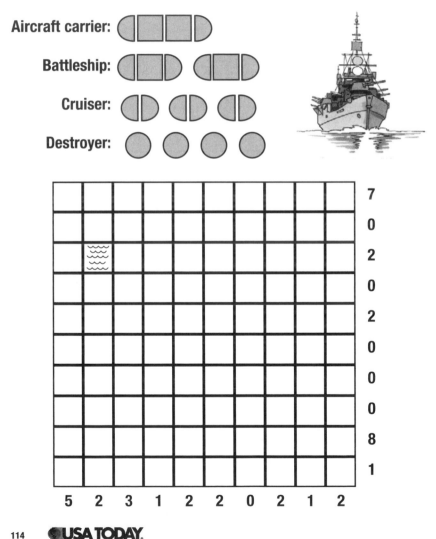

Aircraft carrier:

Battleship:

Cruiser:

Destroyer:

										7
										0
		≈								2
										0
										2
										0
										0
										0
										8
										1
5	2	3	1	2	2	0	2	1	2	

 USA TODAY.

Domino Search

A standard set of dominoes has been laid out, using numbers instead of dots for clarity. Using a sharp pencil and a keen brain, can you draw in the lines to show where each domino has been placed? You may find the check grid useful—crossing off each domino as you find it.

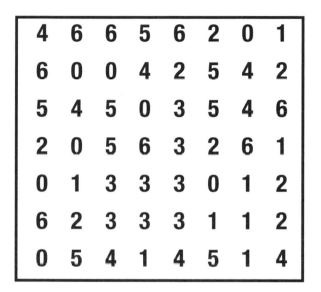

4	6	6	5	6	2	0	1
6	0	0	4	2	5	4	2
5	4	5	0	3	5	4	6
2	0	5	6	3	2	6	1
0	1	3	3	3	0	1	2
6	2	3	3	3	1	1	2
0	5	4	1	4	5	1	4

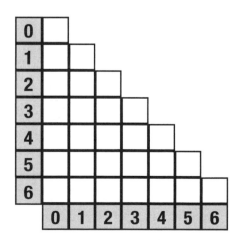

County Girls

Each month *Shire Life,* a British magazine, features a frontispiece photograph of an eligible young lady from the county set and the five girls in this puzzle are featured in this summer's editions. From the information given, can you discover which month's issue contains each girl's photograph, her age, and whose daughter each is?

Clues

1. The issue with the photograph of Phyllis is the month after the 26-year-old is featured, and the month before the Duke of Richworth's daughter.

2. The portrait of Lucinda is in the August issue; she is not the youngest of the five who is not Lord Smart's daughter.

3. Lord and Lady Buck's daughter, who is not Annabel, is featured in May's *Shire Life*.

4. The 25-year-old is in the July issue.

5. Major Weller-Heald's daughter is 23.

6. Samantha is 24 years old.

Month	Girl

	Annabel	Georgina	Lucinda	Phyllis	Samantha	22	23	24	25	26	Hon. Mrs. Broadlands	Lord and Lady Buck	Duke of Richworth	Lord Smart	Major Weller-Heald
May															
June															
July															
August															
September															
Hon. Mrs. Broadlands															
Lord and Lady Buck															
Duke of Richworth															
Lord Smart															
Major Weller-Heald															
22															
23															
24															
25															
26															

	Age	Daughter of

A Week in the Wild

Leading zoologist Gerard Drummle has made a documentary film about his latest expedition to the economically poor but wildlife-rich Tufab region of the African republic of Acirfa, taking his team and the film crew out on each day of one week to a particular part of Tufab in pursuit of a particular endangered species. From the clues below, can you work out where he went each day, what creature he was looking for, and how many specimens of the creature he was able to find and photograph?

Clues

1. On the Thursday of the filmed week, Gerard was looking for the spider-lizard (very much like any other lizard except that it has eight legs); this was later in the week than the trip to Mount Lunku, where Gerard found just 3 specimens.

2. Neither Monday's trip nor the one in pursuit of the rainbow parrot involved a mountain, and both of these trips found fewer specimens than did the one to Mount Borri.

3. The expedition to the D'Kuna Forest was the day after Gerard's team scaled Mount Borri.

4. Gerard's team found more specimens of the ding-bat than of the creature he looked for in the Gwangi Valley.

5. The copper monkey, which takes its name not from its color but from the strange helmet-shaped protrusion on top of its head and its constant cry of "allo, allo, allo," lives only in the trees of the Sporo Plain.

6. Only 2 specimens of the creature being sought on Wednesday were sighted; in contrast, Gerard and his team did photograph and film 9 specimens of the whistling hog.

Day	Area

	D'Kuna Forest	Gwangi Valley	Mount Borri	Mount Lunku	Sporo Plain	Copper monkey	Ding-bat	Rainbow parrot	Spider-lizard	Whistling hog	2	3	6	8	9
Monday															
Tuesday															
Wednesday															
Thursday															
Friday															
2															
3															
6															
8															
9															
Copper monkey															
Ding-bat															
Rainbow parrot															
Spider-lizard															
Whistling hog															

Creature	Number

Codewords

This puzzle has no clues in the conventional sense. Instead, every different number printed in the main grid represents a different letter (with the same number always representing the same letter, of course). For example, if 7 turns out to be a "V," you can write in V wherever a square contains 7. We have completed a very small part of the puzzle to give you a start, but the rest is up to you.

	2	9	20	25	7	12	2	23	12	25		
	1		18		14		7		7		1	
1	22	1	12		18	11	7	11	3	9	11	16
	22		6		1		19		12		23	
22	10	18	7	11	21		4	7	1	12	11	24
	7				7				22			
9	24	10	1	11	3		21	9	21	10	7	3
			6				9				13	
12	1	8	23	12	24		17	23	12	26	9	3
	5		20		15		19		1		10	
19	1	12	1	11	23	9	1		26	12	9	16
			R	**A**	**N**							
	12		3		18		11		26		11	
		20	23	11	21	12	9	6	9	11	16	

A̸ B C D E F G H I J K L M N̸ O P Q R̸ S T U V W X Y Z

1	2	3	4	5	6	7	8	9	10	11	12	13
A										**N**	**R**	
14	15	16	17	18	19	20	21	22	23	24	25	26

TOTALIZED

The 25-second ultimate challenge from **Puzzler Brain Trainer**

Just follow the instructions from top to bottom, starting with the number given to reach an answer at the foot of the ladder.

EASY	MEDIUM	HARDER
9	**54**	**5**
MULTIPLY BY 4	ADD $\frac{1}{2}$ OF IT	TIMES ITSELF
TAKE AWAY 25	DIVIDE BY 9	TIMES ITSELF
MULTIPLY BY 3	MULTIPLY BY 7	TAKE AWAY 94
DOUBLE IT	ADD 13	DIVIDE BY 9
TAKE AWAY 17	ADD $\frac{1}{4}$ OF IT	MULTIPLY BY 3
ADD 6	DIVIDE BY 5	TAKE AWAY 39
DIVIDE BY 5	ADD 39	LESS $\frac{1}{3}$ OF IT
DOUBLE IT	DIVIDE BY 2	DIVIDE BY 4
ADD 49	ADD 14	MULTIPLY BY 7
ANSWER	**ANSWER**	**ANSWER**

Cell Block

Fill the grid by drawing blocks along the grid lines. Each block must contain the number of squares indicated by the digit inside it. Each block must contain only one digit.

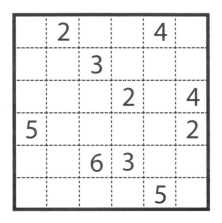

Wordwheel

Using only the letters in the Wordwheel, you have ten minutes to find as many words as possible, none of which may be plurals, foreign words, or proper nouns. Each word must be of three letters or more, all must contain the central letter, and letters can only be used once in every word. There is at least one nine-letter word in the wheel.

Gone Fishin'

The picture below shows Medcalf's Water, a specially created fishing lake, early on a Sunday morning. From the clues below, can you fill in the name of each of the boats on the lake, the name of the angler occupying it, and the number of fish he caught?

Clues

1. Pete Ray has caught 5 fish—although two of them bore a considerable resemblance, and might have been the same fish caught twice!

2. Mick Perch's boat, which has a one-word name, is immediately east of the *Jolly Roger*.

3. The angler in boat D has caught more fish than the man in the *Izaak Walton*, but fewer than Don Bass, who is not in boat A.

4. The angler who has caught just 2 fish is in a boat somewhere east of the *Kitty*.

Boats: *Izaak Walton*; *Jolly Roger*; *Kitty*; *Lorelei*
Anglers: Don Bass; Joe Ling; Mick Perch; Pete Ray
Catches: 2 fish; 3 fish; 4 fish; 5 fish

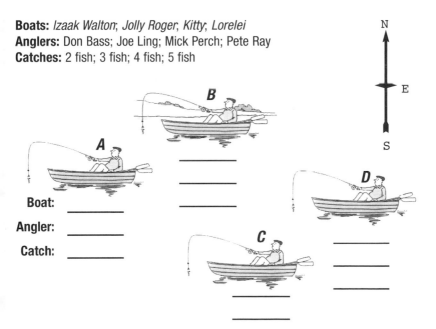

Starting tip: Work out how many fish Don caught.

Five Times Tables

For our daughter's wedding we have arranged the reception seating plan to give a good mix of people at each table, ensuring that there's at least one of the groom's and bride's relations on each table, together with a young friend of the happy couple. From the information given below, can you work out which two relations and friend are at each table?

Clues

1. The bride's Grandma and groom's Uncle Henry are at a table numbered one less than the one where Uncle Frank is sitting.

2. The groom's Auntie Brenda and friend Linda are at a table numbered one less than the one where Grandad is sitting; Grandad is not at the same table as the groom's Uncle Tommy, and the latter is not at table 4.

3. Janet is at table 6 with a relation of the groom whose first name is longer than that of the groom's relation sitting at Mark's table.

4. The bride's Auntie Eileen is at the same table as Ryan, which is not table 3.

5. Uncle Bob is not at the same table as Harriet.

6. Cousin Lou is at table 5.

Table	Bride's relation

	Auntie Eileen	Cousin Lou	Grandad	Grandma	Uncle Frank	Auntie Brenda	Cousin Charles	Uncle Bob	Uncle Henry	Uncle Tommy	Harriet	Janet	Linda	Mark	Ryan
3															
4															
5															
6															
7															
Harriet															
Janet															
Linda															
Mark															
Ryan															
Auntie Brenda															
Cousin Charles															
Uncle Bob															
Uncle Henry															
Uncle Tommy															

Groom's relation	Friend

The Magnificent Six

Shee-La the Golden, peerless swordswoman, and five of her fellow barbarian fantasy heroes (okay, technically Shee-La's a heroine, but does it matter?) are heading
for the city of Port Blackwater to rescue their friend Khull of the Cudgels from the
clutches of Urxxak the Sorcerer. As they're crossing the freezing Icehorn Mountains,
they're all wrapped in warm cloaks, but underneath each of them is disguised as a
member of a respectable Port Blackwater occupation (not that there aren't some
very respectable barbarian fantasy heroes, of course). From the clues given, can
you fill in the name and cognomen (that's the second part of the name) of each
cloaked figure, and say what disguise they're wearing under the cloak?

Clues
1. Topal is immediately right of the warrior known as "the Wolf," who is wearing the
costume of a prosperous merchant under his cloak.

2. The man known as "the Shadow," who specializes in theft and assassination (but
only from and of bad people) is immediately left of the warrior disguised as a shepherd under an all-concealing cloak.

3. Figure C is the exiled Kudrian nobleman named Dionos.

4. Figure D is the warrior known as "the Hawk."

5. The very large barbarian known as "the Colossus," who is not Promero, is somewhere left of the warrior who will enter Port Blackwater in the guise of a peddler.

6. Figure E wears a beggar's rags by way of disguise; the warrior disguised as a
common laborer is somewhere right of the Grizzin tribesman called Lyco.

7. Alarkar is disguised as a Shamarlan cleric under his cloak; he is immediately
right of the warrior whose cognomen is "the Wanderer."

First names: Alarkar; Dionos; Lyco; Promero; Shee-La; Topal
Cognomens: the Colossus; the Hawk; the Golden; the Shadow; the
Wanderer; the Wolf
Disguises: beggar; cleric; shepherd; laborer; merchant; peddler

First name: _____ _____ _____

Cognomen: _____ _____ _____

Disguise: _____ _____ _____

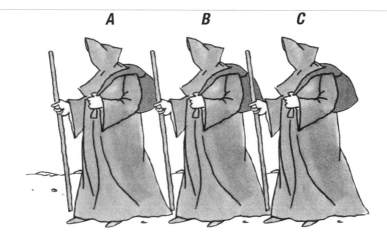

A   B   C

D   E   F

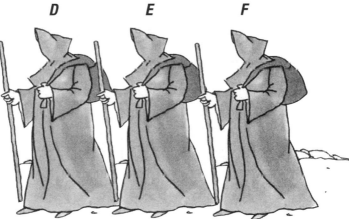

_____ _____ _____

_____ _____ _____

_____ _____ _____

Starting tip: Work out figure F's cognomen.

Pilots

Three people I met the other day were all professional pilots whose main hobby is—what else?—flying. From the clues below, can you work out each one's full name, which aircraft each of them flies professionally, and which one each flies as a hobby?

Clues

1. Bernard is a squadron leader in the RAF, and flies a Tornado for a living; his surname isn't Cayley.

2. Ken's hobby aircraft is a North American Harvard, a trainer from World War II.

3. The pilot who flies a Hercules transport professionally flies a Spitfire for fun.

4. Hannah Wright's father and grandfather were both pilots too.

	Cayley	Maxim	Wright	Boeing 747	Hercules	Tornado	Harvard	Spitfire	Tiger Moth
Bernard									
Hannah									
Ken									
Harvard									
Spitfire									
Tiger Moth									
Boeing 747									
Hercules									
Tornado									

First name	Surname	Work	Hobby

First Night

Four couples who arrived in Portview on the ferry from Bellevue for a vacation spent their first night ashore in adjacent rooms in a local hotel, as shown in the diagram. From the clues given below, can you name the couple in each room and say how each pair spent the following day?

Clues

1. The couple who stayed in the room numbered one lower than Laurens's and Rosa's visited Wilberforce House the following morning and its slave trade exhibition.

2. Magda and her partner stayed in Portview to visit The Deep, and its marine life exhibits.

3. Dirk and his wife, who is not Marijke, were in room 103.

4. The pair in room 104 decided to visit Lincoln Cathedral.

5. Gretchen, whose room bore an even number, was not with Peter.

Males: Dirk; Jan; Laurens; Peter
Females: Gretchen; Magda; Marijke; Rosa
Outings: Beverley Minster; Lincoln Cathedral; The Deep; Wilberforce House

| 101 | 102 | 103 | 104 |

Male: _____ _____ _____ _____

Female: _____ _____ _____ _____

Outing: _____ _____ _____ _____

Starting tip: Begin by naming Dirk's wife.

Find the Lady

Four cards from a standard pack have been laid out in a row on the table in front of four players in the order indicated in the diagram. From the clues given below, can you say to whom each card was dealt?

Clues

1. It's against the odds, but, being a logic problem, no suit or value is repeated, the only court card being a Queen, which is not a Club.

2. Anna's Spade is two places to the right of a 4.

3. Card 3 is three higher than card 1, which wasn't dealt to Katie.

4. The Diamond, dealt to one of the men, is in position 4.

5. The card that is a 10, that was not dealt to Josh, is somewhere to the right of the Heart, but not next to it.

Players: Anna; Josh; Katie; Luke
Suits: Clubs; Diamonds; Hearts; Spades
Cards: 4, 7, 10, Queen

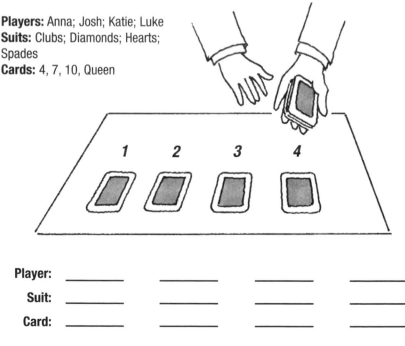

Player:	_____	_____	_____	_____
Suit:	_____	_____	_____	_____
Card:	_____	_____	_____	_____

Starting tip: Start by placing Anna's Spade.

Battleships

Do you remember the old game of battleships? These puzzles are based on that idea. Your task is to find the vessels in the diagram. Some parts of boats or sea squares have already been filled in, and a number next to a row or column refers to the number of occupied squares in that row or column. The boats may be positioned horizontally or vertically, but no two boats or parts of boats are in adjacent squares—horizontally, vertically, or diagonally.

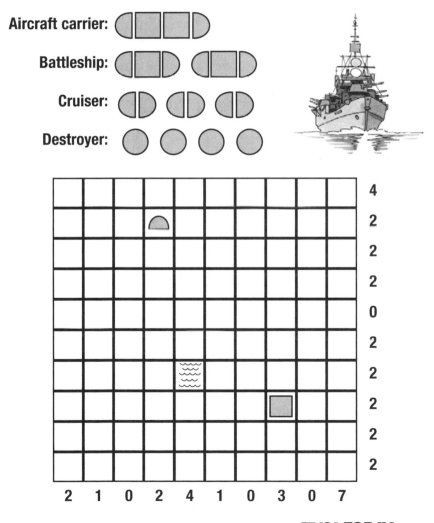

Aircraft carrier:

Battleship:

Cruiser:

Destroyer:

If You Want to Get Ahead

Back in the 1930s, every well-dressed man wore a hat of some kind. The leading man in each of the listed Hollywood movies was no exception. From the clues given below, can you work out which film was made in which year, name its male star, and describe his headgear?

Clues

1. *She Fell for Him* was the name of the film made in 1934.

2. *Coming Home* was shot later than Gene Parker's film, and sometime before the movie whose hero wore a beret.

3. It was, of course, Royston Wallace, star of many western movies, who rode off into the sunset wearing the Stetson he had sported throughout the film.

4. The top hat was worn in the movie made in 1935.

5. The derby, also known as a bowler hat, was worn by the hero of *What's Cooking?*

6. Clark Maybank was the much-admired star of *City Life*, an earlier film than the one whose leading man wore a fedora.

7. Victor O'Sullivan's movie was shot the year before *Stepping Out*.

Year	Movie

	City Life	Coming Home	She Fell for Him	Stepping Out	What's Cooking?	Clark Maybank	Gene Parker	Jefferson Rodgers	Royston Wallace	Victor O'Sullivan	Derby	Fedora	Stetson	Top hat	Beret
1931															
1932															
1933															
1934															
1935															
Derby															
Fedora															
Stetson															
Top hat															
Beret															
Clark Maybank															
Gene Parker															
Jefferson Rodgers															
Royston Wallace															
Victor O'Sullivan															

Hero	Hat

Boys' Toys

Some people, wishing to imply that men never truly mature, say things like "The bigger the boy, the bigger the toy." We're setting out to disprove that here, since all six of the men involved are in their thirties, and the toy they're playing with is quite small—a miniature racetrack that one man's five-year-old got as a present last Christmas. From the clues below, can you fill in on the plan each man's name and occupation, and say which model Grand Prix car he has chosen to use? (On the diagram, A is opposite D, B is opposite E, and C is opposite F.)

Clues

1. Jim, whose car is a BAR, is standing next clockwise from the grocer.

2. The policeman, who is actually the "village constable" for ten villages near Stoneville, is "driving" the Toyota; he is standing immediately clockwise from Phil, who isn't figure A.

3. The electrician is standing diagonally opposite Don.

4. Figure F is Cliff.

5. Figure D is the bricklayer.

6. Figure C is the "driver" of the miniature McLaren; in real life, he is not a professional driver.

7. Ken the cab driver, whose miniature racing car isn't the Renault, is standing immediately counterclockwise from the man with the Williams.

8. Les is standing clockwise next to the truck driver.

Names: Cliff; Don; Jim; Ken; Les; Phil
Occupations: bricklayer; cab driver; electrician; grocer; policeman; truck driver
Car models: BAR; Ferrari; McLaren; Renault; Toyota; Williams

Name: _____

Occupation: _____ _____

Car: _____ _____

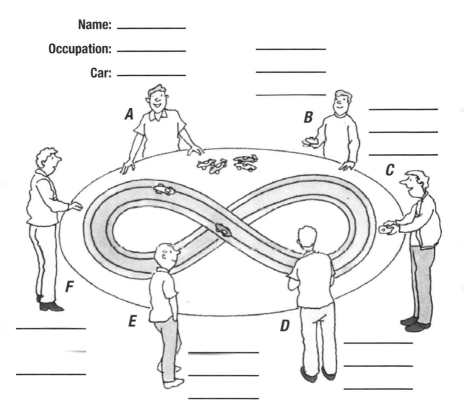

Starting tip: Work out the occupation of figure C.

Domino Search

A standard set of dominoes has been laid out, using numbers instead of dots for clarity. Using a sharp pencil and a keen brain, can you draw in the lines to show where each domino has been placed? You may find the check grid useful—crossing off each domino as you find it.

5	2	0	0	4	6	6	1
1	5	1	2	5	3	1	1
6	6	4	4	3	2	3	3
0	4	3	5	5	5	6	0
0	3	2	3	4	6	2	0
0	5	3	5	4	6	1	0
1	4	6	2	2	1	4	2

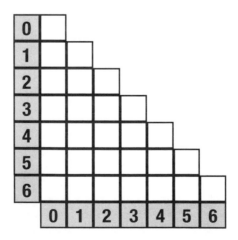

Battleships

Do you remember the old game of battleships? These puzzles are based on that idea. Your task is to find the vessels in the diagram. Some parts of boats or sea squares have already been filled in, and a number next to a row or column refers to the number of occupied squares in that row or column. The boats may be positioned horizontally or vertically, but no two boats or parts of boats are in adjacent squares—horizontally, vertically, or diagonally.

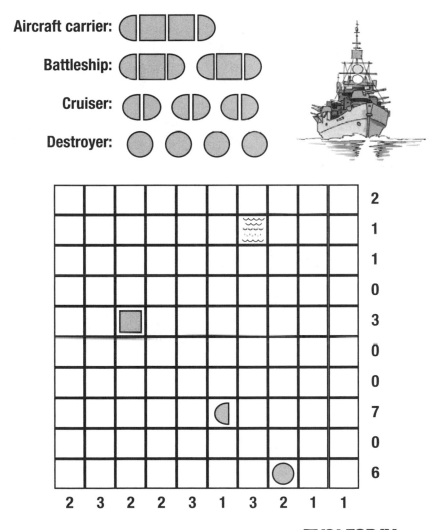

Aircraft carrier:

Battleship:

Cruiser:

Destroyer:

Codewords

This puzzle has no clues in the conventional sense. Instead, every different number printed in the main grid represents a different letter (with the same number always representing the same letter, of course). For example, if 7 turns out to be a "V," you can write in V wherever a square contains 7. We have completed a very small part of the puzzle to give you a start, but the rest is up to you.

	13		20		20	5	17		19		9	
16	3	17	12	5	16		5	16	15	3	18	11
	23		5		5		24		22		10	
20	16 L	5 A	24 P	17	10	5	24		11	12	14	17
	5		16		3		3				16	
15	26	24	5	20	17		23	5	7	23	16	3
26			15						3			7
24	15	18	18	3	23		24	16	5	8	9	3
	20				15		1		4		18	
21	3	10	14		25	15	16	3	18	3	11	11
	13		5		15		14		3		14	
11	14	2	17	3	18		18	14	11	15	16	1
	6		11		22	5	11		11		23	

A̸ B C D E F G H I J K L̸ M N O P̸ Q R S T U V W X Y Z

| 1 | 2 | 3 | 4 | 5 A | 6 | 7 | 8 | 9 | 10 | 11 | 12 | 13 |
| 14 | 15 | 16 L | 17 | 18 | 19 | 20 | 21 | 22 | 23 | 24 P | 25 | 26 |

138 ■USA TODAY.

TOTALIZED

The 25-second ultimate challenge from **Puzzler Brain Trainer**

Just follow the instructions from top to bottom, starting with the number given to reach an answer at the foot of the ladder.

EASY	MEDIUM	HARDER
6	**28**	**17**
MULTIPLY BY 8	DIVIDE BY 7	MULTIPLY BY 4
ADD 17	TIMES ITSELF	ADD 50% OF IT
DIVIDE BY 5	ADD $\frac{1}{4}$ OF IT	TAKE AWAY 46
MULTIPLY BY 10	MULTIPLY BY 6	ADD 75% OF IT
TAKE AWAY 40	DIVIDE BY 12	DIVIDE BY 7
DIVIDE BY 5	MULTIPLY BY 7	TIMES ITSELF
ADD 36	ADD $\frac{1}{2}$ OF IT	TAKE AWAY 72
ADD 45	DIVIDE BY 6	DIVIDE BY 4
DIVIDE BY 9	MULTIPLY BY 3	MULTIPLY BY 6
ANSWER	**ANSWER**	**ANSWER**

Cell Block

Fill the grid by drawing blocks along the grid lines. Each block must contain the number of squares indicated by the digit inside it. Each block must contain only one digit.

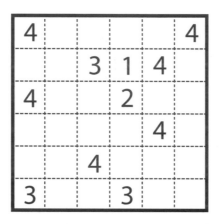

Wordwheel

Using only the letters in the Wordwheel, you have ten minutes to find as many words as possible, none of which may be plurals, foreign words, or proper nouns. Each word must be of three letters or more, all must contain the central letter, and letters can only be used once in every word. There is at least one nine-letter word in the wheel.

Battleships

Do you remember the old game of battleships? These puzzles are based on that idea. Your task is to find the vessels in the diagram. Some parts of boats or sea squares have already been filled in, and a number next to a row or column refers to the number of occupied squares in that row or column. The boats may be positioned horizontally or vertically, but no two boats or parts of boats are in adjacent squares—horizontally, vertically, or diagonally.

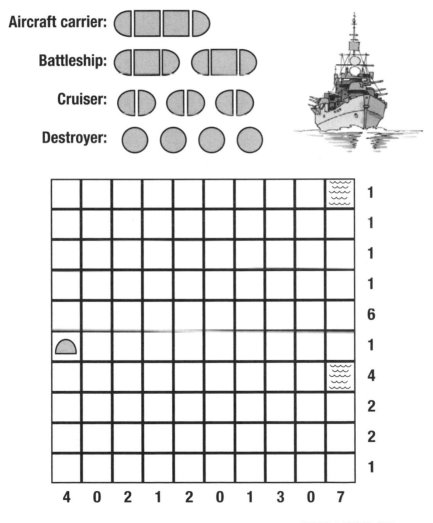

Aircraft carrier:

Battleship:

Cruiser:

Destroyer:

Babylon Valley

Over the years, Australian wines have built up quite a reputation, and recently six wines produced by vineyards along the Babylon Valley have been attracting particular attention. From the clues given, can you fill in on the map the name of each vineyard, the name of the wine produced there, and the type of wine it is?

Clues

1. The vineyard that produces the wine called Southern Sceptre lies due north of the one called Gurrambidgee.

2. The Forest Hill vineyard, which produces a notable dry red wine, is indicated by an even number on the map.

3. The dry white wine comes from vineyard 6, which has a two-word name.

4. The sweet red wine called Eric the Red—it has a Viking on the label—comes from the vineyard immediately east of Cootimumbah.

5. The King's Rock vineyard is indicated by a higher number than the one that produces the sparkling white wine they're not allowed to call champagne, which isn't produced at Platypus Park.

6. The Black Dog vineyard makes the wine called Chateau d'If; it is on the same bank of the River Babylon as the vineyard that produces Horn of Plenty.

7. Vineyard 1 makes the wine called Old Nick, which is apparently smooth but very strong.

8. The vineyard producing the sweet white wine is south of the river.

9. The vineyard producing Horn of Plenty and the one where the medium red is made are in line on the north-south axis.

Vineyards: Black Dog; Cootimumbah; Forest Hill; Gurrambidgee; King's Rock; Platypus Park
Wine names: Bandicoot; Chateau d'If; Eric the Red; Horn of Plenty; Old Nick; Southern Sceptre
Wine types: dry red; dry white; medium red; sparkling white; sweet red; sweet white

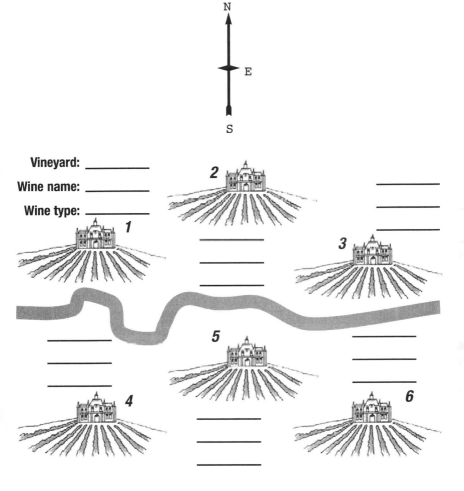

N

E

S

Vineyard: _____
Wine name: _____
Wine type: _____

1

2

3

4

5

6

Captain Gore's Last Stand

The late 18th-century pirate Captain Gore was fierce and merciless when dealing with unarmed merchantmen; but if he ever sighted a vessel that could have made a fight against his *Sea Demon*, he ran away. Then one morning, his four lookouts each sighted something that told him he had upset too many people too often. From the clues can you fill in on the chart the name of each lookout, what he saw approaching, and what flag it was flying?

Clues

1. The pirate lookout called "Hook-hand Harry" was looking in the opposite direction to the man who spotted a British frigate approaching, with her guns run out ready for action.

2. The warship flying the (almost brand-new) American flag was approaching the *Sea Demon* from the west; the vessel bearing down from the north wasn't showing the tricolor of France.

3. "Dirty Dan" was keeping a lookout southward.

4. "Scarface Sam" was looking out in a direction ninety degrees counterclockwise from that from which the 76-gun ship of the line (whose broadsides eventually sent the *Sea Demon* to Davy Jones's locker) was approaching.

5. The armed brig observed by "Mad Malachi" wasn't coming from the east.

Lookouts: "Dirty Dan"; "Hook-hand Harry"; "Mad Malachi"; "Scarface Sam"
Approaching vessels: brig; frigate; ship of the line; sloop
Flags: American; British; French; Spanish

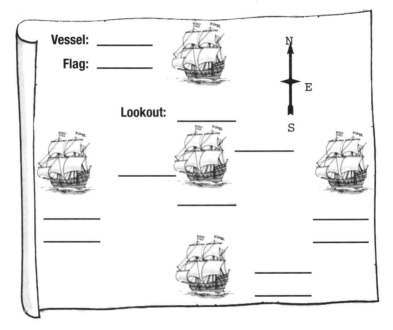

Vessel: _____
Flag: _____

Lookout: _____

N
E
S

Starting tip: Which flag was flown on the northern ship?

Mix and Match

Four neighbors on the same street each had occasion to visit a different one of four shops on the same block the other day. From the clues given below, can you work out who lives at which house, and locate and describe the shop she patronized?

Clues

1. Gill's neighbor in the other half of her duplex visited the grocer's, which is in the same relative position in the line as Eileen's house on the street.

2. Lesley lives at number 7.

3. Tina visited the florist; she is the only one of the four who patronized a shop in the same position in the line as her own house.

4. The woman from number 1 went to have her hair styled at a shop farther left in the block than the one visited by her friend from number 5.

Names: Eileen; Gill; Lesley; Tina
Shops: florist; grocer; hairdresser; health food store

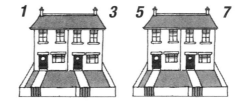

Name: _____ _____   _____ _____

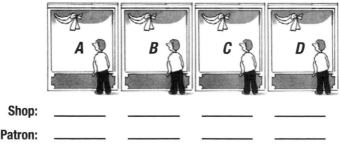

Shop: _____ _____ _____ _____

Patron: _____ _____ _____ _____

Starting tip: Start by identifying shop D.

Bus Stop

Three people are waiting at the High Street West bus stop in Buffalo Town Center, each waiting for a different bus. From the clues given, can you work out each person's full name, their destination, and which number bus they're waiting for?

Clues

1. Carol is waiting for a bus numbered seven above the service that Mrs. Dennis is intending to catch.

2. Penny isn't waiting for the number 14 bus.

3. The 28 service runs from the town center out to Lovel Park.

4. Mrs. Scammell, who is on the way to visit her friend Mandy in the City Hospital, isn't Joan.

	Dennis	Foden	Scammell	City Hospital	Lovel Park	Victoria Bridge	14	21	28
Carol									
Joan									
Penny									
14									
21									
28									
City Hospital									
Lovel Park									
Victoria Bridge									

First name	Surname	Destination	Bus

Dick the Driver

Dick the driver delivers furniture for Madewells Ltd. of Chicago, and yesterday he had three deliveries to make in suburbs not far from town. From the clues below, can you work out the name of each of the ladies he was delivering to, the suburb in which she lives, what time Dick was due there, and what he was delivering?

Clues

1. At 1:00 p.m. Dick, who always keeps strictly to time, delivered the bed, but not in Bolingbrook.

2. Dick delivered a wardrobe to Mrs. Adams, who does not live in Wheaton.

3. Dick visited Wheaton before delivering to Mrs. Bruce's home.

4. Mrs. Cook received her delivery at 11:30 a.m. on the dot.

	Oak Park	Wheaton	Bolingbook	10:00 a.m.	11:30 a.m.	1:00 p.m.	Bed	Dressing table	Wardrobe
Mrs. Adams									
Mrs. Bruce									
Mrs. Cook									
Bed									
Dressing table									
Wardrobe									
10:00 a.m.									
11:30 a.m.									
1:00 p.m.									

Customer	Suburb	Time	Item

Twitchers

Four bird-watchers of the variety known as "twitchers"—who would rather catch a fleeting glimpse of an exotic bird than spend time observing an ordinary one—are crouching in a hide on the Munsmere Marshes nature reserve, doing what they love best. From the clues given, can you fill in each ornithologist's full name and the name of the very unusual bird they're watching?

Clues

1. Robin, who is watching the seldom-seen mud warbler, is next clockwise from Gull.

2. Twitcher B is a Quail, though not, of course, the winged variety.

3. The man in position D was named Jonathan by his parents, but prefers to be known as Jay.

4. Figure A is observing a rare blue swan (it's from the Arctic and hasn't warmed up yet); he or she isn't Mavis, whose surname isn't Finch.

5. Twitcher Wren is not watching an unusual owl-duck, which looks like a cross between—well, I suppose you can imagine.

First names: Jay; Mavis; Mynah; Robin
Surnames: Finch; Gull; Quail; Wren
Birds: blue swan; mud warbler; owl-duck; reedpiper

First name: _____
Surname: _____
Bird: _____

Starting tip: Begin by positioning Robin.

Battleships

Do you remember the old game of battleships? These puzzles are based on that idea. Your task is to find the vessels in the diagram. Some parts of boats or sea squares have already been filled in, and a number next to a row or column refers to the number of occupied squares in that row or column. The boats may be positioned horizontally or vertically, but no two boats or parts of boats are in adjacent squares—horizontally, vertically, or diagonally.

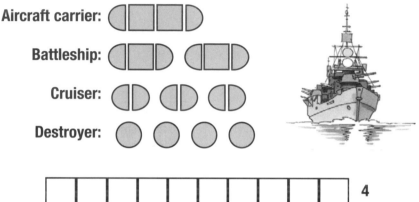

Aircraft carrier:

Battleship:

Cruiser:

Destroyer:

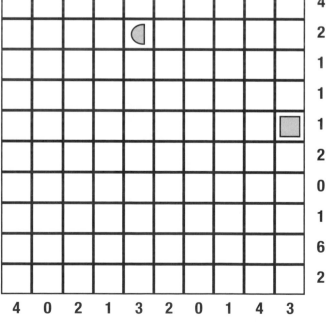

Domino Search

A standard set of dominoes has been laid out, using numbers instead of dots for clarity. Using a sharp pencil and a keen brain, can you draw in the lines to show where each domino has been placed? You may find the check grid useful—crossing off each domino as you find it.

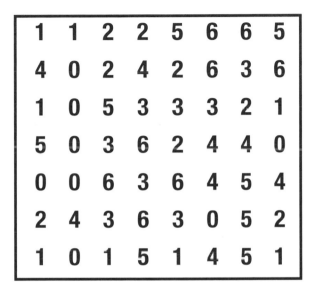

1	1	2	2	5	6	6	5
4	0	2	4	2	6	3	6
1	0	5	3	3	3	2	1
5	0	3	6	2	4	4	0
0	0	6	3	6	4	5	4
2	4	3	6	3	0	5	2
1	0	1	5	1	4	5	1

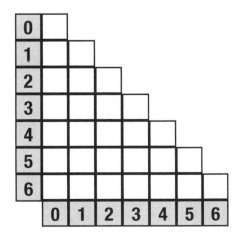

Busy Morning in Black Rock

The Wild West town of Black Rock, Arizona, was generally pretty quiet, but on one memorable morning in the spring of 1881, local lawman Marshal Jed Bigler made no fewer than four arrests of wanted men, thus earning himself considerable fame—and quite a lot in reward money, too! From the clues given, can you work out who he arrested at each of the listed times, what crime the man was wanted for, and where Jed made the arrest?

Clues

1. At 9:50 a.m., Jed arrested the notorious "Red" O'Leary.

2. Jed arrested the rustler while he was having a shave in Mason's Barber Shop, an hour after he had captured "Dutchy" Kruger, who wasn't wanted for bank robbery.

3. The crime for which Nat Diamond was wanted appears in the alphabetical list immediately after the one for which Jed arrested the outlaw he found in the Four Aces Saloon.

4. Jake Morgan, the train robber, wasn't arrested at 11:50 a.m., and wasn't the man the Marshal found in the blacksmith's forge, waiting for his big palomino stallion to be reshod.

Time	Name

	"Dutchy" Kruger	Jake Morgan	Nat Diamond	"Red" O'Leary	Bank robber	Horse thief	Rustler	Train robber	Blacksmith's forge	Doolin's Store	Four Aces Saloon	Mason's Barber Shop
8:50 a.m.												
9:50 a.m.												
10:50 a.m.												
11:50 a.m.												
Blacksmith's forge												
Doolin's Store												
Four Aces Saloon												
Mason's Barber Shop												
Bank robber												
Horse thief												
Rustler												
Train robber												

Crime	Place

Codewords

This puzzle has no clues in the conventional sense. Instead, every different number printed in the main grid represents a different letter (with the same number always representing the same letter, of course). For example, if 7 turns out to be a "V," you can write in V wherever a square contains 7. We have completed a very small part of the puzzle to give you a start, but the rest is up to you.

15		15		13		11		5		14		6
1	20	7	18	20	7	15	8	4		15	11	20
17		7 **R**		22		13		22		24		22
5	17	4 **E**	8	3		26	12	17	8	24	4	5
3		3 **S**		20		12		13				4
	3	8	7	20	19	4	5		23	15	17	7
25		4		22				2		18		3
10	22	5	20		3	23	7	17	13	18	3	
15				3		17		3		4		26
16	12	20	10	8	4	5		1	15	22	20	4
16		7		10		17		20		5		15
4	26	26		5	21	22	15	3	8	17	4	3
5		3		21		11		4		9		8

A B C D E̷ F G H I J K L M N O P Q R̷ S̷ T U V W X Y Z

1	2	3 **S**	4 **E**	5	6	7 **R**	8	9	10	11	12	13
14	15	16	17	18	19	20	21	22	23	24	25	26

TOTALIZED

*The 25-second ultimate challenge from **Puzzler Brain Trainer***

Just follow the instructions from top to bottom, starting with
the number given to reach an answer at the foot of the ladder.

EASY ▼	MEDIUM ▼	HARDER ▼
17	**26**	**11**
ADD 35	LESS 50% OF IT	TIMES ITSELF
DIVIDE BY 4	MULTIPLY BY 3	MULTIPLY BY 5
TAKE AWAY 8	ADD 37	TAKE AWAY 287
MULTIPLY BY 11	DIVIDE BY 4	LESS $^2/_3$ OF IT
TAKE AWAY 27	MULTIPLY BY 6	ADD $^1/_2$ OF IT
DIVIDE BY 7	DIVIDE BY 3	TAKE AWAY 75
MULTIPLY BY 9	ADD 87	DIVIDE BY 4
ADD 33	DIVIDE BY 5	TIMES ITSELF
DIVIDE BY 3	ADD 60% OF IT	TAKE AWAY 65
▼	▼	▼
ANSWER	**ANSWER**	**ANSWER**

Cell Block

Fill the grid by drawing blocks along the grid lines. Each block must contain the number of squares indicated by the digit inside it. Each block must contain only one digit.

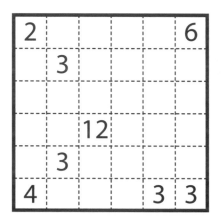

Wordwheel

Using only the letters in the Wordwheel, you have ten minutes to find as many words as possible, none of which may be plurals, foreign words, or proper nouns. Each word must be of three letters or more, all must contain the central letter, and letters can only be used once in every word. There is at least one nine-letter word in the wheel.

Curtain Calls

Four women visited the curtains department of a large store at roughly hourly intervals the other day. From the clues given below, can you name the customer at each time, say for which room she was buying new curtains, and work out the predominant color of the material each chose?

Clues

1. The yellow material was selected for her child's bedroom by a later customer than Sally.

2. Louise visited the store's curtain department at 10:30 that morning.

3. The green curtains were not bought by Joanne, nor were they for use in a living room.

4. Marie purchased some new curtains for her dining room.

5. The curtains for one woman's main bedroom, which were not blue, were selected at 12:30.

Names: Joanne; Louise; Marie; Sally
Rooms: child's bedroom; dining room; living room; main bedroom
Colors: beige; blue; green; yellow

9:30	10:30	11:30	12:30

Name: _____   _____   _____   _____

Room: _____   _____   _____   _____

Color: _____   _____   _____   _____

Starting tip: Begin by naming the 12:30 customer.

Roadside Census

The diagram shows four drivers and their cars, which have been waved over on a busy road to take part in a census to help future road alterations. From the clues given below, can you name the driver of each of cars 1 to 4, say roughly how many miles each is intending to travel, and name the student who took details from each driver?

Clues

1. Bridget interviewed the driver immediately behind the one who was covering 150 miles.

2. The driver of car 3 in the pull-off is Edward, who was not traveling as long a distance as Susan.

3. Ruth, who was not questioned by Daniel, was intending to travel farther than the driver interviewed by Tom, who was not in car 4.

4. George was on a longer journey than the driver immediately behind him in the pull-off.

5. Alison questioned the driver next but one either behind or in front of the one making the shortest trip, who is the same sex as her interviewee.

Drivers: Edward; George; Ruth; Susan
Distances: 25 miles; 90 miles; 150 miles; 200 miles
Students: Alison; Bridget; Daniel; Tom

	1	2	3	4
Driver:	_____	_____	_____	_____
Distance:	_____	_____	_____	_____
Student:	_____	_____	_____	_____

Starting tip: First identify the driver traveling 25 miles.

Halloween Visitors

Our diagram shows a group of four children in costumes paying a trick-or-treat visit to the home of a neighbor on Halloween. From the clues given, can you fully identify the child in each position in the group and describe his or her Halloween costume?

Clues

1. Lewis is on the other side of the neighbor's front door from the child named Walker, who is dressed as a witch.

2. Position 3 is occupied by the youngster named Farmer.

3. Drewery's first name is not Jonathan, while Kirstie is located next but one in the group from the child in the red demon costume.

4. Visitor number 1 is disguised in a sheet to represent a ghost.

5. The "skeleton" is the left-hand neighbor on the doorstep of the child named Coles, who has a longer first name.

First names: Jonathan; Kirstie; Lewis; Miranda
Surnames: Coles; Drewery; Farmer; Walker
Costumes: demon; ghost; skeleton; witch

First name: ————— ————— ————— —————
Surname: ————— ————— ————— —————
Costume: ————— ————— ————— —————

Starting tip: Start by working out the position occupied by Coles.

Metro Musicians

At intervals along a tunnel linking sections of a busy Paris Metro station sit four musicians earning money by entertaining the passing travelers. From the clues given below, can you fully identify the musicians in positions 1 to 4 along the subway, and say which instrument each plays?

Clues

1. As you walk along the subway from left to right, Alphonse is the next musician you encounter after Lemoine, and the next before the accordion player.

2. Didier Charpentier, who does not play the harmonica, is not in position 3.

3. Jean is not Gautier, whose instrument is the guitar.

4. Marcel plays the violin, but his surname is not Fourneau.

First names: Alphonse; Didier; Jean; Marcel
Surnames: Charpentier; Fourneau; Gautier; Lemoine
Instruments: accordion; guitar; harmonica; violin

First name: _____ _____ _____ _____

Surname: _____ _____ _____ _____

Instrument: _____ _____ _____ _____

Starting tip: Begin by placing Didier.

Battleships

Do you remember the old game of battleships? These puzzles are based on that idea. Your task is to find the vessels in the diagram. Some parts of boats or sea squares have already been filled in, and a number next to a row or column refers to the number of occupied squares in that row or column. The boats may be positioned horizontally or vertically, but no two boats or parts of boats are in adjacent squares—horizontally, vertically, or diagonally.

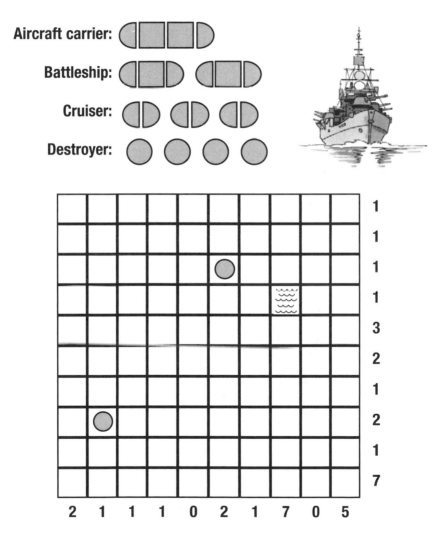

Aircraft carrier:

Battleship:

Cruiser:

Destroyer:

1 1 1 1 3 2 1 2 1 7

2 1 1 1 0 2 1 7 0 5

Domino Search

A standard set of dominoes has been laid out, using numbers instead of dots for clarity. Using a sharp pencil and a keen brain, can you draw in the lines to show where each domino has been placed? You may find the check grid useful—crossing off each domino as you find it.

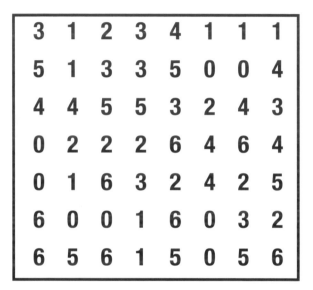

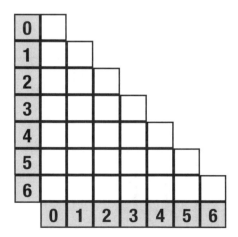

USA TODAY.

Mixed Doubles

The diagram shows a bird's-eye view of a tennis mixed doubles match in the local park. From the clues given below, can you fully identify the players numbered 1 to 4, and say at which aspect of the game each particularly excels?

Clues

1. Unfortunately for Clive, whose strength is his return of serve, he is not player 3, who is about to receive service at the moment depicted in our diagram.

2. Dick and Miss Deuce are doubles partners in the ongoing game.

3. Acey, the player whose passing shots are much admired, is indicated by a number half that denoting Letts.

4. Forehand shots are the best part of the game of player 1, shown about to serve, whose first name is not Suzanne.

> **First names:** Clive; Dick; Melanie; Suzanne
> **Surnames:** Acey; Deuce; Letts; Lobb
> **Best shots:** backhand; forehand; passing shot; return of serve

First name: _____   _____

Surname: _____   _____

Shot: _____   _____

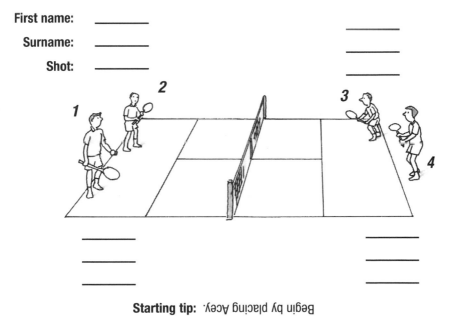

Starting tip: Begin by placing Acey.

Battleships

Do you remember the old game of battleships? These puzzles are based on that idea. Your task is to find the vessels in the diagram. Some parts of boats or sea squares have already been filled in, and a number next to a row or column refers to the number of occupied squares in that row or column. The boats may be positioned horizontally or vertically, but no two boats or parts of boats are in adjacent squares—horizontally, vertically, or diagonally.

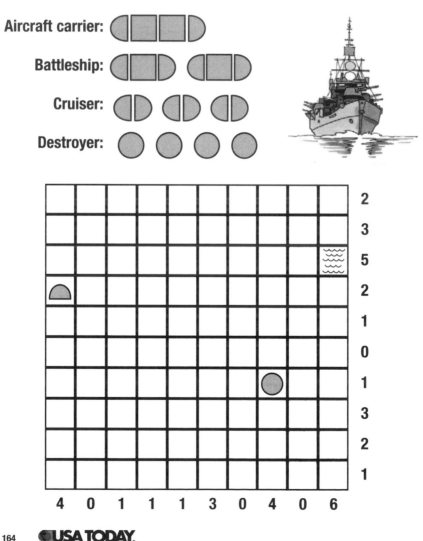

Aircraft carrier:

Battleship:

Cruiser:

Destroyer:

Domino Search

A standard set of dominoes has been laid out, using numbers instead of dots for clarity. Using a sharp pencil and a keen brain, can you draw in the lines to show where each domino has been placed? You may find the check grid useful—crossing off each domino as you find it.

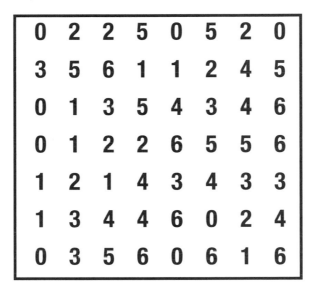

0	2	2	5	0	5	2	0
3	5	6	1	1	2	4	5
0	1	3	5	4	3	4	6
0	1	2	2	6	5	5	6
1	2	1	4	3	4	3	3
1	3	4	4	6	0	2	4
0	3	5	6	0	6	1	6

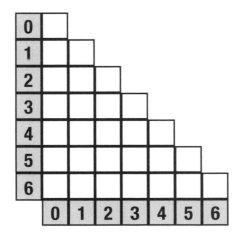

Don't Eat the Bar Snacks!

The picture on the following page shows a sort of street in the fantasy town of Kroprom, where four low-quality taverns stand side by side; it's generally known as Rat Poison Alley, which says it all. From the clues below, can you work out the name of each tavern, the name of its owner, and the one thing they serve there that probably won't kill you? (But if you visit any of them, whatever you do, don't eat the bar snacks!)

Clues

1. The tavern that serves a strong ale that is just about drinkable is immediately left of the notorious Blue Ferret.

2. Hob Stonybroke, who is actually one of the wealthiest men in Kroprom, imports a rum that is generally believed to be nontoxic, although definitely not good for the drinker's general health!

3. The Fox and Werewolf is somewhere to the right of the Dented Drum, which belongs to Egbert Snakehugger (no, don't ask!).

4. Tavern 2 is the Skull and Bones.

5. Tavern 3, which sells quite a pleasant white "wine" (real wine, of course, is made with grapes), doesn't belong to the sinister widow known ironically as Mother Hood.

Taverns: Blue Ferret; Dented Drum; Fox and Werewolf; Skull and Bones

Owners: Clem Grimmett; Egbert Snakehugger; Hob Stonybroke; Mother Hood

Drinks: ale; brandy; rum; wine

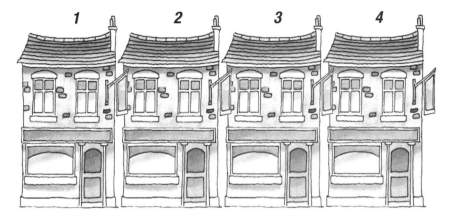

	1	2	3	4
Tavern:	_____	_____	_____	_____
Owner:	_____	_____	_____	_____
Drink:	_____	_____	_____	_____

Starting tip: Decide which numbered tavern serves ale.

Battleships

Do you remember the old game of battleships? These puzzles are based on that idea. Your task is to find the vessels in the diagram. Some parts of boats or sea squares have already been filled in, and a number next to a row or column refers to the number of occupied squares in that row or column. The boats may be positioned horizontally or vertically, but no two boats or parts of boats are in adjacent squares—horizontally, vertically, or diagonally.

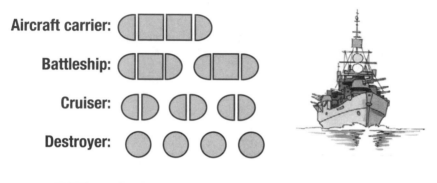

Aircraft carrier:

Battleship:

Cruiser:

Destroyer:

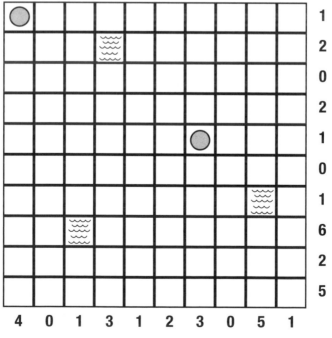

Staff Shortages

This morning, three trains that should have left MaidenRail's Dukes Road Station in Washington DC at 8:30 a.m. failed to do so because of what were announced as "staff shortages"—the drivers didn't turn up. From the clues given, can you work out the full name of each driver, when he eventually turned up, and the reason he was so late?

Clues

1. Mr. Gresley's all-electric home had suffered a power cut, leaving his family without light, heat, cooking facilities—or even an alarm clock!

2. Brian got to work later than Mr. Bulleid, who wasn't the driver delayed by being stuck in traffic.

3. Nick Stanier is one of MaidenRail's top-ranked drivers.

4. One driver couldn't get in until 10:00 a.m. because his rabbit had been taken ill overnight and he had to make sure it was all right before setting out for work.

	Rabbit taken ill	Power cut	Stuck in traffic	9:45 a.m.	10:00 a.m.	10:15 a.m.	Bulleid	Gresley	Stanier
Brian									
Nick									
Victor									
Bulleid									
Gresley									
Stanier									
9:45 a.m.									
10:00 a.m.									
10:15 a.m.									

First name	Surname	Arrival time	Reason

Codewords

This puzzle has no clues in the conventional sense. Instead, every different number printed in the main grid represents a different letter (with the same number always representing the same letter, of course). For example, if 7 turns out to be a "V," you can write in V wherever a square contains 7. We have completed a very small part of the puzzle to give you a start, but the rest is up to you.

22		9		19		21		13		12		21
20	4	14	24	10	23	16		21	1	2	4	16
4		24		6		17		7		4		22
6	21	6	6	3		20	21	2	17	4	26	
24		17		2		25		10				22
25	21	10	6		25	21	12	6	4	16	10	21
4		4		9				4		8		23
6	21	14	14	21	17	24	14		18	11	6	15
			R	A	T							
21				10		2		7		21		20
	16	6	24	14	4	26		14	21	26	10	24
21		4		10		4		10		14		14
12	14	21	5	4		16	10	17	23	24	25	16
4		14		16		17		16		6		4

~~A~~ B C D E F G H I J K L M N O P ~~Q~~ ~~R~~ S ~~T~~ U V W X Y Z

1	2	3	4	5	6	7	8	9	10	11	12	13
14	15	16	17	18	19	20	21	22	23	24	25	26
R			T				A					

TOTALIZED

The 25-second ultimate challenge from **Puzzler Brain Trainer**

Just follow the instructions from top to bottom, starting with the number given to reach an answer at the foot of the ladder.

EASY	MEDIUM	HARDER
4	**9**	**27**
MULTIPLY BY 8	MULTIPLY BY 4	MULTIPLY BY 9
DOUBLE IT	ADD $\frac{1}{2}$ OF IT	LESS $33\frac{1}{3}$ OF IT
TAKE AWAY 22	ADD 30	ADD 28
DIVIDE BY 7	DIVIDE BY 12	LESS $\frac{3}{5}$ OF IT
MULTIPLY BY 12	TIMES ITSELF	ADD $\frac{3}{4}$ OF IT
TAKE AWAY 23	MULTIPLY BY 3	ADD 47
DIVIDE BY 7	TAKE AWAY 63	$\frac{5}{9}$ OF IT
MULTIPLY BY 8	LESS 25% OF IT	DIVIDE BY 4
ADD 27	DIVIDE BY 7	TIMES ITSELF
ANSWER	**ANSWER**	**ANSWER**

Cell Block

Fill the grid by drawing blocks along the grid lines. Each block must contain the number of squares indicated by the digit inside it. Each block must contain only one digit.

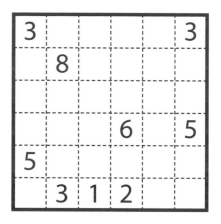

Wordwheel

Using only the letters in the Wordwheel, you have ten minutes to find as many words as possible, none of which may be plurals, foreign words, or proper nouns. Each word must be of three letters or more, all must contain the central letter, and letters can only be used once in every word. There is at least one nine-letter word in the wheel.

Battleships

Do you remember the old game of battleships? These puzzles are based on that idea. Your task is to find the vessels in the diagram. Some parts of boats or sea squares have already been filled in, and a number next to a row or column refers to the number of occupied squares in that row or column. The boats may be positioned horizontally or vertically, but no two boats or parts of boats are in adjacent squares—horizontally, vertically, or diagonally.

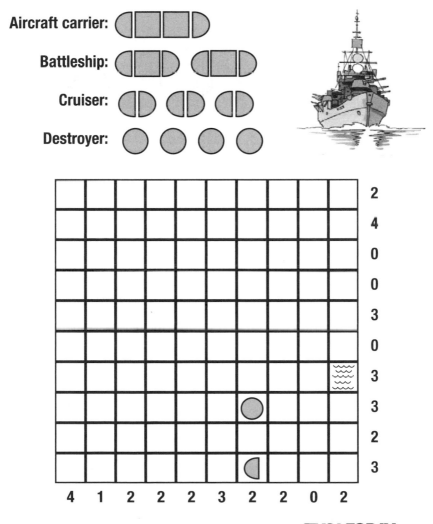

Aircraft carrier:

Battleship:

Cruiser:

Destroyer:

										2
										4
										0
										0
										3
										0
										3
										3
										2
										3
4	1	2	2	2	3	2	2	0	2	

Battleships

Do you remember the old game of battleships? These puzzles are based on that idea. Your task is to find the vessels in the diagram. Some parts of boats or sea squares have already been filled in, and a number next to a row or column refers to the number of occupied squares in that row or column. The boats may be positioned horizontally or vertically, but no two boats or parts of boats are in adjacent squares—horizontally, vertically, or diagonally.

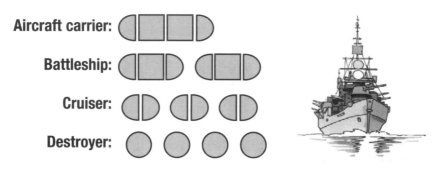

Aircraft carrier:

Battleship:

Cruiser:

Destroyer:

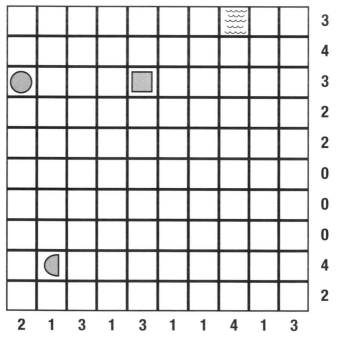

3
4
3
2
2
0
0
0
4
2

2 1 3 1 3 1 1 4 1 3

USA TODAY.

Fathers and Sons

They had a "Bring Your Child to Work" day at Albion-TV the other day, and the picture below shows four male Albion employees with their sons outside the studios at lunch time. From the clues given, can you work out the name of each man, his job with Albion-TV, and his son's name?

Clues

1. The newsreader is adult C in the picture; his son isn't called Brendan.

2. Ken Spooner, who brought his 10-year-old Toby to work with him, isn't an engineer.

3. Ian Wilsher and his son are immediately left of the studio fireman and his 9-year-old Harry.

4. The pair at A are Terry Lucas and his son.

Fathers: Eddie Price; Ian Wilsher; Ken Spooner; Terry Lucas
Occupations: cameraman; engineer; fireman; newsreader
Sons: Brendan; Harry; Paul; Toby

Father:	_____	_____	_____	_____
Occupation:	_____	_____	_____	_____
Son:	_____	_____	_____	_____

Starting tip: Decide in which position Harry is standing.

Police News

Today's issue of the *New Lincoln Post-Herald*, the daily newspaper of that city, contains news stories about four members of the New Lincoln Police Department— or "New Lincoln's Finest," as they like to be known. From the clues below, can you work out each man's name and rank, which of the city's precincts he's attached to, and the nature of the story featured in the paper?

Clues

1. Gil Fernandez features in a story of how he rescued a baby from a car sinking in the city's West River after a traffic accident on Riverside Drive; Detective Harvey McCuen is not the cop reported to be recovering in the hospital after a heart attack.

2. Bernie Carlson, whose rank is not Patrolman, is attached to the 24th Precinct, over in the Midtown area.

3. The Sergeant, who does not have a six-letter first name, made the headlines by arresting the jewel thief known as "the Broadway Burglar."

4. Ollie Stein's precinct, which is not the 10th, has a lower number than the one to which the police officer who has been charged with corruption is attached.

Name	Rank

	Detective	Lieutenant	Patrolman	Sergeant	10th	14th	24th	27th	Arrested burglar	Corruption charges	Heart attack	Rescued baby
Bernie Carlson												
Gil Fernandez												
Harvey McCuen												
Ollie Stein												
Arrested burglar												
Corruption charges												
Heart attack												
Rescued baby												
10th												
14th												
24th												
27th												

Precinct	Story

My Guests This Evening

Perry McGee started out as a comedian, then became a successful singer as well; now he has his own TV show, which features many international guest stars—none of whom sing or tell jokes. From the clues below, can you work out the details of the guests on his show last week—the full name of the person who filled each of the five guest slots and what it is that they do?

Clues

1. Perry's first guest, whose first name was not Tristan, was a juggler in the grand tradition.

2. The third guest was surnamed Karrol; Lauren, who took the fourth guest spot, is not Bergin.

3. Matt appeared immediately after Chang and immediately before the illusionist, who finished by making a young lady disappear from a plastic ball suspended in midair.

4. Bergin isn't the pianist, who at least got to duet with Perry—playing while the great man sang.

5. Finley is an incredibly skilled impressionist, reproducing the voices of all kinds of celebrities, politicians, and real people—but, on this occasion, no comedians or singers.

6. Dominic Hepburn flew over from his home in Switzerland specially to do the show.

Spot	First name

	Cheryl	Dominic	Lauren	Matt	Tristan	Bergin	Chang	Finley	Hepburn	Karrol	Illusionist	Impressionist	Juggler	Pianist	Tap dancer
First															
Second															
Third															
Fourth															
Fifth															
Illusionist															
Impressionist															
Juggler															
Pianist															
Tap dancer															
Bergin															
Chang															
Finley															
Hepburn															
Karrol															

Surname	Act

Relics of the Railroad

At a railroad museum, eight locomotives are on display on a turntable, in the positions shown in the diagram. From the clues given below, can you work out the name carried by each train, and name the exact year in which it was built?

Clues

1. *Prairie King* occupies a diametrically opposite position on the turntable from the engine built in 1857.

2. *Cowpuncher* was built in the same decade as the loco in position 6.

3. *Apache* bears a number in the diagram two lower than the loco built in 1861.

4. *Stampede* was the name given to loco 2 on the turntable because of its effect in the early days as it steamed across cow country; it was not built in the 1870s.

5. *Little Lucy* was constructed for switching duties in 1869.

6. The most recently built loco, dating from 1893, is in position 8.

7. The nameplate of loco 5, which was not built in 1886, carries fewer letters than that of loco 1, which is the immediate predecessor datewise of *Iron Maiden*.

8. *Goliath*'s position is indicated by a number half that denoting the loco built in 1878.

Locomotives: *Apache; Cowpuncher; Goliath; Iron Maiden; Leviathan; Little Lucy; Prairie King; Stampede*
Years built: 1857; 1861; 1869; 1874; 1878; 1886; 1890; 1893

Locomotive: _____
Year built: _____

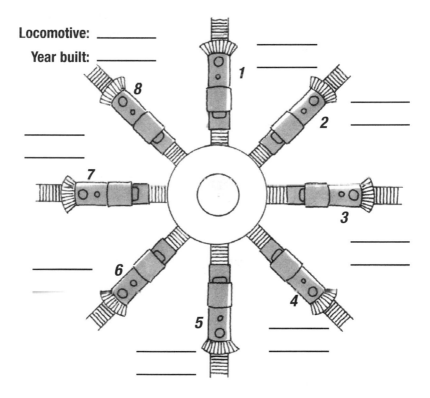

Starting tip: Begin by placing *Goliath.*

Poker Faces

At a top casino in Monaco, six of the world's most successful poker players are competing for the Monte Carlo Trophy and, more importantly, prize money of one million dollars. At this stage of the game, each of the six has a hand that could be a winner. From the clues given, can you fill in on the plan the name of each player, the city where they're normally resident these days, and what potentially winning hand they're holding?

Clues

1. Tony Morgan from Manchester is not the player in seat F.

2. Sam Cleary is sitting directly opposite the player based in Singapore, who is holding "threes"—in this case the sixes of clubs, hearts, and diamonds; the latter's seat is indicated by an earlier letter of the alphabet.

3. The player from Atlantic City, New Jersey, occupies a seat indicated by an earlier letter of the alphabet than that marking the position of the person holding a "straight," meaning five cards in sequence regardless of suit, which in this case are the eight of clubs, seven and six of spades, five of diamonds, and four of hearts.

4. Ernie Lambros is occupying seat B.

5. The player in seat A is holding a "full house"—that is, three cards of one denomination and two of another, in this case the twos of clubs, hearts, and diamonds, and the fives of spades and clubs.

6. Stu Fontana, who is holding "fours"—the nines of all four suits, is sitting alongside the London-based player on the same side of the table.

7. Player C, who comes from, and, indeed, owns a casino in, Las Vegas, Nevada (won with three kings and a perfect poker face), who is not the player holding "two pairs" of kings and threes, is not Leo Kang; the player in seat E does not live in Vancouver, Canada.

Players: "Dandy" Penn; Ernie Lambros; Leo Kang; Sam Cleary; Sto Fontana; Tony Morgan

Hometowns: Atlantic City; Las Vegas; London; Manchester; Singapore; Vancouver

Hands (in ascending order of value): two pairs; threes; straight; full house; fours; royal flush

Player: _____

Home: _____

Hand: _____

Starting tip: Work out where the player from Singapore is sitting.

Battleships

Do you remember the old game of battleships? These puzzles are based on that idea. Your task is to find the vessels in the diagram. Some parts of boats or sea squares have already been filled in, and a number next to a row or column refers to the number of occupied squares in that row or column. The boats may be positioned horizontally or vertically, but no two boats or parts of boats are in adjacent squares—horizontally, vertically, or diagonally.

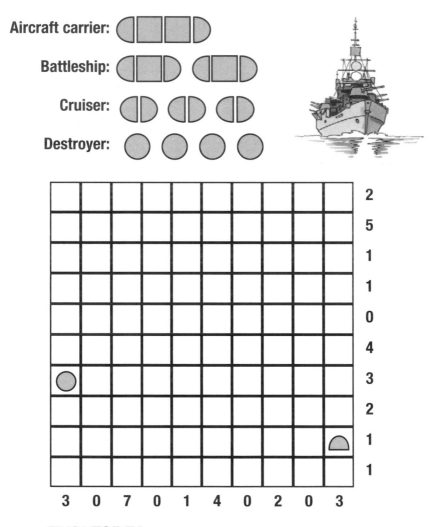

Aircraft carrier:

Battleship:

Cruiser:

Destroyer:

Domino Search

A standard set of dominoes has been laid out, using numbers instead of dots for clarity. Using a sharp pencil and a keen brain, can you draw in the lines to show where each domino has been placed? You may find the check grid useful—crossing off each domino as you find it.

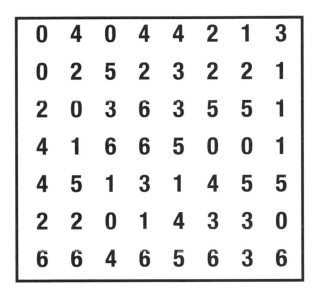

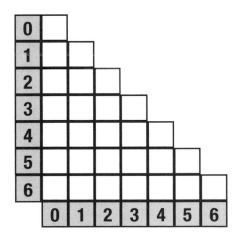

Romantic Writers

Five female romantic novelists are busily working on their latest titles for publisher Moon and Bills. From the information given below, can you work out where each likes to work while writing, the number of words each aims to produce each day, and the title of each author's latest romantic novel?

Clues

1. Virginia Champion is working on *Hearts Are Trumps*, and aims to write more words daily than Amanda Fancy.

2. Miss Fancy does not work in her conservatory; neither the writer who does, nor the one who uses her library, is the author producing 2,000 words a day toward *For Love or Money*.

3. The writer who works in her library is neither the one writing 3,000 words a day nor the one working on *Change of Heart*.

4. The author working away in her study produces 2,000 more words a day than the one writing *A Summer Affair*.

5. The highest output comes from the writer in the summerhouse.

6. Betty Sansom aims to write 4,000 words daily, while Maria Darcy works in a converted room above her garage.

Novelist	Work room

	Conservatory	Library	Room over garage	Study	Summerhouse	2,000	3,000	4,000	5,000	6,000	Change of Heart	For Love or Money	Hearts Are Trumps	The House on the Green	A Summer Affair
Virginia Champion															
Maria Darcy															
Amanda Fancy															
Candida Moore															
Betty Sansom															
Change of Heart															
For Love or Money															
Hearts Are Trumps															
The House on the Green															
A Summer Affair															
2,000															
3,000															
4,000															
5,000															
6,000															

Words per day	Latest novel

Codewords

This puzzle has no clues in the conventional sense. Instead, every different number printed in the main grid represents a different letter (with the same number always representing the same letter, of course). For example, if 7 turns out to be a "V," you can write in V wherever a square contains 7. We have completed a very small part of the puzzle to give you a start, but the rest is up to you.

14		12		5		2		18		8		26
26	3	5	6	19		24	25	17	5	19	26	19 **S**
15		1		2		18		10		22		4 **P**
5	15	1	17	11	14	26		4	22	2	6	2 **O**
26		11		8		13				25		17
	16	26	15	6		6	17	15	15	26	11	19
12				26				5				26
8	13	13	17	19	26	1		13	2	2	19	
24		2				25		26		1		23
25	5	4	26	15		2	17	6	19	5	7	26
5		5		2		23		5		2		11
13	8	15	9	2	15	19		26	20	17	8	11
19		14		21		9		19		19		19

A B C D E F G H I J K L M N Ø P Q R Ŗ T U V W X Y Z

1	2 **O**	3	4 **P**	5	6	7	8	9	10	11	12	13
14	15	16	17	18	19 **S**	20	21	22	23	24	25	26

TOTALIZED

*The 25-second ultimate challenge from **Puzzler Brain Trainer***

Just follow the instructions from top to bottom, starting with
the number given to reach an answer at the foot of the ladder.

EASY	MEDIUM	HARDER
11	**17**	**13**
MULTIPLY BY 8	MULTIPLY BY 4	MULTIPLY BY 14
TAKE AWAY 37	ADD 137	ADD 50% OF IT
DIVIDE BY 3	DIVIDE BY 5	TAKE AWAY 84
MULTIPLY BY 5	ADD 33	LESS $\frac{5}{9}$ OF IT
TAKE AWAY 28	ADD $\frac{1}{2}$ OF IT	ADD $\frac{2}{3}$ OF IT
MULTIPLY BY 2	MULTIPLY BY 3	DIVIDE BY 28
TAKE AWAY 49	DIVIDE BY 9	CUBE IT
DIVIDE BY 5	MULTIPLY BY 6	TAKE AWAY 30
ADD 42	ADD $\frac{1}{2}$ OF IT	LESS $\frac{1}{5}$ OF IT
▼	▼	▼
ANSWER	**ANSWER**	**ANSWER**

Cell Block

Fill the grid by drawing blocks along the grid lines. Each block must contain the number of squares indicated by the digit inside it. Each block must contain only one digit.

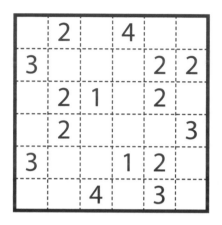

Wordwheel

Using only the letters in the Wordwheel, you have ten minutes to find as many words as possible, none of which may be plurals, foreign words, or proper nouns. Each word must be of three letters or more, all must contain the central letter, and letters can only be used once in every word. There is at least one nine-letter word in the wheel.

Sea View

Four female senior citizens of Brighton braved the gale-force winds on New Year's Day to take their regular stroll along the promenade, stopping off as usual to rest in a seafront shelter and make conversation while watching the seagulls, who had no choice about facing up to the forces of nature. From the clues given below, can you name each of the women in positions 1 to 4 on the seat, and work out their respective ages?

Clues

1. The woman in position 2 is the immediate junior of Nora.

2. Doris is older than her friend in position 1 on the seat, but younger than Mrs. Viggar.

3. As you look at the picture, Madge is sitting immediately to the right of Mrs. Allweather, who is not as old as her.

4. Mrs. Stout is the immediate senior of the four to Lottie, who is seated between her and the woman aged 83 on the bench in the shelter.

First names: Doris; Lottie; Madge; Nora
Surnames: Allweather; Hardy; Stout; Viggar
Ages: 77; 79; 83; 85.

First name: _____   _____   _____   _____

Surname: _____   _____   _____   _____

Age: _____   _____   _____   _____

Starting tip: First name the youngest woman.

On Patrol

Our diagram shows four patrol cars that have just set off from the police station on Letsby Avenue, each heading in a different direction. From the clues given below, can you fully identify the driver of each car, and work out the first name of his partner in the passenger seat?

Clues

1. Sergeant Sargent and his partner are not the crew of the car heading west.

2. Bradley is not Elmett, whose passenger is Wayne, and another of the cars is manned by Kevin and Alan.

3. Colin is driving due south.

4. Lewis Cuff is driving the car heading in exactly the opposite direction from the one in which Joe is traveling.

5. The car driven by Pincham is going due east.

Drivers' first names: Bradley; Colin; Kevin; Lewis
Surnames: Cuff; Elmett; Pincham; Sargent
Partners: Alan; Daniel; Joe; Wayne

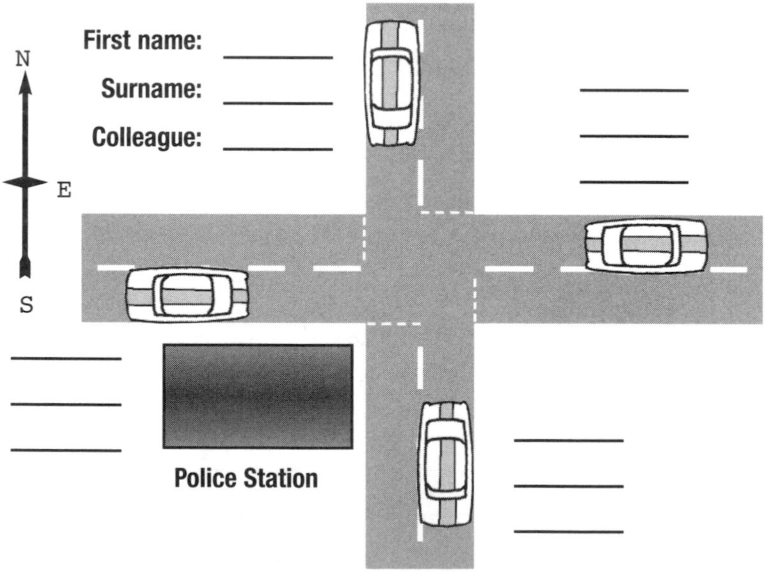

First name: _____
Surname: _____
Colleague: _____

N

E

S

Police Station

Starting tip: Begin by naming Cuff's partner.

Battleships

Do you remember the old game of battleships? These puzzles are based on that idea. Your task is to find the vessels in the diagram. Some parts of boats or sea squares have already been filled in, and a number next to a row or column refers to the number of occupied squares in that row or column. The boats may be positioned horizontally or vertically, but no two boats or parts of boats are in adjacent squares—horizontally, vertically, or diagonally.

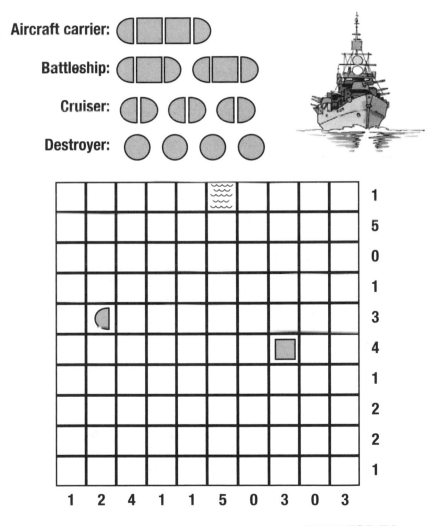

Aircraft carrier:

Battleship:

Cruiser:

Destroyer:

				~						1
										5
										0
										1
										3
										4
										1
										2
										2
										1
1	2	4	1	1	5	0	3	0	3	

Showing This Week

What used to be the Athenaeum Cinema in Redding has just become a multi-screen—well, a triple-screen, anyway. From the clues below, can you work out which film is currently showing on each of the three and the names of its male and female stars?

Clues

1. *Assassin*, the action-adventure movie starring Ben Tyrrell, isn't showing on Screen 1.

2. *Star Ranger*, the science-fiction blockbuster showing on Screen 2, is not the movie starring Steve Jay and his real-life partner Marion Du Nord.

3. Candy Kaine does not appear in the film showing on Screen 3.

	Assassin	14th Street	Star Ranger	Ben Tyrrell	Nic Decker	Steve Jay	Candy Kaine	Marion Du Nord	Tina St. John
Screen 1									
Screen 2									
Screen 3									
Candy Kaine									
Marion Du Nord									
Tina St. John									
Ben Tyrrell									
Nic Decker									
Steve Jay									

Screen	Film	Male star	Female star

Couples

Three co-workers from PennyCorp's St. Louis administration center are taking their wives to a costume party at the company's social club. From the clues below, can you work out the first names and surname of each couple, and which famous couple they've decided to dress as for the dance?

Clues

1. Howard is not Mr. Mason, who has hired Romeo and Juliet costumes for himself and his wife to wear to the dance.

2. Susan Smith and her husband have only been married for a year.

3. Mark and his wife are going to the dance as Caesar and Cleopatra.

4. Judy and her husband are going to the dance as Sonny and Cher.

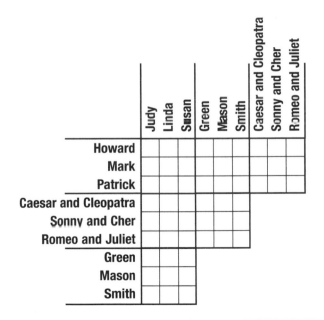

Husband	Wife	Surname	Costume

Superheroes

Miracle Comics has just introduced four new superhero titles, each featuring the usual mild-mannered average citizen who has somehow acquired unusual abilities and decided to become a costumed crime-fighter, taking on the bad guys in and around their hometown. From the clues given, can you work out each one's real name and occupation, the secret superhero identity they've adopted, and the fictional town in which they're based?

Clues

1. It is, of course, Patsy Ryan who turns into superstrong Powerwoman—that would be rather too good a disguise for a male crime fighter!

2. The superhero based in San Marco (a fictitious California town based on San Francisco) works as a film critic for a city newspaper in his or her normal identity.

3. The hero known as Blue Flash, who has a number of electricity-based abilities, operates in Ocean City, an East Coast community based on Atlantic City, New Jersey; his real name isn't Bill Colman.

4. The Champion, whose superpowers relate to skills with all kinds of weapons, is a songwriter when he's not fighting crime; the librarian is not Shadowman, who has the power to disappear in anything less than the brightest light.

5. Ray Salvio, who couldn't write a song to save his life, pursues his career as a costumed crimefighter in the Nevada city of Las Piedras, which is based on Las Vegas.

Real name	Occupation

  **USA TODAY.**

	Film critic	Gem cutter	Librarian	Songwriter	Blue Flash	Powerwoman	Shadowman	The Champion	Crescent Falls	Las Piedras	Ocean City	San Marco
Bill Colman												
Jack Kreski												
Patsy Ryan												
Ray Salvio												
Crescent Falls												
Las Piedras												
Ocean City												
San Marco												
Blue Flash												
Powerwoman												
Shadowman												
The Champion												

Superhero	City

The Arena of Death

In the course of her latest quest, Shee-La the Golden, peerless swordswoman of the fantasy realm, has found herself sentenced to fight to the death in the arena at Xarkaz against four champion gladiators. (Don't worry—she survives.) The picture below shows the arena at the start of the combat; from the clues given, can you work out the name of each of Shee-La's opponents, where he's from, and his chosen weapon or weapons?

Clues

1. The Pellian fighter is armed with the traditional short-stabbing spear of his people; the man with the battle-axe is not from Auzakia.

2. Sebru the Dagonian comes, not too surprisingly, from the mountains of Dagonia; Orklaga, who is not gladiator A, is armed with the classic net and trident.

3. Gladiator C is carrying a sword and round shield.

4. Gladiator D, Garogh, is not from Pellia.

First names: Garogh; Orklaga; Sebru; Thespius
Homelands: Auzakia; Dagonia; Pellia; Sogdia
Weapons: battle-axe; net and trident; spear; sword and shield

Name: _____ _____
Homeland: _____ _____
Weapon: _____

A

D

B

C

Starting tip: Begin by placing Orklaga.

Battleships

Do you remember the old game of battleships? These puzzles are based on that idea. Your task is to find the vessels in the diagram. Some parts of boats or sea squares have already been filled in, and a number next to a row or column refers to the number of occupied squares in that row or column. The boats may be positioned horizontally or vertically, but no two boats or parts of boats are in adjacent squares—horizontally, vertically, or diagonally.

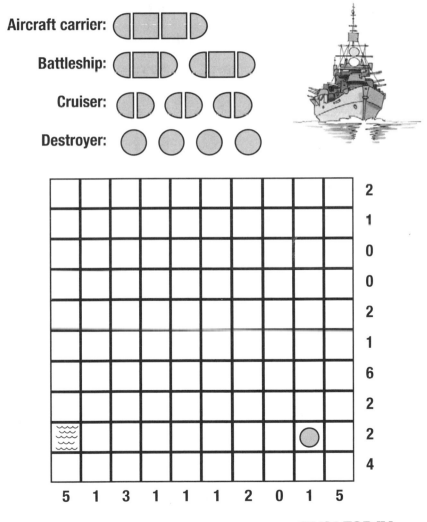

Aircraft carrier:

Battleship:

Cruiser:

Destroyer:

										2
										1
										0
										0
										2
										1
										6
										2
≈							○			**2**
										4
5	**1**	**3**	**1**	**1**	**1**	**2**	**0**	**1**	**5**	

Wanted Men

The poster on the following page was issued by the Sheriff of Calder County, Arizona, back in 1878, following a raid on the Cattleman's Bank there and the shooting of two citizens by the notorious Hole in the Rock Gang. From the clues given, can you fill in on the poster the first name, nickname, and surname of each of the wanted men?

Clues

1. The outlaw nicknamed Windy is pictured immediately above Samuel Mitchell.

2. Tiger is shown immediately to the right of Clayton.

3. The man in picture 4, who was nicknamed Cheyenne after his home town in Wyoming, had a first name more than six letters long.

4. Jonathan wasn't Rawlins, who was the youngest member of the gang.

5. The outlaw nicknamed Gato—Spanish for cat—is shown somewhere vertically below the veteran badman Greeley.

6. Picture 3 shows the army deserter surnamed Lubbock.

7. Dickinson's picture appears immediately above Bartholomew's.

8. Nathaniel, who preferred to be known as Ace, is shown in the picture numbered immediately below Lester's; Lester and David are pictured in different columns on the poster.

First names: Bartholomew; David; Jonathan; Lester; Nathaniel; Samuel
Nicknames: Ace; Cheyenne; Gato; Snake; Tiger; Windy
Surnames: Clayton; Dickinson; Greeley; Lubbock; Mitchell; Rawlins

First name: _____
Nickname: _____
Surname: _____

First name: _____
Nickname: _____
Surname: _____

First name: _____
Nickname: _____
Surname: _____

_____
_____
_____

_____
_____
_____

_____
_____
_____

Starting tip: Begin by positioning Samuel Mitchell.

Codewords

This puzzle has no clues in the conventional sense. Instead, every different number printed in the main grid represents a different letter (with the same number always representing the same letter, of course). For example, if 7 turns out to be a "V," you can write in V wherever a square contains 7. We have completed a very small part of the puzzle to give you a start, but the rest is up to you.

24		2		14		16		3		2		26
4	4	16	9	16		9	16	6	2	20	8	24
15		23		26		22		12		26		15
23	6	8	8	5	15	5	18		24	2	16	5
23				11		18		19		13		18
8	2	4	16	15	6		24	20	8	4	17	
11		16		2				8		8		3
	1	26	15	8	19		23	22	5	11	8	6
21		5		11		19		6				15
4	16	11	12		11	15	25	15	5	15	5	18
15		8		22		23			24		9		18
19	26	6	19	4	8	24		8	7	23	8	4
	U	**R**	**T**									
10		24		11		12		24		24		12

A B C D E F G H I J K L M N O P Q ~~R~~ S ~~T~~ ~~U~~ V W X Y Z

1	2	3	4	5	6 **R**	7	8	9	10	11	12	13
14	15	16	17	18	19 **T**	20	21	22	23	24	25	26 **U**

TOTALIZED

The 25-second ultimate challenge from **Puzzler Brain Trainer**

Just follow the instructions from top to bottom, starting with the number given to reach an answer at the foot of the ladder.

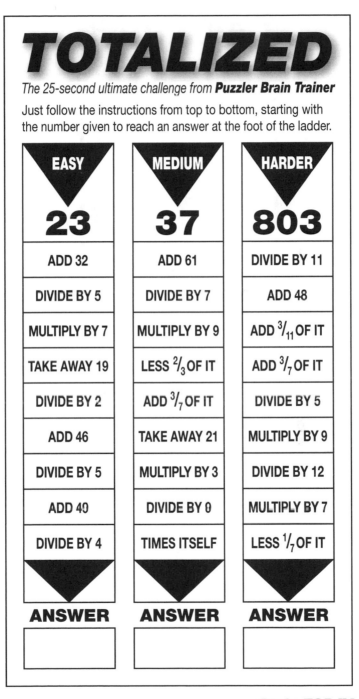

EASY	MEDIUM	HARDER
23	**37**	**803**
ADD 32	ADD 61	DIVIDE BY 11
DIVIDE BY 5	DIVIDE BY 7	ADD 48
MULTIPLY BY 7	MULTIPLY BY 9	ADD $^3/_{11}$ OF IT
TAKE AWAY 19	LESS $^2/_3$ OF IT	ADD $^3/_7$ OF IT
DIVIDE BY 2	ADD $^3/_7$ OF IT	DIVIDE BY 5
ADD 46	TAKE AWAY 21	MULTIPLY BY 9
DIVIDE BY 5	MULTIPLY BY 3	DIVIDE BY 12
ADD 40	DIVIDE BY 0	MULTIPLY BY 7
DIVIDE BY 4	TIMES ITSELF	LESS $^1/_7$ OF IT
ANSWER	**ANSWER**	**ANSWER**

Cell Block

Fill the grid by drawing blocks along the grid lines. Each block must contain the number of squares indicated by the digit inside it. Each block must contain only one digit.

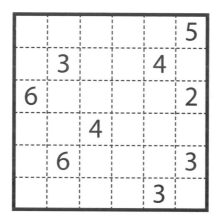

Wordwheel

Using only the letters in the Wordwheel, you have ten minutes to find as many words as possible, none of which may be plurals, foreign words, or proper nouns. Each word must be of three letters or more, all must contain the central letter, and letters can only be used once in every word. There is at least one nine-letter word in the wheel.

Walking the Dog

Three friends from Labrador Road in Memphis take their dogs for a walk down on the fields by the Mississippi River every evening. From the clues given, can you work out each man's full name, and the breed and name of his canine companion?

Clues

1. None of the dogs has a name beginning with the same letter as his or her master's first name.

2. Mr. Pye's corgi isn't called Sally.

3. Sam's dalmatian isn't called Muffin.

4. Mr. Gunn's dog isn't called Bingo.

	Gunn	Pye	Toye	Boxer	Corgi	Dalmatian	Bingo	Muffin	Sally
Bill									
Mick									
Sam									
Bingo									
Muffin									
Sally									
Boxer									
Corgi									
Dalmatian									

First name	Surname	Breed	Name

The Location Man

Miles Tugo is a location scout for a big movie company and spends his time traveling around the world to search out specific locations for the company's forthcoming productions. (It's a tough job but somebody's got to do it.) Last year, he visited five major cities in the course of his work; from the clues given, can you say which city he visited in each of the listed months and the title and type of film for which he scouted locations there?

Clues

1. Miles was in Moscow, scouting locations for a tough crime drama, two months after he worked on locations for *Nameless*.

2. In March, Miles was checking out locations for *Wild Honey*, but not in Rio de Janeiro.

3. The locations in and around Bangkok weren't required for the comedy.

4. In May, Miles flew to Dublin, but not to select locations for the horror film *Oblivion*.

5. September was the month when Miles was busy finding locations for the science-fiction spectacular.

6. It was *Starlight* that used locations in and around Sydney.

Month	City

  USA TODAY.

	Bangkok	Dublin	Moscow	Rio de Janeiro	Sydney	Brotherhood	Nameless	Oblivion	Starlight	Wild Honey	Comedy	Crime drama	Horror	Romance	Science fiction
March															
May															
July															
September															
November															
Comedy															
Crime drama															
Horror															
Romance															
Science fiction															
Brotherhood															
Nameless															
Oblivion															
Starlight															
Wild Honey															

Title	Type

San Guinari Nights

The South American republic of San Guinari is most famous for its frequent and violent changes of government, and one of its main exports is ex-presidents clearing off with large chunks of the national treasury. However, when actress Cindy Dolle visited the country to promote her latest movie *The Model and the Monster* (guess which she plays!) she met a number of the country's best-looking and most eligible bachelors, and was invited out by a different one of them on each of the five evenings she was there. From the clues given, can you work out who she went out with on each evening, what he was, and what they did?

Clues

1. Ricardo Ortiz, a prominent politician tipped to be either the next El Presidente or the victim of an unfortunate accident, didn't date Cindy on Tuesday.

2. On Monday, Cindy spent the evening—and quite a lot of the night, actually—with Tomas Bartolo, who wasn't the local movie star who took Cindy to the premiere of his latest movie *El Pistolero*.

3. Cindy was taken to the traditional carnival on the evening of St. Guinarius's Day, which was the day after she went out with the arms dealer (a respected and indeed essential member of San Guinarian society), who didn't take her to a night club, and the day before she spent her evening with Luis Vargas.

4. Angel Salinas took Cindy for dinner on his private yacht, which is just a little smaller than the coastal gunboats that make up the bulk of the local navy.

5. On Tuesday night, Cindy's escort—who wasn't the army officer—took her to a local night club, which turned out to be rather wilder than anything in Los Angeles.

Day	Name

	Angel Salinas	Julio Diaz	Luis Vargas	Ricardo Ortiz	Tomas Bartolo	Arms dealer	Army officer	Judge	Movie star	Politician	Carnival	Dinner on yacht	Film premiere	Night club	Party at home
Monday															
Tuesday															
Wednesday															
Thursday															
Friday															
Carnival															
Dinner on yacht															
Film premiere															
Night club															
Party at home															
Arms dealer															
Army officer															
Judge															
Movie star															
Politician															

Occupation	Activity

Domino Search

A standard set of dominoes has been laid out, using numbers instead of dots for clarity. Using a sharp pencil and a keen brain, can you draw in the lines to show where each domino has been placed? You may find the check grid useful—crossing off each domino as you find it.

5	5	6	3	6	0	0	6
4	4	6	5	6	6	5	0
5	4	3	3	5	5	0	5
2	2	6	4	4	4	4	1
1	6	3	3	3	0	1	4
2	2	1	2	0	1	3	2
1	1	0	0	1	2	2	3

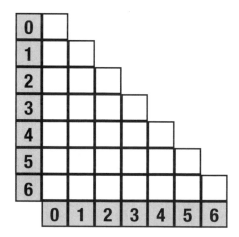

Snow Fun

After a heavy snowfall, the children in each of four neighboring houses built a snowman in the backyard, and each rounded off his or her work with a different type of headgear. From the clues given below, can you name the maker of the snowman at each address (shown before the crowning glory was added) and describe the final touch added by each child?

Clues

1. The black top hat was worn by the snowman in the yard of the house sharing a duplex with Kelly's.

2. Oliver lives at number 3.

3. The bobble-hat was chosen for the snowman at number 7.

4. Brown was the color of the item Jayne placed on the head of her snowman, which was not in the backyard at number 5.

5. The green headgear was on display at a higher-numbered house than the cloth cap, but a lower-numbered one than Andrew's home.

Children: Andrew; Jayne; Kelly; Oliver
Colors: black; blue; brown; green
Headgear: beret; bobble-hat; cloth cap; top hat

	1	3	5	7
Child:				
Color:				
Headgear:				

Starting tip: Work out first who lives at number 5.

Battleships

Do you remember the old game of battleships? These puzzles are based on that idea. Your task is to find the vessels in the diagram. Some parts of boats or sea squares have already been filled in, and a number next to a row or column refers to the number of occupied squares in that row or column. The boats may be positioned horizontally or vertically, but no two boats or parts of boats are in adjacent squares—horizontally, vertically, or diagonally.

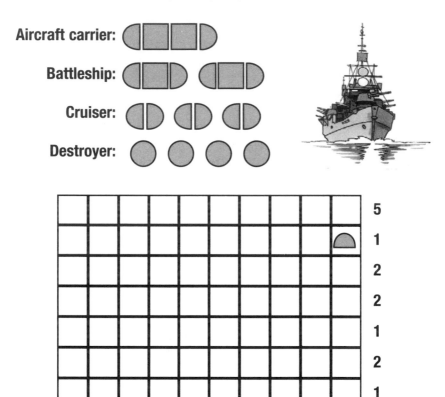

Aircraft carrier:

Battleship:

Cruiser:

Destroyer:

Dropping In

The rescue helicopter had a busy time last week, as a number of climbers got into difficulties in a range of mountains during severe winter weather. From the clues given below, can you name the four notorious peaks lettered A to D, say on which day the helicopter was required on each, and work out how many climbers were winched to safety on each occasion?

Clues

1. The double-pronged peak known as the Devil's Pitchfork, marked A on the plan, was the scene of the rescue the day following the one when four climbers had to be lifted off one hillside.

2. Peak Perilous is next clockwise on the plan from the site of the Monday incident, which involved a larger number of climbers.

3. Heartbreak Crags was the location to which the helicopter was summoned the day after the rescue on peak B.

4. Two climbers got into difficulties during a blizzard on Mount Dastardly.

Peaks: Devil's Pitchfork; Heartbreak Crags; Mount Dastardly; Peak Perilous
Days: Monday; Tuesday; Wednesday; Thursday
Climbers: 1; 2; 3; 4

Peak:	_____	_____	_____	_____
Day:	_____	_____	_____	_____
Climbers:	_____	_____	_____	_____

Starting tip: First identify the peak from which four climbers were rescued.

Men and Mounts

Our two-part picture shows four cowboys from the Lazy Critter ranch playing cards during an off-duty period at the Lucky Horseshoe saloon, with their horses tethered outside. From the clues given, your task is to fully identify the men numbered 1 to 4 in the saloon and match them with their mounts outside, lettered A to D.

Clues

1. None of the letters denoting the horses is the alphabetical equivalent of the number denoting its owner.

2. Lou is directly across the table from Herd as they sit playing poker.

3. Hank's horse is tethered immediately to the left of the one belonging to the cowboy in seat 3 as you look at the picture.

4. Lariatt is the surname of the cowhand in position 4 at the table, while Frank has a lower-numbered position than Roper, whose horse is not next to his in the line.

5. Horse C belongs to Jesse, while the owner of horse D is not the man sitting in position 2, whose surname is not Stockman.

First names: Frank; Hank; Jesse; Lou
Surnames: Herd; Lariatt; Roper; Stockman

Owner: _____

Owner: _____

Owner: _____

Owner: _____

First name: _____

Surname: _____

Starting tip: First work out the position of the horse owned by cowboy 3.

Sunk!

My Uncle Frank was in the Merchant Navy during the Second World War, and three times the ship in which he was serving was sunk by enemy action. From the clues below, can you work out what type of ship each vessel was, and how and in which year it was sunk?

Clues

1. It was a collier on which Uncle Frank was serving as bosun that was sunk by shell fire from a submarine's deck gun.

2. The tanker went down two years earlier than the *White Knight*.

3. The freighter was sunk in 1940.

4. The *Alston Castle* went down some years after one of Frank's ships was torpedoed by an E-boat.

	Collier	Freighter	Tanker	Bombed	Shelled	Torpedoed	1940	1942	1944
Alston Castle									
North Cape									
White Knight									
1940						
1942						
1944						
Bombed			
Shelled			
Torpedoed			

Ship	Type	How sunk	Year

Codewords

This puzzle has no clues in the conventional sense. Instead, every different number printed in the main grid represents a different letter (with the same number always representing the same letter, of course). For example, if 7 turns out to be a "V," you can write in V wherever a square contains 7. We have completed a very small part of the puzzle to give you a start, but the rest is up to you.

	1		26		4	24	4		2		16	
12	2	21	23	8	21		17	21	21	7	25	3
	21		10		17		18		21		3	
9	10	6	4	10	24	14	22		4	17	21	19
	17		16		23		21				17	
21	1	1	10	19	1		11	21	26	18	1	21
22			9						10			17
11	25	9	3	21	11		1	5	24	8	21	17
	20				21		21		17		18	
5	19	6	22		26	17	24	21	22	11	23	19
	14		25		12		13		21		25	
1	21	15	18	21	23		21	22 (N)	1 (S)	24 (I)	14	22
	22		22		19	21	1		1		19	

A B C D E F G H ~~I~~ J K L M ~~N~~ O P Q R ~~S~~ T U V W X Y Z

1 **S**	2	3	4	5	6	7	8	9	10	11	12	13
14	15	16	17	18	19	20	21	22 **N**	23	24 **I**	25	26

TOTALIZED

*The 25-second ultimate challenge from **Puzzler Brain Trainer***

Just follow the instructions from top to bottom, starting with
the number given to reach an answer at the foot of the ladder.

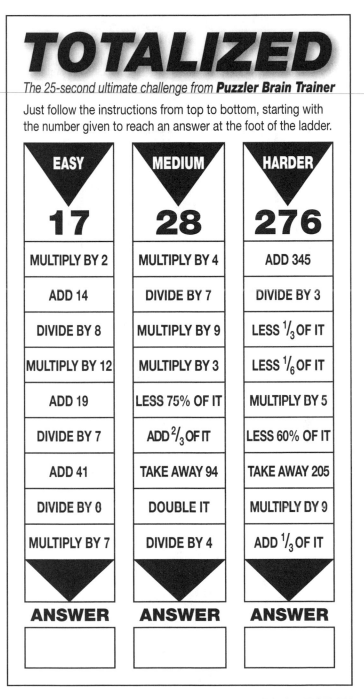

EASY	MEDIUM	HARDER
17	**28**	**276**
MULTIPLY BY 2	MULTIPLY BY 4	ADD 345
ADD 14	DIVIDE BY 7	DIVIDE BY 3
DIVIDE BY 8	MULTIPLY BY 9	LESS $\frac{1}{3}$ OF IT
MULTIPLY BY 12	MULTIPLY BY 3	LESS $\frac{1}{6}$ OF IT
ADD 19	LESS 75% OF IT	MULTIPLY BY 5
DIVIDE BY 7	ADD $\frac{2}{3}$ OF IT	LESS 60% OF IT
ADD 41	TAKE AWAY 94	TAKE AWAY 205
DIVIDE BY 0	DOUBLE IT	MULTIPLY DY 9
MULTIPLY BY 7	DIVIDE BY 4	ADD $\frac{1}{3}$ OF IT
ANSWER	**ANSWER**	**ANSWER**

Cell Block

Fill the grid by drawing blocks along the grid lines. Each block must contain the number of squares indicated by the digit inside it. Each block must contain only one digit.

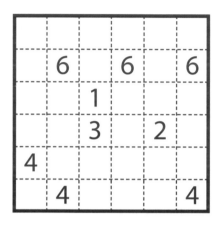

Wordwheel

Using only the letters in the Wordwheel, you have ten minutes to find as many words as possible, none of which may be plurals, foreign words, or proper nouns. Each word must be of three letters or more, all must contain the central letter, and letters can only be used once in every word. There is at least one nine-letter word in the wheel.

Battleships

Do you remember the old game of battleships? These puzzles are based on that idea. Your task is to find the vessels in the diagram. Some parts of boats or sea squares have already been filled in, and a number next to a row or column refers to the number of occupied squares in that row or column. The boats may be positioned horizontally or vertically, but no two boats or parts of boats are in adjacent squares—horizontally, vertically, or diagonally.

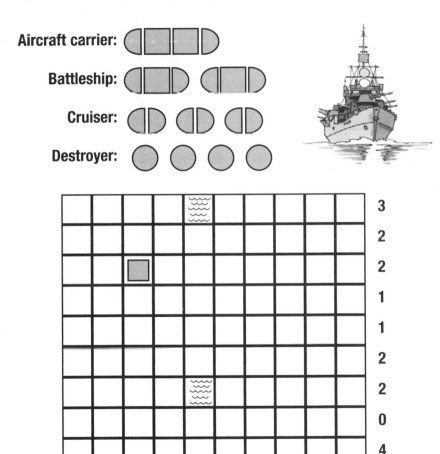

Aircraft carrier:

Battleship:

Cruiser:

Destroyer:

Domino Search

A standard set of dominoes has been laid out, using numbers instead of dots for clarity. Using a sharp pencil and a keen brain, can you draw in the lines to show where each domino has been placed? You may find the check grid useful—crossing off each domino as you find it.

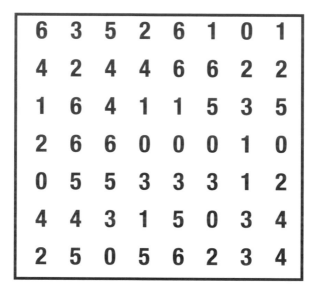

6	3	5	2	6	1	0	1
4	2	4	4	6	6	2	2
1	6	4	1	1	5	3	5
2	6	6	0	0	0	1	0
0	5	5	3	3	3	1	2
4	4	3	1	5	0	3	4
2	5	0	5	6	2	3	4

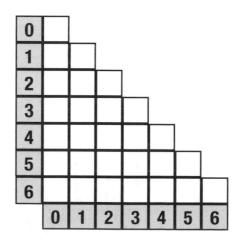

Learn the Lingo

Polly Glott loves going on vacation abroad, and always likes to teach herself the language before setting off. On her bookshelf, picked out and numbered 1 to 4 in the diagram, are four volumes that have assisted her in recent years. From the clues given, can you work out which language each book tackles, identify its cover color, and say in which year Polly used it to good effect?

Clues

1. The red book is somewhere to the right of the one on Greek, and somewhere to the left of the tome from which Polly taught herself in 2000.

2. The most recently acquired of the four books can be seen in position 3; it was not the one from which Polly became fluent in Spanish, which is farther left on the shelf and does not have a blue cover.

3. The yellow book was used two years after the one from which Polly learned Swedish.

4. Book 1 on the shelf was used to good effect two years prior to the green one, whose subject is not Russian.

5. Book 2 was a later acquisition than the blue one.

Subjects: Greek; Russian; Spanish; Swedish
Covers: blue; green; red; yellow
Years: 1998; 2000; 2002; 2004

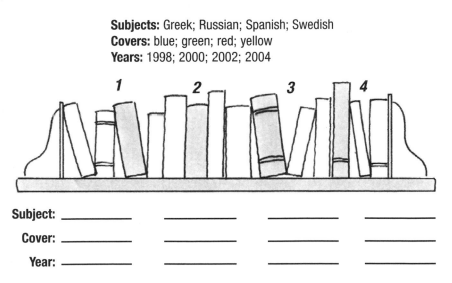

Subject: _____   _____   _____   _____

Cover: _____   _____   _____   _____

Year: _____   _____   _____   _____

Starting tip: Start by working out the position of the book Polly used in 2000.

Windows of the Devil's Castle

The Devil's Castle (or el Castello del Diablo, as it's known to the locals) stands in San Guinari City, capital of the South American republic; the Spanish built it as a fortress and prison in the 17th century, and El Presidente continues to use it as a jail today. From the clues below, can you work out whose cell lies behind each of the windows shown, what position he formerly held, and how long he's been in there so far?

Clues

1. The man who has only been in jail for 10 years is one of the two neighbors of former army general Anibal del Campo, who tried to stage a coup and failed.

2. The one-time police general who has been in jail for 22 years after failing to prevent an unsuccessful attempt on El Presidente's life is in the cell next door but one to Cesar Flores's.

3. The man who has been in jail for 18 years is in one of the end cells, next to that of the one-time Minister of Finance who tried to steal the contents of the national treasury.

4. The man whose cell is behind window C has not occupied it for 13 years.

5. The former Prime Minister—jailed for negotiating with a neighboring country behind El Presidente's back—is not called Diego Mendez.

Names: Anibal del Campo; Cesar Flores; Diego Mendez; Jorge Rubio
Former positions: army general; Minister of Finance; police general; Prime Minister
Periods of imprisonment: 10 years; 13 years; 18 years; 22 years

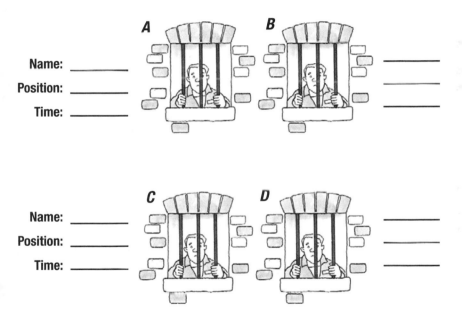

A

Name: _____
Position: _____
Time: _____

B

_____
_____
_____

C

Name: _____
Position: _____
Time: _____

D

_____
_____
_____

Starting tip: Place Anibal del Campo in his correct cell.

Family on the Phone

On Saturday morning, while trying to get his garden dug, Nigel Bell received three phone calls from female relatives. From the clues below, can you work out the name and relationship to Nigel of the caller at each time and the topic of her call?

Clues

1. Joanne phoned some time after the relative who had called to report a lottery win—though, sadly, only a $10 one.

2. Sylvia is Nigel's sister.

3. Nigel's mother called at 11:45 a.m.

4. Dorothy, who isn't Nigel's cousin, wasn't the woman who called to ask advice about the trouble she was having with her car.

	Dorothy	Joanne	Sylvia	Cousin	Mother	Sister	Car trouble	Family reunion	Lottery win
9:00 a.m.									
10:15 a.m.									
11:45 a.m.									
Car trouble									
Family reunion									
Lottery win									
Cousin									
Mother									
Sister									

Time	Name	Relation	Topic

Battleships

Do you remember the old game of battleships? These puzzles are based on that idea. Your task is to find the vessels in the diagram. Some parts of boats or sea squares have already been filled in, and a number next to a row or column refers to the number of occupied squares in that row or column. The boats may be positioned horizontally or vertically, but no two boats or parts of boats are in adjacent squares—horizontally, vertically, or diagonally.

Aircraft carrier:

Battleship:

Cruiser:

Destroyer:

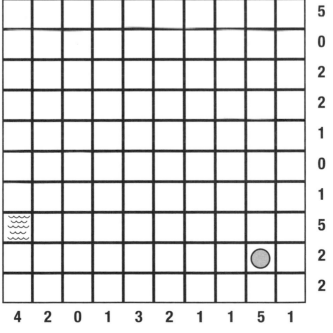

Domino Search

A standard set of dominoes has been laid out, using numbers instead of dots for clarity. Using a sharp pencil and a keen brain, can you draw in the lines to show where each domino has been placed? You may find the check grid useful—crossing off each domino as you find it.

2	1	1	5	5	6	6	6
1	1	1	0	6	5	5	4
6	4	6	0	1	2	5	4
1	5	4	0	0	0	6	4
3	2	5	0	3	0	3	4
1	2	4	2	6	0	4	5
2	2	2	3	3	3	3	3

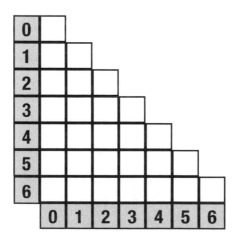

Musical Lives

The Lute sisters are all concert-standard musicians, playing different instruments, and all have recently married men who are also involved in the music business. From the clues below, can you work out the name of each sister, the instrument she plays, the name of her husband, and his occupation?

Clues

1. Daphne, who plays the violin, is not married to Paul Rebec.

2. Angela is married to Ray Sacbut, who is not the composer of TV and movie scores.

3. Gloria, who doesn't play the piano, is married to a music publisher.

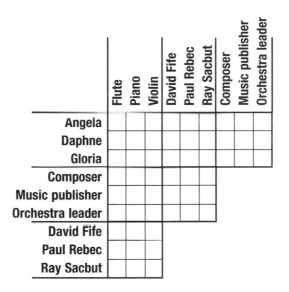

Sister	Instrument	Husband	Occupation

Battleships

Do you remember the old game of battleships? These puzzles are based on that idea. Your task is to find the vessels in the diagram. Some parts of boats or sea squares have already been filled in, and a number next to a row or column refers to the number of occupied squares in that row or column. The boats may be positioned horizontally or vertically, but no two boats or parts of boats are in adjacent squares—horizontally, vertically, or diagonally.

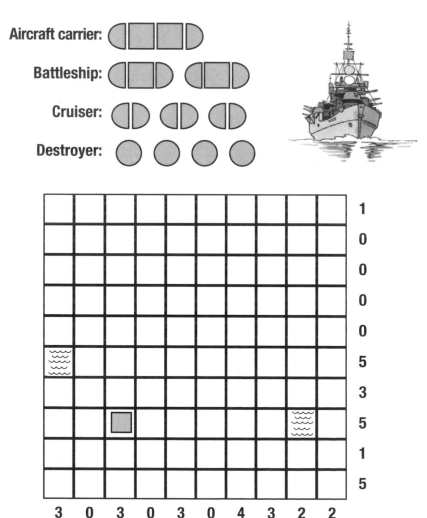

Changing Times

Four former cinemas in the town center were converted some time ago to new uses. From the clues given below, can you work out the former name of the cinemas at locations 1 to 4, say what purpose they now serve, and name the year in which each transformation took place?

Clues

1. The mosque was opened four years after the Plaza started its new role at a point farther east.

2. The Palace was in the next location west from the site where the change of use took place in 1986.

3. By the time the auction rooms commenced trading, site 1 had already been transformed, while the former Carlton cinema was the next to be adapted.

4. The sports hall opened some time after the new project at location 2.

5. The change of use at location 3 was not the first, but did precede the new venture at the site of the Roxy, which was not the cinema in location 1.

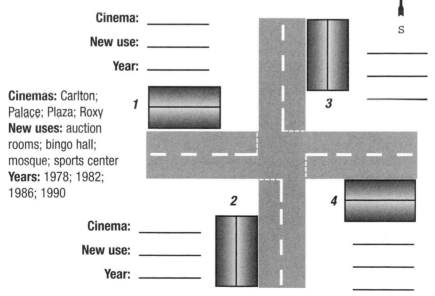

Cinema: _____
New use: _____
Year: _____

Cinemas: Carlton; Palace; Plaza; Roxy
New uses: auction rooms; bingo hall; mosque; sports center
Years: 1978; 1982; 1986; 1990

Cinema: _____
New use: _____
Year: _____

Starting tip: Decide first which new venture opened in 1978.

Lots of Pictures

Four pictures are shown on display at the presale viewing session at an auction room. From the clues given below, can you name the pictures that will be listed as lots 53 to 56, and say who painted each in roughly what year?

Clues

1. Belgian artist Basil Brusch painted the picture next right from the seascape, which is an earlier work.

2. The hunting scene is the subject of lot 53, which is the next most recent work after the one by Pallet.

3. The Parisian street scene is a later painting than the one offered as lot 54.

4. Hoyles is the man whose work is listed in the auction catalog as lot 55; it was painted more recently than the picture by Frame.

Pictures: hunting scene; landscape; Parisian street scene; seascape
Artists: Brusch; Frame; Hoyles; Pallet
Approximate years painted: 1775; 1835; 1870; 1900

Lot 53   **Lot 54**   **Lot 55**   **Lot 56**

Picture: _____   _____   _____   _____

Artist: _____   _____   _____   _____

Year: _____   _____   _____   _____

Starting tip: First identify the lot number of the painting by Brusch.

Enjoying the Open Air

Four young ladies who work at the multinational Penny Corporation's Belton complex decided to go for a country walk on a bright Saturday morning—but, before they got home again, they were already regretting it. From the clues below, can you fill in on the drawing the name of each walker, where in PennyCorp she works, and why she was wishing she had stayed at home?

Clues

1. The draftsperson from research & development (R&D) got a black eye from a tree branch.

2. The young lady who was stung on the shoulder by a wasp is shown somewhere ahead of the secretary from advertising.

3. Nina Price, a stock control supervisor in the stores, is shown somewhere behind the girl who was limping because of her blistered heel.

4. Figure 2, who isn't Terri Vyne, operates a plastic molding machine in the PennyCorp factory.

5. The girl whose ankles and lower legs were extensively stung when she carelessly walked into a patch of nettles is immediately behind Joan Lacey.

Names: Carol Ellis; Joan Lacey; Nina Price; Terri Vyne
Works in: advertising; factory; R&D; stores
Misfortunes: black eye; blistered heel; nettle stings; wasp sting

	1	**2**	**3**	**4**
Name:	_____	_____	_____	_____
Works in:	_____	_____	_____	_____
Misfortune:	_____	_____	_____	_____

Starting tip: Decide where walker 1 works.

Domino Search

A standard set of dominoes has been laid out, using numbers instead of dots for clarity. Using a sharp pencil and a keen brain, can you draw in the lines to show where each domino has been placed? You may find the check grid useful—crossing off each domino as you find it.

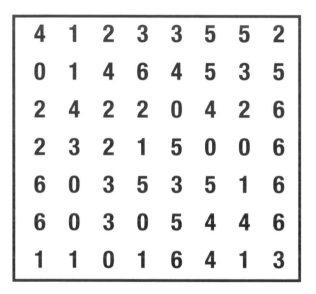

4	1	2	3	3	5	5	2
0	1	4	6	4	5	3	5
2	4	2	2	0	4	2	6
2	3	2	1	5	0	0	6
6	0	3	5	3	5	1	6
6	0	3	0	5	4	4	6
1	1	0	1	6	4	1	3

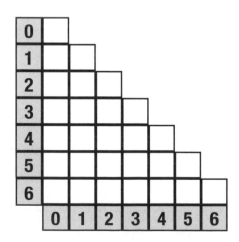

Desperados

The Mannick brothers, the four sons of a respectable Texas businessman, were notorious outlaws in the old Wild West; the picture below shows them a few weeks before they tried to rob the First Republican Bank in Green Valley, California, in 1885, and ended up shooting it out with the citizenry. From the clues given, can you fill in on the picture each brothers' real name, the name by which he was known, and the year of his birth?

Clues

1. Enoch Elijah Mannick was born two years after his brother who was nicknamed "Bull," who is not figure 4 in the picture.

2. Figure 1 is "Laredo" Mannick; he wasn't the brother whose real forename is Nathaniel Noah, who was older than Jeremiah Jude.

3. As we look at the picture, "Rocky" Mannick is standing immediately to the right of his brother who was born in 1854.

4. As we look at the picture, Reuben Raphael Mannick is immediately right of the brother who was nicknamed "Preacher"; "Preacher" was younger by two years than Reuben.

Real names: Enoch Elijah; Jeremiah Jude; Nathaniel Noah; Reuben Raphael
Nicknames: "Bull"; "Laredo"; "Preacher"; "Rocky"
Years of births: 1854; 1856; 1858; 1860

Real name: _____   _____   _____   _____

Nickname: _____   _____   _____   _____

Birth: _____   _____   _____   _____

Starting tip: Work out the nickname of figure 4.

Answers

Codewords, p. 1

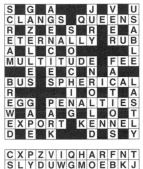

S		G		A				J		V		U
C	L	A	N	G	S		Q	U	E	E	N	S
R		Z		E		S		R		E		A
E	T	E	R	N	A	L	L	Y		R	U	B
A		L		C		O						L
M	U	L	T	I	T	U	D	E		F	E	E
		E		E		C		N		A		
B	U	S		S	P	H	E	R	I	C	A	L
R						I		O		T		A
E	G	G		P	E	N	A	L	T	I	E	S
W		A		A		G		L		O		T
E	X	P	O	R	T		K	E	N	N	E	L
D		E		K				D		S		Y

C	X	P	Z	V	I	Q	H	A	R	F	N	T
S	L	Y	D	U	W	G	M	O	E	B	K	J

Totalized, p. 2

Easy: 29, Medium: 144, Harder: 115

Cell Block, p. 3

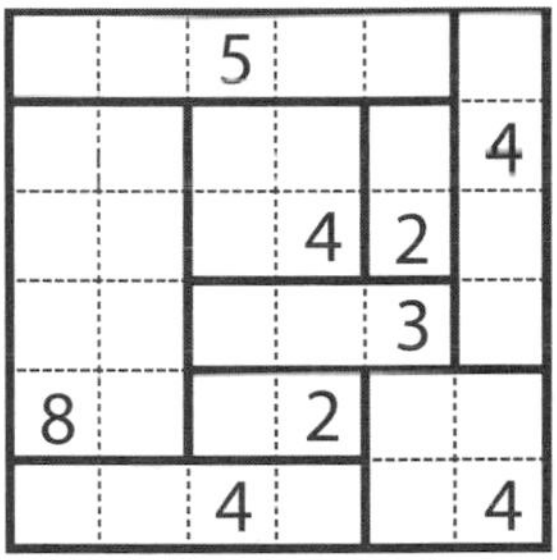

Wordwheel, p. 3

The nine-letter word is GALLIVANT.

Extras, p. 4

Lynne has four days' work (clue 2), so Kevin, who has secured an even number of days' work that isn't ten (clue 4), must have six days and therefore he must be working on the sci-fi film (clue 5). From clue 4, the extra on the Paddy Britt film must therefore have seven days' work (clue 4). The "romcom" involves three more days' work than the Jodie Dent film (clue 1), so it is not ten days, since the seven days of work is on the Paddy Britt picture. Therefore Sarah's romcom must be giving her seven days' work and the Jodie Dent film must be providing Lynne with four days' work. Kevin is not appearing in the Donny Jepp costume drama (clue 6) or the Harry Fordson film, which is Danny (clue 3), so it must be the Keeley Knight movie. Therefore, by elimination, Vic must be the extra in the Donny Jepp film. As Danny does not have five days' work (clue 3), it must be ten, leaving the five days as Vic's booking. Finally, Lynne's four days are not on the crime film (clue 2), so it must be the thriller, leaving the crime picture as the Harry Fordson film.

Danny, crime, Harry Fordson, 10.
Kevin, sci-fi, Keeley Knight, 6.
Lynne, thriller, Jodie Dent, 4.
Sarah, romcom, Paddy Britt, 7.
Vic, costume drama, Donny Jepp, 5.

Battleships, p. 6

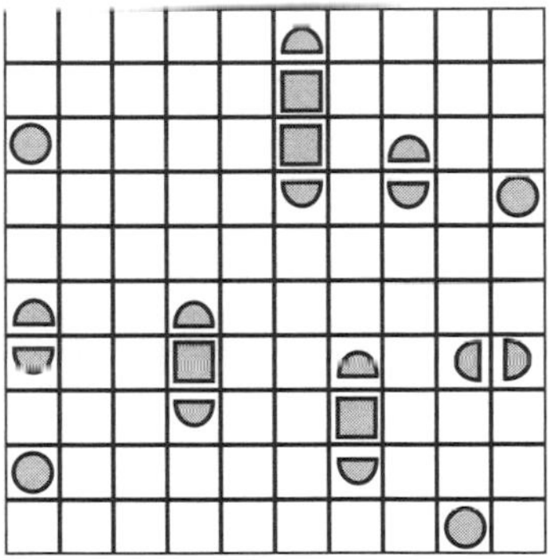

On Your Bike, p. 7

The 20-minute ride was not made by Mary (clue 1), Dorothy (clue 2), or Noel (clue 4), so it must have been Jack's. The 32-minute ride was not to Frameleigh (clue 1), Chainford (clue 2), or Spokesby, which is due east (clue 4), so it must have been to Peddleham. So, from clue 3, the 28-minute journey

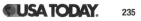

was made by the rider cycling due north. We know this is not to Spokesby or Peddleham. If it were to Chainford, from clue 2, Dorothy would have ridden for 32 minutes due east, but we know that is to Spokesby, and it was Peddleham that is 32 minutes away, so Chainford cannot be due north, and Frameleigh must be. So, from clue 1, Mary headed due south, and rode for 32 minutes, so that must be the direction of Peddleham. By elimination, Chainford must be due west, so, from clue 2, Dorothy must have headed north to Frameleigh, cycling for 28 minutes, and the time taken to reach Chainford was therefore 24 minutes (clue 2). So the rider who went there was not Jack, and must have been Noel, and, by elimination, Jack's 20-minute ride must have taken him due east to Spokesby.

North, Frameleigh, Dorothy, 28 minutes.
East, Spokesby, Jack, 20 minutes.
South, Peddleham, Mary, 32 minutes.
West, Chainford, Noel, 24 minutes.

The Lifestory Channel, p. 8

Sir Coward de Custarde's the subject of the 10:00 p.m. program (clue 5) so, from clue 1, Cyril's program about Uramis can't be at 6:00 p.m., 9:00 p.m., or 11:00 p.m., so must be at 8:00 p.m. The same clue now tells us that de Grey, who's presenting the program about Rupert de Grey, must be on air at 9:00 p.m. As Bulford's forename is Winston (clue 2), he's not the 8:00 p.m. presenter, and neither is either Milliken or Pinhorn (clue 3), so Cyril must be Scrobby. We now know Bulford's and Scrobby's full names: as neither Milliken nor Pinhorn is Lucien (clue 3), that must be de Grey's forename. Clue 2 tells us that Winston Bulford can't be presenting at 6:00 p.m. or 11:00 p.m., so, as we already know the 8:00 p.m. and 9:00 p.m. presenters, he must be presenting the 10:00 p.m. show about Sir Coward and, from the same clue, Milliken is the 11:00 p.m. presenter, leaving the 6:00 p.m. one as Pinhorn. Therefore Pinhorn isn't Magnus (clue 4), so must be Desmond, leaving Magnus as Milliken, the 11:00 p.m. presenter. Therefore his subject isn't Beau Nydel (clue 4) and must be Miss Raffles, leaving Beau Nydel as the subject of Desmond Pinhorn's 6:00 p.m. show.

6:00 p.m., Desmond Pinhorn, Beau Nydel.
8:00 p.m., Cyril Scrobby, Uramis.
9:00 p.m., Lucien de Grey, Rupert de Grey.
10:00 p.m., Winston Bulford, Sir Coward de Custarde.
11:00 p.m., Magnus Milliken, Miss Raffles.

Strangers in Town, p. 10

Arm 4 points to the museum (clue 3), so Jack and his wife, who visited the castle, cannot have followed arm 3 (clue 5). Since Hannah followed arm 1 (clue 4), clue 4 rules out the botanical gardens as the legend on arm 3, which therefore, by elimination, must be the riverside walk. So, from clue 5, the castle visited by Jack must have been indicated on arm 2, which leaves arm 1, followed by Hannah, as showing the way to the botanical gardens. So clue 1 tells us Lewis and Maxine followed arm 3, to the riverside walk. Since we now know Josie did not head in direction 3, clue 2 rules out direction 4, to the museum, for Peter, so he must have headed for the botanical gardens with Hannah, and Josie therefore followed arm 4 to the museum (clue 2). So her partner was not Jack, and must have been Adrian, leaving Jack's wife as Eileen.

1, botanical gardens, Peter and Hannah.
2, castle, Jack and Eileen.
3, riverside walk, Lewis and Maxine.
4, museum, Adrian and Josie.

Domino Search, p. 11

0	3	0	6	5	6	3	5
2	4	1	1	4	5	1	2
3	3	2	5	6	4	0	4
6	6	3	4	0	3	1	1
2	4	4	2	1	2	2	3
5	5	5	0	4	1	0	0
6	0	6	6	5	1	3	2

Codewords, p. 12

P	A	C	K	A	G	E	S			A	M	E	N
O		O		L		X			B		U		U
W	A	N	T	S		H	E	L	P	F	U	L	
E		Q		O		O		U		T		L	
R	O	U	X		G	R	A	F	F	I	T	I	
		E		C		T		F					F
T	H	R	I	L	L		J	E	R	S	E	Y	
A			A		V		R		T				
C	H	O	I	R	B	O	Y			Z	I	P	S
T		W		I		O		A		M			L
F	L	I	R	T	E	D		S	A	U	N	A	
U		N		Y		O		K		L			N
L	O	G	S			B	O	O	S	T	I	N	G

U	E	Z	C	V	P	Y	F	T	R	N	K	S
W	L	D	M	X	B	H	J	G	A	O	I	Q

Totalized, p. 13
Easy: 43, Medium: 67, Harder: 99

Cell Block, p. 14

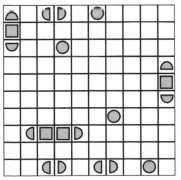

Wordwheel, p. 14
The nine-letter word is PROGNOSIS.

Battleships, p. 15

Cats' Chorus, p. 16
The long-haired cat lives at #12 (clue 6), so the one from #4, who serenades from the shed roof and that is not the brindle or the tabby (clue 4), or the calico (clue 5), must be the black cat, Sooty (clue 1). Therefore, from clue 5 the cat that wails from the garage roof must live at #6 and the calico must live at #10. The former is not the brindle (clue 3), so it must be the tabby. By elimination, Daisy from #8 (clue 1) must be the brindle cat. It does not wail from outside the back door (clue 3) or outside the bedroom window, which is Cleo (clue 2), so it must be from the garden wall. Bubble is not the tabby (clue 2), so she does not live at #6, and as her house number is less than that of Cleo (also clue 2), it is not #12, so it must be #10, and Bubble must therefore be the calico. Therefore Cleo must be the cat from #12 who wails outside the bedroom window (clue 2), and must be the long-haired cat (clue 6). By elimination, the tabby must be called Prince, and Bubble must be the cat from #10 who caterwauls from outside the back door.

Bubble, calico, #10, outside back door.
Cleo, long-haired, #12, outside bedroom window.
Daisy, brindle, #8, garden wall.
Prince, tabby, #6, garage roof.
Sooty, black, #4, shed roof.

Breakdown Breakdown, p. 18
The 10-minute repair was effected after a wait of 27 minutes (clue 3) so, from clue 2, the repairman who took 37 minutes to reach the car with the broken clutch cable must have taken 20 minutes to fix it. Also from clues 2 and 3, Mrs. Langford must have had to wait 27 minutes and, from clue 1, Mr. Hedley must have had his dead battery fixed in just 5 minutes. So Mr. Hedley hadn't waited 22 minutes (clue 4), or 43 minutes, which was Mr. Hawkins's wait (clue 5), so it must have been 35 minutes. The member who waited 22 minutes took longer to get on the road again than the member who waited 43 minutes (clue 4), the former repair must have taken 25 minutes and the latter 15 minutes. The broken clutch cable wasn't suffered by Mr. Mills (clue 2), so it must have been Mr. Robson, and, by elimination, the person who waited 22 minutes for the 25-minute repair must have been Mr. Mills. The

call-out to the overheating car did not take 22 or 27 minutes (clue 3), so it must have been Mr. Hawkins's problem, entailing a wait of 43 minutes. As the misfire took longer to fix than the fuel blockage (clue 6), the former must have taken 25 minutes, after a 22-minute wait, and the latter 10 minutes, after a 27-minute wait.

Mr. Hawkins, overheating, 43, 15.
Mr. Hedley, dead battery, 35, 5.
Mrs. Langford, fuel blockage, 27, 10.
Mr. Mills, misfire, 22, 25.
Mr. Robson, broken clutch cable, 37, 20.

Night on the Plains, p. 20

Since the Hatch family wagon is opposite the one with 9 passengers (clue 5), the former must have 6 passengers (clue 1). From clues 1 and 4, Draper, who's a smith, must have 7 passengers in his wagon, which is therefore opposite the one with 8 passengers. From clue 4 again, the carpenter's wagon can't have 5 or 6 passengers; we know it doesn't have 7, and, since the Willards' wagon doesn't have 6 or 7, the carpenter's can't have 8 or 9, so it must have 10 passengers and the Willards' wagon 8. The Logans' wagon can't have 9 or 10 passengers (clue 3), so must have 5. The gunsmith's wagon can't have 6 on board (clue 2), so the Ogdens' wagon opposite (clue 2 again) can't have 9 passengers (clue 1), so must have 10, and is therefore the carpenter's, with the gunsmith's wagon having 5 on board (clue 1) and the gunsmith therefore being Logan. Monroe, who is not a smith (clue 6), can't be the farmer, as he has fewer children than the blacksmith (clue 3), so must be the saddler. Therefore wagon C must be the Willards', with 8 passengers. The Hatch family wagon, with 6 passengers, must therefore be wagon D (clue 5). From the same clue, Monroe, the saddler's family, must be in wagon A, and the tinsmith's in wagon F, which must have 7 on board (clue 6), and they are therefore the Drapers. Finally, Ogden, the carpenter's family, must be in wagon E, and the gunsmith must be Logan, with 5 passengers on his wagon (clue 2), and, from clue 3, the Willards must be in wagon C and the Hatch family in wagon D.

A, Monroe, 9, saddler.
B, Logan, 5, gunsmith.
C, Willard, 8, blacksmith.
D, Hatch, 6, farmer.
E, Ogden, 10, carpenter.
F, Draper, 7, tinsmith.

Brought to Book, p. 22

Davidson was booked in the 22nd minute, and he wore a shirt numbered lower than #12, who was booked for verbal dissent (clue 1). #9 was booked in the 10th minute (also clue 1), and #4's surname didn't begin with D (clue 3), so Davidson must have been #7. He wasn't booked for not retreating the full ten yards, which happened in the 73rd minute (clue 2), and the player who faked injury didn't have a surname beginning with D (clue 3), so Davidson must have held on to his opponent. The player who didn't retreat far enough in the 73rd minute was not #4 (clue 3), #7, #9, or #12, so it must have been #15. Therefore Perrin must have been #9, booked in the 10th minute (clue 1). This was not for the hard foul, which was Elstow, so it must have been for faking injury. By elimination, Elstow must have been wearing #4. We now know that Da Costa must have been wearing #12 and Linnell #15 (clue 4). Since Elstow's hard foul took place earlier than Da Costa's booking (clue 3), it must have been in the 41st minute, and Davidson must have been shown the yellow card for holding his opponent in the 22nd minute.

#4, Elstow, hard foul, 41st minute.
#7, Davidson, holding opponent, 22nd minute.
#9, Perrin, faking injury, 10th minute.
#12, Da Costa, verbal dissent, 58th minute.
#15, Linnell, not retreating fully, 73rd minute.

Dinner with Friends, p. 24

The guest who had apple pie for dessert didn't have lamb with herbs or sole in orange sauce for main course (clue 4), and, since he or she had salmon terrine as a starter (clue 4 again), the main course chosen can't have been veal piccata, which went with the soup starter (clue 6), or chimichangas, which went with the cheesecake dessert (clue 5) so must have been muckalica. This diner was not Rebecca (clue 2), Arnold, whose main course was lamb with herbs (clue 3), Graham, whose dessert was the torte (clue 1), or Martin, who started with chicken and bacon salad (clue 1), so must have been Tracey. We know that Arnold's starter wasn't salmon terrine or chicken and bacon salad, nor was it the soup, which went with the veal piccata; as the lamb with herbs didn't follow the melon salad (clue 3), he must have had the goat's cheese. Therefore his dessert wasn't apple pie, torte, or cheesecake; the goat's cheese wasn't on the same person's order as the fruit salad (clue 2), so Arnold's dessert must have been strawberry shortcake. Rebecca's dessert wasn't fruit salad (clue 2), so it must have been cheesecake, and her main course was therefore chimichangas. By elimination, the fruit salad dessert must have been ordered by Martin, whose starter was the chicken and bacon salad. His main course wasn't veal piccata, which followed the soup, so, by elimination it must have been sole in orange sauce. Therefore the soup and veal piccata must have been ordered by Graham, whose dessert was the torte, and Rebecca's starter to go with her chimichangas and cheesecake must have been melon salad.

Arnold, goat's cheese, lamb with herbs, strawberry shortcake.

Graham, soup, veal piccata, raspberry torte.

Martin, chicken and bacon salad, sole in orange, fruit salad.

Rebecca, melon salad, chimichangas, cheesecake.

Tracey, salmon terrine, muckalica, apple pie.

March Hare's Tea Party, p. 26

The third person to entertain recited (clue 4). The fourth to perform cannot have done magic tricks (clue 1), or danced (clue 3), so this must have been the dormouse, who snored a song in his sleep (clue 1). Neither Alice (clue 3), nor the host, the March Hare (clue 5), performed first, so the Mad Hatter must have done so. We know he did not snore a song or recite, and, since his hat was borrowed as a prop (clue 1), he cannot have performed the magic tricks, so he must have danced the jig. Therefore, by elimination, the second performer must have done the tricks, and was therefore in seat 4 (clue 2). We know the host, the March Hare, was not the first or fourth to perform,

and clue 5 now rules him out for the third performance, the recitation, since the person in seat 3 did not perform second, so, by elimination, he must have done the tricks and occupied seat 4. By elimination, it must have been Alice who recited. Clue 5 now places the Hatter in seat 3, so, from clue 3, Alice must have been in seat 2, leaving the dormouse in seat 1.

1, Dormouse, snored song, fourth.

2, Alice, recited, third.

3, Mad Hatter, danced, first.

4, March Hare, magic tricks, second.

Feet of Clay, p. 27

The Church Hall in Northtown isn't the venue where Lucy's seeing 8 patients (clue 1), nor can it be where she's seeing 7 patients on Friday (clues 1 and 3), so there must be 6 patients there. As she's at the Village Hall on Wednesday (clue 2), the venue on Friday must be the Parish Rooms, and she must be at the Church Hall, Northtown, on Monday. Since the venue in Plighwood isn't the Village Hall (clue 2), it must be the Parish Rooms on Friday with 7 patients booked, leaving the Village Hall as the venue in Goosebury, where, by elimination, Lucy must have 8 patients booked.

Monday, Church Hall, Northtown, 6 patients.

Wednesday, Village Hall, Goosebury, 8 patients.

Friday, Parish Rooms, Plighwood, 7 patients.

Codewords, p. 28

Totalized, p. 29

Easy: 74, Medium: 73, Harder: 819

Cell Block, p. 30

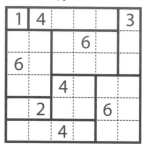

Wordwheel, p. 30
The nine-letter word is EMBROIDER.

Pet Shop Boys, p. 31
Customer 2 bought the dog collar and leash (clue 4). Clue 1 rules out positions 3 and 4 for the purchaser of the hamster wheel, so he must be number 1. Oliver has two neighbors in the diagram (clue 3), so he cannot be number 4, and, since he bought the fish food (clue 3), he is not 1 or 2, so he must be number 3. By elimination, number 4 must have bought the toy for the bird. Oliver cannot have been served third or fourth (clue 3), and Marcus was served second (clue 2), so Oliver must have been served first. Daniel's position cannot be 1 or 4 (clue 1), so he must be number 2, who bought the dog collar and leash. Nor was he served fourth (clue 1). So he must have been served third, and, from clue 1, the boy in position 4 must have been served fourth. So this was not Marcus, and must have been Craig, leaving Marcus as number 1, who bought the hamster wheel.

1, Marcus, hamster wheel, second.
2, Daniel, dog collar and leash, third.
3, Oliver, fish food, first.
4, Craig, toy for bird, fourth.

Hand-Reared, p. 32
Patsy is raising Toto (clue 4), and Denise is raising a vulture (clue 1), so the young woman raising Prince the jaguar, who isn't Yvonne (clue 2), must be Karen. Patsy, who's raising Toto, isn't Ms. Kirk, who's raising the chimpanzee (clue 4), so Toto must be the alligator, and, by elimination, Ms. Kirk

must be Yvonne. She's not rearing Sasha, which is Ms. Ross's assignment (clue 3), and we know she isn't rearing Prince or Toto, so she must be rearing Gemma. By elimination, Ms. Ross, who's rearing Sasha, must be Denise, and Sasha is thus the vulture. Karen, who's rearing Prince, isn't Ms. Fleming (clue 2), so her surname must be Thomas, and, by elimination, Ms. Fleming must be Patsy, who's rearing Toto the alligator.

Denise Ross, Sasha, vulture.
Karen Thomas, Prince, jaguar.
Patsy Fleming, Toto, alligator.
Yvonne Kirk, Gemma, chimpanzee.

Domino Search, p. 34

0	3	0	0	1	1	5	4
2	0	2	6	2	2	4	5
4	5	3	5	3	3	6	2
6	6	1	4	4	4	0	2
3	1	6	3	5	5	3	1
0	2	5	2	6	6	3	1
5	4	4	1	0	0	1	6

Battleships, p. 35

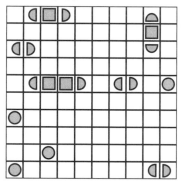

Further Cases, p. 36
Broken Man is by Alec MacDonald (clue 2) and the episode featuring Jack the Ripper is by Robert St. Simon (clue 6), so *Beggar's Book*, which features

Cecil Rhodes and is also by a male writer (clue 4) must be by Jonathan Small. Episode 3 is by Laura Lyons (clue 5), so *Stolen Sword* is not episode 1, featuring Sir Robert Baden-Powell (clues 1 and 3); nor is that episode *Red Queen* (clue 3) or *Broken Man* (clue 2), so it must be *Dying Lion*, and, by elimination, must have been written by Nancy Devoy. Alec MacDonald's *Broken Man* doesn't feature Winston Churchill (clue 2), so must feature Oscar Wilde, leaving Winston Churchill as the real-life character in Laura Lyons's episode 3. From clue 2, Oscar Wilde must feature in episode 4, so episode 3 must be *Stolen Sword*, and episode 5 must feature Cecil Rhodes (clue 1). Therefore *Stolen Sword* features Winston Churchill, and, by elimination, Robert St. Simon's episode featuring Jack the Ripper must be episode 2 in the series and must be called *Red Queen*.

1, *Dying Lion*, Nancy Devoy, Sir Robert Baden-Powell.
2, *Red Queen*, Robert St. Simon, Jack the Ripper.
3, *Stolen Sword*, Laura Lyons, Winston Churchill.
4, *Broken Man*, Alec MacDonald, Oscar Wilde.
5, *Beggar's Book*, Jonathan Small, Cecil Rhodes.

The Old School, p. 38

The girls' number 1 is surnamed Pembroke (clue 3), so the boys' number 1 can't be Archie (clue 1). Nor can he be Simon (clue 4) or Jack Darwin (clue 6), so he must be Len. Therefore Simon is the boys' number 2 (clue 4). Pembroke isn't Mary (clue 3), nor can she be Elsie (clue 5), or, since we know Jack Darwin isn't the boys' number 2, Hattie (clue 6), so she must be Amy. Since we know Amy Pembroke is the girls' number 1, the boys' number 4 can't be Keble or Wadham (clue 2), so, from clue 7, the girls' number 2 can't be Linacre; we know she isn't Darwin or Pembroke, nor can she be Keble or Wadham (clue 2), while Merton is male (clue 5); nor can the girls' number 2 be Clare (clue 7), so she must be Hall. Thus, from clue 7, the boys' number 4 must be Jack Darwin. Therefore, from clue 6, Hattie must be the girls' number 3. Now, by elimination, Archie must be the boys'

number 3, so, from clue 1, Clare must be the girls' number 3. Elsie can't be the girls' number 2 (clue 5), so must be their number 4, and Simon is therefore Merton (clue 5). Now, by elimination, Hall must be Mary. Len's surname, which we know isn't Pembroke, must be Wadham (clue 4), so, from clue 2, Keble must be Elsie, the girls' number 4, which leaves Archie, by elimination, as Linacre.

Boys:
1, Len Wadham.
2, Simon Merton.
3, Archie Linacre.
4, Jack Darwin.

Girls:
1, Amy Pembroke.
2, Mary Hall.
3, Hattie Clare.
4, Elsie Keble.

B-Movie Heroes, p. 40

Doyle Embury made a series of 10 films (clue 4), and the actor playing Jay Dyson made 14 (clue 7), so, from clue 6, John Kramer, who played Nick Delaney and didn't make 17 or 19 films, must have made 22 films. The actor who played Gil Dane wasn't Tony Vernon and can't have been Doyle Embury (clue 1), and we know he wasn't John Kramer; since his character was a soldier of fortune (clue 1), he can't have been Mike Norris, who played a Texas Ranger (clue 2), so, by elimination, he must have been Alan Belson. So we know he didn't make 10, 14, or 22 films; from clue 5, he can't have made 19 either, so he must have made 17. Therefore there were 19 Mac McGee films (clue 5), so that was not Doyle Embury's character, who must therefore have been Rob Farmer. Mac McGee, who was in 19 films, can't have been played by Tony Vernon (clue 1), so, by elimination, he must have been played by Mike Norris, and was therefore a Texas Ranger, leaving Tony Vernon as the man who played Jay Dyson in 14 films. The doctor was neither Doyle Embury's Rob Farmer nor John Kramer's Nick Delaney, hero of 50 films (clue 3), so must have been Tony Vernon's Jay Dyson. Therefore, from clue 3, Nick Delaney, played by John Kramer in 22 films, was a private eye, leaving Rob Farmer, played by Doyle Embury in 10 films, as a federal agent.

Alan Belson, Gil Dane, soldier of fortune, 17.
Doyle Embury, Rob Farmer, federal agent, 10.
John Kramer, Nick Delaney, private eye, 22.
Mike Norris, Mac McGee, Texas Ranger, 19.
Tony Vernon, Jay Dyson, doctor, 14.

It Must Be True . . . , p. 42

The 11:00 sighting was in Paris (clue 3). The one at 11:30 cannot have been in the Helsinki sauna (clue 1), nor was it reported from Rome by Tanya Tittle (clue 2), and clue 4 rules it out for Munich, so, by elimination, it must have been in London. Clue 1 rules out this report for Hugh Codham's column, and we know it was not reported by Tanya Tittle. Clue 4 rules out Tina Tattle and it was Whelan Ventitt who reported the sighting at 9:30 (clue 5), so, by elimination, Lotta Drivell must have detailed the London sighting, which was therefore at the rave (clue 7). We know the report from Paris did not refer to the sauna or the rave, nor was its location the hotel (clue 3). The meeting in the restaurant was recorded as taking place at 10:00 (clue 6), so, by elimination, the Paris report must have referred to the nightclub. The column in which this appeared cannot have been by Hugh Codham (clue 2), and we know it was not by any of Whelan Ventitt, Tanya Tittle, or Lotta Drivell, so it must have appeared in Tina Tattle's column. We have matched three locations with times, and clue 1 now rules out the one in the sauna for 10:30, so it must have been at 9:30, and was recorded by Whelan Ventitt, which tells us Hugh Codham reported the 10:00 meeting in the restaurant (clue 1). By elimination, the alleged sighting in Rome must have been in a hotel at 10:30, and it must have been in Munich that Hugh Codham stated that the celebrity had been seen.

Hugh Codham, Munich, restaurant, 10:00.
Lotta Drivell, London, rave, 11:30.
Tanya Tittle, Rome, hotel, 10:30.
Tina Tattle, Paris, nightclub, 11:00.
Whelan Ventitt, Helsinki, sauna, 9:30.

Codewords, p. 44

Totalized, p. 45

Easy: 42, Medium: 3, Harder: 900

Cell Block, p. 46

	2		4	
		3	6	3
5				
			4	4
	5			

Wordwheel, p. 46

The nine-letter word is REFRESHED.

Battleships, p. 47

Conspiracy Theories, p. 48

Chickweed's name wasn't Oswald (clue 5), nor was he Ambrose or Zachary, who must both have had seven-letter surnames (clue 6), so, as Egbert was Sleary (clue 4), Chickweed must have been Lancelot, and his pen name was therefore Warlock (clue 3). His article wasn't about the *Titanic* sinking (clue 3) or UFOs (clue 5); it was Colossus who wrote about the Bermuda Triangle (clue 2), and Ambrose wrote about diabetes (clue 6), so Lancelot Chickweed's subject must have been the Kennedy assassination. We know that Mercurius wasn't Lancelot Chickweed, nor was he Meagles (clue 1) or Egbert Sleary (clue 4); Blimber was Spyglass (clue 2), so Mercurius must have been Jeddler. We now know the subjects about which Ambrose and Lancelot Chickweed wrote; Oswald didn't write about the *Titanic* sinking (clue 3) or UFOs (clue 5), so his subject must have been the Bermuda Triangle, and his pen name was therefore Colossus. From his forename, Oswald can't have been Chickweed or Sleary, and his pen name tells us he wasn't Blimber or Jeddler, so he must have been Meagles. The man who wrote about UFOs wasn't Mercurius (clue 1) or Soothsayer (clue 5), so must have been Spyglass, who was Mr. Blimber. The information we now have tells us he wasn't Ambrose, Egbert, Lancelot, or Oswald, so he must have been Zachary. By elimination, Egbert Sleary must have written about the *Titanic* sinking, and Ambrose, who wrote about diabetes, must have been Jeddler, alias Mercurius, leaving Egbert Sleary's pen name as Soothsayer.

Ambrose Jeddler, Mercurius, diabetes.
Egbert Sleary, Soothsayer, *Titanic* sinking.
Lancelot Chickweed, Warlock, Kennedy assassination.
Oswald Meagles, Colossus, Bermuda Triangle.
Zachary Blimber, Spyglass, UFOs.

Out of Space, p. 50

The class introduced in 2400 was too complex (clue 1), so, from clue 6, the Emerald light transport can't have been introduced in 2385 or 2400; the Kilorik was introduced in 2355 (clue 7) and the survey ship in 2340 (clue 4), so the Emerald must have been introduced in 2370, and the ship scrapped because of its short range must have been introduced in 2385 (clue 5). We now know either the purpose or reason for scrapping to go with four years, so the patrol ship that broke up at speed (clue 2) must have been the Kilorik, introduced in 2355. The escort can't have been the too-complex ship introduced in 2400 (clue 5), so, by elimination, must have been the short-ranged ship introduced in 2385, leaving the ship introduced in 2400 as the transport. Clue 5 now tells us it was the Prahun. Now, from clue 3, the underpowered ship must have been the survey ship introduced in 2340, leaving the Emerald light transport, introduced in 2370, as the ship that was unstable. The underpowered survey ship wasn't the Tiger (clue 3), so must have been the Firebird, leaving the Tiger as the short-ranged escort introduced in 2385.

2340, Firebird, survey ship, underpowered.
2355, Kilorik, patrol ship, broke up at speed.
2370, Emerald, light transport, unstable.
2385, Tiger, escort, short range.
2400, Prahun, transport, too complex.

Chopper Cabs, p. 52

Jenny Kite can only have 3 or 4 passengers (clue 2), and so can Roy Swan (clue 3). Since Vince Wren can't have 3 passengers (clue 4), Roy Swan can't have 4 (clue 5), so he must have 3 and Jenny Kite 4. Vince Wren accordingly has 2 (clue 5), and Sue Teal, by elimination, just 1. The pilot heading for Hyannis Port must have been male (clue 2), but since, from the same clue this helicopter couldn't have had 3 passengers, its pilot must have been Vince Wren. The pilot of helicopter A isn't Jenny Kite (clue 2), and, from the numbers of passengers, can't be Sue Teal (clue 1) or Roy Swan (clue 4), so must be Vince Wren. His number of passengers puts Jenny Kite in helicopter B (clue 2). We know that helicopter B has 4 passengers, so Roy Swan can't be the pilot of helicopter C (clue 3), and must be helicopter D, with C piloted by Sue Teal. Jenny Kite is thus flying to the Hamptons (clue 1). Roy Swan's destination can't be Martha's Vineyard (clue 4), so must be Woodstock, leaving Sue Teal's destination as Martha's Vineyard.

A, Vince Wren, 2, Hyannis Port.
B, Jenny Kite, 4, the Hamptons.
C, Sue Teal, 1, Martha's Vineyard.
D, Roy Swan, 3, Woodstock.

Days Out, p. 53

The bus trip was on Wednesday (clue 4). The car trip wasn't on Monday (clue 1), so that must have been the day they went to the Natural History Museum by train (clue 2), and the car trip must have been on Friday. So Kansas City, which was visited two days before the car trip (clue 1), must have been the Wednesday location visited by bus. We know that the Natural History Museum was visited by train, so travel to the Louisberg Cider Mill in Parkville (clue 3), must have been by car on Friday. By elimination, the bus trip to Kansas City on Wednesday must have been to the zoo, and the Natural History Museum visited on Monday must have been in Lawrence.

Monday, Natural History Museum, Lawrence, train.
Wednesday, Zoo, Kansas City, bus.
Friday, Louisberg Cider Mill, Parkville, car.

Vacation Reading, p. 54

Not for Love is by Melissa Reveling (clue 2). *King of Love* isn't by Honoria Blount (clue 3), so it must be by Anna Estensen, and Honoria Blount must have written *False and True Love*. *King of Love* has an Elizabethan setting (clue 4), so *False and True Love*, which has 200 pages (clue 1) and so can't be set in the Civil War (clue 3), must be set in Regency times. The Civil War book, which, from clue 3, must have 250 pages, must therefore be *Not for Love* by Melissa Reveling. By elimination, *King of Love*, Anna Estensen's Elizabethan romance, must have 300 pages.

***False and True Love*, Honoria Blount, Regency, 200 pages.**
***King of Love*, Anna Estensen, Elizabethan, 300 pages.**
***Not for Love*, Melissa Reveling, Civil War, 250 pages.**

Getting an Eiffel, p. 55

The Bakers are at the first stage (clue 4). From clue 1, the Cleggs are not at the summit or at ground level, so they must be at the second platform. Therefore, from clue 1, Martin must be at the summit. His companion there is not Helena (clue 1), or Victoria (clue 2), and Leonie is married to Oliver (clue 3), so Martin's wife must be Daphne. Their surname cannot be Gibson (clue 3), so it must be Wylie, which places the Gibsons at ground level. Now, from clue 2, Victoria must be Mrs. Clegg. From clue 3, Oliver and Leonie must be the Bakers at the first stage of the tower. Mr. Gibson is not Thomas (clue 1), so he must be Andrew, leaving Thomas as Mr. Clegg at the second stage.

Ground level, Andrew and Helena Gibson.
First stage, Oliver and Leonie Baker.
Second stage, Thomas and Victoria Clegg.
Summit, Martin and Daphne Wylie.

Coffee Break, p. 56

Nurse Otley works on Kennerly Ward (clue 1), and Diane's surname is Milligan (clue 4), so Sally from Penryn Ward, who isn't Nurse Parsons (clue 2), must be Baxter, who is figure C (clue 3). So, from clue 2, figure A is Nurse Parsons. Diane Milligan can't be figure D (clue 4); we know she's not figure C, and her surname rules out figure A, so she must be figure B. Helen can't be figure A (clue 4), who must therefore be Nancy, leaving Helen as figure D. By elimination, Helen must be Nurse Otley from Kennerly Ward. Nancy Parsons doesn't work in A&E (clue 5), so she must be on Sackville Ward, leaving the A&E nurse as Diane Milligan, figure B.

A, Nancy Parsons, Sackville.
B, Diane Milligan, A&E.
C, Sally Baxter, Penryn.
D, Helen Otley, Kennerly.

Battleships, p. 57

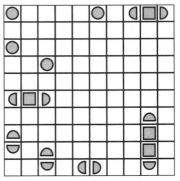

Domino Search, p. 61

1	4	2	5	0	0	1	1
5	3	6	5	4	4	0	2
1	3	6	2	3	5	0	1
4	5	2	3	3	3	1	6
5	6	6	2	0	5	1	0
2	2	4	4	1	6	6	3
4	6	5	0	4	0	3	2

Codewords, p. 58

Totalized, p. 59

Easy: 64, Medium: 20, Harder: 72

Cell Block, p. 60

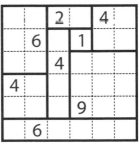

Wordwheel, p. 60

The nine-letter word is HORSEBACK.

2020 Visions, p. 62

Michael is Burroughs (clue 6), so the man surnamed Rocklynne, who isn't Donald (clue 1), must be Stephen. Joanne wrote *The Horsemen* (clue 3), so she can't be Wells, who wrote *Judgment* (clue 5), nor is she Leinster (clue 3), so she must be Smith, and her story is therefore about an alien invasion (clue 2). *Dog Days*, about toxic pollution, isn't by Stephen Rocklynne (clue 4), nor is his story called *Endgame* (clue 1), so it must be *Red Sky*. It can't feature the famine, which is in Abigail's story (clue 2), nor the plague (clue 6), so the problem it deals with must be nuclear war. Michael Burroughs's story doesn't feature the plague (clue 5), so must feature toxic pollution, and is therefore called *Dog Days* (clue 4). Donald's story isn't *Endgame* (clue 1), so it must be *Judgment*, and Donald must therefore be Wells; by elimination, it must feature the plague. Also by elimination, Abigail must be Leinster, and her story about the famine must be *Endgame*.

Abigail Leinster, *Endgame*, famine.
Donald Wells, *Judgment*, plague.
Joanne Smith, *The Horsemen*, alien invasion.
Michael Burroughs, *Dog Days*, toxic pollution.
Stephen Rocklynne, *Red Sky*, nuclear war.

Special Requirements, p. 64

Lurimeg's been assigned cabin 5 (clue 7), so, from clue 1, the methane atmosphere can't be needed for cabin 1, 4, or 5; it's cabin 3 that has to have no water vapor (clue 5), so, by elimination, the methane atmosphere must be for cabin 2.

Therefore, from clue 1, Bodi-Nadi must have cabin 3, with no water vapor, and cabin 1 must be the Pimtrians. We now know that Sinuwei hasn't been assigned cabin 3 or 5, and clue 3 now rules out cabins 1 and 4, so Sinuwei must have cabin 2, with the methane atmosphere. So, from clue 3, cabin 1, the Pimtrian's, has the subzero temperature. The Pimtrian isn't Y'Alidan (clue 4), so must be Hravpak, leaving Y'Alidan with cabin 4. That cabin isn't being provided with low gravity (clue 4), so must require total darkness, and Y'Alidan is therefore Gunitrian (clue 2). By elimination, cabin 5, Lurimeg's, is getting low gravity. From his cabin number, Lurimeg can't be Ordolase or Dravian, so he must be Jirrizic. Clue 6 now tells us the Ordolase is Sinuwei in cabin 2, and Bodi-Nadi in cabin 3 is Dravian.

Cabin 1, Hravpak, Pimtrian, subzero temperature.
Cabin 2, Sinuwei, Ordolase, methane atmosphere.
Cabin 3, Bodi-Nadi, Dravian, no water vapor.
Cabin 4, Y'Alidan, Gunitrian, total darkness.
Cabin 5, Lurimeg, Jirrizic, low gravity.

Wilde Types, p. 66

Hector is having one week's vacation (clue 5) and Alexander is not heading for a European destination (clue 1), so the brother spending two weeks in Austria (clue 3), who is not Sebastian or Ranulph, the pony-trekker (clue 3), must be Ferdinand. He will be neither pony-trekking nor cycling, which is the five-week vacation (clue 5), nor will he be diving, which is the Seychelles vacation (clue 6), and the climbing vacation is not in Europe (clue 1), so the Austrian vacation must be hiking. The five-week cycling vacation is not being taken by Alexander (clue 1), so it must be Sebastian. Therefore the Mexican vacation must be Hector's one-week activity (clue 5) that, by elimination, must be climbing, leaving the diving vacation as Alexander's. Now, from clue 2, Ranulph must be going to the Pyrenees and Sebastian to Brazil. Alexander's vacation is shorter than the one being taken in the Pyrenees (clue 1), so it must be three weeks, and Ranulph must be spending four weeks pony-trekking in the Pyrenees.

Alexander, Seychelles, diving, 3 weeks.
Ferdinand, Austria, hiking, 2 weeks.
Hector, Mexico, climbing, 1 week.
Ranulph, Pyrenees, pony-trekking, 4 weeks.
Sebastian, Brazil, cycling, 5 weeks.

Bust Up, p. 68

Room 4 cannot be the music room (clue 2), or the lounge (clue 3), and clue 4 tells us it is not the dining area, so, by elimination, it must be the library, where the bust sits on a bookshelf (clue 1), so, from that clue, Beethoven's bust must be in room 3. We know the bust on the sideboard is not in room 4, and clue 3 rules it out for both room 1 and room 2, so, by elimination, it must support Beethoven in room 3. Clue 3 tells us the bust of Bach must be in either room 3 or room 4. We know it is not in room 3, so it must be in room 4. Since Mozart sits atop an occasional table (clue 4), by elimination, Chopin's bust must be on the mantelpiece. This is not in room 1 (clue 3), so it must be in room 2, leaving Mozart in room 1. So room 2, with its bust on the mantelpiece, is not the lounge (clue 3), nor is it the music room (clue 2), so it must be the dining area. So the music room, which is not number 2 (clue 2), must be room 1 (clue 2), leaving room 3 as the lounge, with a bust of Beethoven on the sideboard.

1, music room, Mozart, occasional table.
2, dining area, Chopin, mantelpiece.
3, lounge, Beethoven, sideboard.
4, library, Bach, bookshelf.

Battleships, p. 69

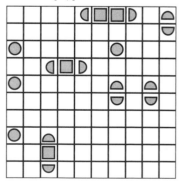

Giving Up, p. 70

One of the men has not smoked for seven weeks (clue 3), but it's not Dai Coffin, who has given up for less than six weeks (clue 1) and from clue 3 we know that Jackie is female, so it must be Bernard Ash. The 10-a-day smoker has not had one for eight weeks (clue 6), and Eileen Hale has not smoked for four weeks (clue 3), so 40-a-day Jackie Tinn, who has not been smoke-free for five weeks (clue 3), must have given up so far for two weeks, and therefore is the one who used nicotine patches (clue 5). Dai Coffin isn't the ex-smoker who gave up eight weeks ago (clue 1), so it must be five weeks, leaving Virginia Hook as the 10-a-day smoker who hasn't smoked for eight weeks, and who must have used hypnotism to help (clue 4). The 20-a-day smoker used sponsorship to give up (clue 5), but that person didn't give up seven or five weeks ago (clue 2), so it must be four weeks, and it must be Eileen Hale. Dai Coffin didn't use nicotine gum (clue 1), so it must have been willpower alone, leaving the gum-user as Bernard Ash, who has given up for seven weeks. Finally, Dai Coffin's willpower didn't cure him of a 15-a-day habit (clue 5), so he must have smoked 30 a day, leaving Bernard Ash as the former smoker of 15 cigarettes a day.

Bernard Ash, 15 a day, 7 weeks, nicotine gum.
Dai Coffin, 30 a day, 5 weeks, willpower.
Eileen Hale, 20 a day, 4 weeks, sponsorship.
Jackie Tinn, 40 a day, 2 weeks, nicotine patches.
Virginia Hook, 10 a day, 8 weeks, hypnotism.

Clubbing Coppers, p. 72

The club Inspector Mullen is to raid isn't the Equator (clue 2), Foxx's (clue 2 again), the Chicago, which is to be raided by Inspector Carter (clue 6), or the Aztec, which is to be raided by a sergeant (clue 1), so must be Mr. Hyde on Forsyth Street (clue 3). He won't be looking for forged credit cards (clue 2), stolen cash (clue 3), drugs, which Sergeant Pomeroy's squad will be searching for (clue 4), or stolen goods, which will be searched for in the club on Walpole Lane (clue 1), so he must be going to look for guns. The club Inspector Harvey will be raiding isn't on Walpole Lane or Lincoln Street (clue 1), and we know he isn't raiding Mr. Hyde on Forsyth Street; Sergeant Lyndon will be raiding the club on Erskine Street (clue 5), so Inspector Harvey must be going to raid the club on Buckland Street. Sergeant Pomeroy's men will be looking for drugs; the club on Walpole Lane, where stolen goods will be sought, must be the Chicago, to be searched by Inspector Carter. By elimination, the club on Lincoln Street must be going to be searched by Sergeant Pomeroy, seeking drugs. This club isn't the Aztec (clue 1), so that must be the club on Erskine Street to be raided by Sergeant Lyndon. The Equator isn't on Lincoln Street either (clue 2), so must be on Buckland Street and due for a raid by Inspector Harvey, and, as he won't be looking for forged credit cards (clue 2), he'll be seeking stolen cash. By elimination, the club on Lincoln Street that will be raided by Sergeant Pomeroy, looking for drugs, must be Foxx's, and Sergeant Lyndon will be searching the Aztec for forged credit cards.

Aztec, Erskine Street, Sergeant Lyndon, forged credit cards.
Chicago, Walpole Lane, Inspector Carter, stolen goods.
Equator, Buckland Street, Inspector Harvey, stolen cash.
Foxx's, Lincoln Street, Sergeant Pomeroy, drugs.
Mr. Hyde, Forsyth Street, Inspector Mullen, guns.

Codewords, p. 74

Totalized, p. 75

Easy: 31, Medium: 29, Harder: 21

Cell Block, p. 76

```
┌───┬───┬───┬───┬───┐
│ 2 │   │   │ 4 │   │
├───┼───┼───┼───┼───┤
│   │   │ 2 │   │   │
├───┼───┼───┼───┼───┤
│   │ 2 │   │ 1 │ 2 │
├───┼───┼───┼───┼───┤
│ 3 │   │ 2 │   │ 5 │
├───┼───┼───┼───┼───┤
│   │ 3 │   │ 3 │   │
├───┼───┼───┼───┼───┤
│ 2 │   │ 2 │   │ 3 │
└───┴───┴───┴───┴───┘
```

Wordwheel, p. 76

The nine-letter word is BOYFRIEND.

Fully Furnished, p. 77

The street light is outside number 5 (clue 3). Since Allen lives at number 15 (clue 4), clue 2 rules out the bus stop as the item outside Terry's house at number 11 (clue 4), and that clue rules out the manhole cover, so, by elimination, the fire hydrant must be outside number 11. Since Nathan Pickles does not live at number 5 (clue 3), he must live at number 3. From clue 1, Anna cannot be Allen, at number 15, nor is she Norton, so she must be Byers, and she must live at number 5, the house near the street light. So clue 2 places the bus stop outside Nathan's house, number 3. By elimination, Allen must be Myra's surname, and the manhole cover must be outside her house, number 15, and Terry's surname must be Norton.

3, Nathan Pickles, bus stop.
5, Anna Byers, street light.
11, Terry Norton, fire hydrant.
15, Myra Allen, manhole cover.

Park and Ride, p. 78

Three people were in car 4 (clue 3), and two were aboard the Rover (clue 1). The Hyundai in space 2 was not carrying just one person (clue 2), so, by elimination, four people must have been in it. Car 4 is not the Saab (clue 3), and we know it is not the Hyundai. Since Janine used space 3 (clue 4), clue 1 rules out space 4 for the Rover, so it must contain the Jaguar. Therefore, from clue 5, Steve's car is the Rover, carrying two people. We know he

did not park in space 3, and that the Rover is not in spaces 2 or 4, so it must be in space 1. So, from clue 1, Carole's car is the Hyundai in space 2. Now, by elimination, the Jaguar in space 4 must have been driven by Luke, and Janine must have used space 3 for the Saab, of which she must have been the sole occupant.

1, Rover, Steve, 2 people.
2, Hyundai, Carole, 4 people.
3, Saab, Janine, 1 person.
4, Jaguar, Luke, 3 people.

To the Clinic, p. 79

Dolittle's appointment is on Friday (clue 4), so, from clue 1, Kildare's must be on Wednesday and Jekyll's on Monday. Jekyll is Ivy (clue 3), so the woman surnamed Dolittle (clue 4), who can't be Arnold, must be Edna, leaving Arnold's surname as Kildare. From clue 1, Ivy Jekyll must be going to the Arthritis Clinic, and, from clue 2, Edna Dolittle will be attending the Diabetes Clinic. This leaves Arnold Kildare visiting the Cardiac Clinic.

Arnold Kildare, Cardiac, Wednesday.
Edna Dolittle, Diabetes, Friday.
Ivy Jekyll, Arthritis, Monday.

Call Me Lucky, p. 80

The Asian incident was in September (clue 6). The event in January 1966 wasn't in Africa or North America (clue 1), nor South America (clue 4), so it must have been in Europe, and was therefore the pirate attack (clue 3). Since it wasn't in 1924, the South American incident (clue 4) can't have been in May, and must have been in July, and the 1924 event must have been in March. It wasn't in Africa (clue 1), so must have been in North America. By elimination, the shipwreck in May (clue 5) must have been in Africa. It wasn't in 1949 (clue 1) or 1953, the year of the airship crash (clue 3), so must have been in 1937. The volcanic eruption was not in North America (clue 2), so wasn't in March, and, as it was earlier in the year than the airship crash (clue 2 again), it wasn't in September, so it must have been the July incident in South America. Therefore the airship crash must have been in September 1953 (clue 2), and must have happened in Asia. By elimination, it must have been in North America in March 1924 that "Lucky" survived a landslide, and the volcanic eruption in South America must have been in July 1949.

Airship crash, Asia, September, 1953.
Landslide, North America, March, 1924.
Pirate attack, Europe, January, 1966.
Shipwreck, Africa, May, 1937.
Volcanic eruption, South America, July, 1949.

Grumbly Old Codgers, p. 82

Billy Aker is 52 (clue 3), and Terry Bull is over 55 (clue 4), so the 49-year-old, who is not Malcolm Tent (clue 2) or Saul Dyer (clue 3), must be comedian Ivor Growse (clue 1). He is not irritated by computers (clue 2), body piercing (clue 1), fast food, which is the 58-year-old (clue 5), or speed cameras, which is the singer (clue 2), so it must be reality TV. The 53-year-old is not the singer or actor (clue 2), nor can he be the 56-year-old DJ (clue 6), so he must be the novelist. By elimination, the singer complaining about speed cameras must be 52-year-old Billy Aker and the 58-year-old must be the actor. This is not Terry Bull (clue 4), so he must be the 56-year-old DJ. Malcolm Tent is not the actor (clue 2), so he must be the 53-year-old novelist grumbling about body piercing. This leaves the actor as Saul Dyer, and Terry Bull as the computer hater.

Billy Aker, singer, 52, speed cameras.
Terry Bull, DJ, 56, computers.
Saul Dyer, actor, 58, fast food.
Ivor Growse, comedian, 49, reality TV.
Malcolm Tent, novelist, 53, body piercing.

Battleships, p. 84

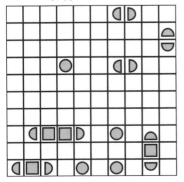

Stepping Down, p. 85

Since Westward Ho! has 48 steps (clue 4), it cannot be Richard's house, nor is Clifftops (clue 1), while Jeremy's is named Shangri-La (clue 3), so Richard must own Windyridge. Angela's house, which has 39 steps (clue 2), cannot be Westward Ho!, so it must be Clifftops. Therefore, from clue 1, Windyridge, owned by Richard, must have 37 steps, leaving Jeremy's Shangri-La with 43. Also, by elimination, Westward Ho! must be Glenda's house. It is not number 1 (clue 4), nor can Angela's Clifftops be (clue 2), and clue 1 rules out Richard's Windyridge, so house 1 must be Jeremy's Shangri-La. Clue 2 now places Clifftops as house 2. Clue 3 tells us Windyridge is not number 3, so it must be house 4, leaving Westward Ho! in position 3.

1, Shangri-La, Jeremy, 43 steps.
2, Clifftops, Angela, 39 steps.
3, Westward Ho!, Glenda, 48 steps.
4, Windyridge, Richard, 37 steps.

Cowboy Heroes, p. 86

McCoy operated in California (clue 2), and Steele was a gunfighter (clue 4), so the U.S. Marshal operating in Arizona, who wasn't Wyler (clue 6), must have been Flynn. The gambler's horse was Prince (clue 3), so he can't have been Wyler (clue 6), and must have been McCoy, who operated in California. By elimination, Wyler, Randy's rider, must have been a wandering cowboy. Now, from clue 4, Dusty, whose horse was Buck, who can't have been Steele, the gunfighter, must have been Flynn, who operated in Arizona. By elimination, Steele the gunfighter's horse must have been Warrior. Dusty Flynn's not in picture C (clue 4), and can't be in picture A (clue 6): Bowie's in picture D (clue 5), so Dusty Flynn must be in picture B, and, from clue 6, Wyler, the wandering cowboy, must be in picture A. Therefore Wyler can't have been Lucky (clue 1), and we know that Bowie's in picture D, so Wyler must have been Johnny. Therefore he didn't operate in Texas (clue 1), and must have operated in Montana. By elimination, the man who operated in Texas must have been Steele the gunfighter. We now know the names of the men in three pictures, so Lucky must be in picture C. Therefore he wasn't Steele, the gun-

fighter (clue 4), and must have been McCoy the gambler, leaving Bowie in picture D as Steele the gunfighter.

A, Johnny Wyler, wandering cowboy, Randy, Montana.
B, Dusty Flynn, U.S. Marshal, Buck, Arizona.
C, Lucky McCoy, gambler, Prince, California.
D, Bowie Steele, gunfighter, Warrior, Texas.

Hollywood Hopefuls, p. 88

The girl who would be Imogen Valentine arrived in Hollywood in 1930 (clue 4), the girl from Illinois became Sabrina Banks (clue 1), and Simone Lamont arrived later than the girl from Missouri (clue 3), so the girl from Ohio who moved west in 1929, and who didn't become Meryl Day (clue 2), must have been Grace Horne, and therefore had been born Grace Waghorn (clue 6). Therefore the year that the girl from Louisiana arrived in Hollywood, which was the year after Audrey Mullett (clue 3), cannot have been 1930 or 1932. Hyacinth Mudge arrived in 1932 (clue 5), so the aspiring actress from Louisiana who also didn't arrive in 1933, must have done so in 1934. Therefore Audrey Mullett must have traveled to "Tinseltown" in 1933 (clue 3). As Eunice Wigg was from New York (clue 1), she didn't travel west in 1932 or 1933, so it must have been 1930, and she must have become Imogen Valentine. Simone Lamont wasn't from Missouri (clue 3), so she must have moved from Louisiana in 1934, and, by elimination, the girl from Missouri must have become Meryl Day. So she must have arrived in Hollywood in 1932, and been born Hyacinth Mudge (clue 5), and Audrey Mullett, arriving in 1933, must have been the Illinois girl who became Sabrina Banks, leaving Janice Allibone as the Louisiana girl who went to Hollywood in 1934 and found fame as actress Simone Lamont.

1929, Ohio, Grace Waghorn, Grace Horne.
1930, New York, Eunice Wigg, Imogen Valentine.
1932, Missouri, Hyacinth Mudge, Meryl Day.
1933, Illinois, Audrey Mullett, Sabrina Banks.
1934, Louisiana, Janice Allibone, Simone Lamont.

Codewords, p. 90

Totalized, p. 91
Easy: 119, Medium: 8, Harder: 75

Cell Block, p. 92

Wordwheel, p. 92
The nine-letter word is WHISPERED.

Domino Search, p. 93

3	3	6	4	2	1	1	5
2	2	2	4	3	6	5	1
1	1	4	4	0	0	0	0
2	6	5	6	4	3	1	5
6	6	1	3	5	2	3	5
0	0	4	6	6	0	1	5
3	3	0	5	4	2	4	2

Dump It!, p. 94

Mr. Thrower is getting rid of 10 items or bundles (clue 5) and Mrs. Heap drives a Ford (clue 3), so the 5 items in the Fiat, which do not belong to Mr. Sachs (clue 1) or Mr. Binnett (clue 3) must be Mrs. Riddings's bundles of paper (clue 6). 6 bags of garden waste are going into the green waste dumpster (clue 2), so the amount of metal in the back of the Chevrolet (clue 1) must be at least 8 items or bundles and, from clue 1, Mr. Sachs must have 12 items for the recyclers. Mr. Sachs doesn't drive a Toyota (clue 2), so it must be the Volvo. The 6 bags of garden waste are not in the back of the Toyota (clue 2), so they must be in Mrs. Heap's Ford. By elimination, the 8 items must belong to Mr. Binnett. The car at the household waste dumpster is not the Toyota (clue 2), so it must be the Volvo with the 12 items. Finally, the number of items being thrown into the wood dumpster is not 8 (clue 4), so it must be Mr. Thrower's 10 items, and, by elimination, he must be the owner of the Toyota. This leaves Mr. Binnett's 8 items as those being thrown into the metals dumpster.

Green waste, Mrs. Heap, 6, Ford.
Household, Mr. Sachs, 12, Volvo.
Metal, Mr. Binnett, 8, Chevrolet.
Paper, Mrs. Riddings, 5, Fiat.
Wood, Mr. Thrower, 10, Toyota.

Under Par, p. 96

The Canadian is figure D (clue 2), so, from clue 1, the golfer from the United States must be either figure A or figure B. Since he is 4 under par (clue 1), clue 3 rules out figure A, so the American player must be figure B and Don Magnus from Australia figure C (clue 1). By elimination, figure A must be from England. Now, from clue 4, figure B, the American, must be Rick Simons. The leader, who's 7 under par, isn't Shane Hardie (clue 3) or Glen Boyd (clue 5), so he must be Don Magnus from Australia, figure C. Figure D, the Canadian, can't be Glen Boyd (clue 5), so must be Shane Hardie, leaving Glen Boyd as figure A from England. Finally, from clue 3, Glen Boyd must be 6 under par, and Shane Hardie 5 under par.

A, Glen Boyd, England, 6 under par.
B, Rick Simons, United States, 4 under par.
C, Don Magnus, Australia, 7 under par.
D, Shane Hardie, Canada, 5 under par.

Battleships, p. 97

Elevated Art, p. 98

Since Arsène lived at number 25 (clue 2), clue 1 places Pierre at number 23, and Lacoste at number 21. We now know Grègoire must have lived at either number 21 or number 27, so Mercier, the abstract painter, must have lived at 23 or 25 (clue 4). We know Lacoste did not live at 27, nor did Dupont (clue 5), so Robert must have done. He was not Grègoire (clue 4), so he must have been Yves, and, by elimination, Grègoire was Lacoste at number 21. Clue 3 now tells us Arsène, at 25, painted portraits, so, by elimination, Mercier, the abstract painter, must have been Pierre, at number 23, and Arsène's surname must be Dupont. From clue 1, the landscape painter cannot have been Grègoire Lacoste, so the latter must have painted still lifes, and Yves Robert must have been the landscape artist.

21, Grègoire Lacoste, still life.
23, Pierre Mercier, abstract.
25, Arsène Dupont, portrait.
27, Yves Robert, landscape.

Sporting Stars, p. 99

Karen goes to Hillside (clue 2) and Cooper is at Windsor Green (clue 3), so Diane Piggott (clue 1) must be at St. Peter's, and is therefore in the high jump (clue 4). This leaves Karen from Hillside as Stewart. She's not in the 400m hurdles (clue 2), so must be in the 100m. Now, by elimination, Cooper's forename must be Shelley, and she must be in the 400m hurdles.

Diane Piggott, St. Peter's, high jump.
Karen Stewart, Hillside, 100m.
Shelley Cooper, Windsor Green, 400m hurdles.

On the Red-eye, p. 100

Terry Wiles is going to Minneapolis (clue 3) and Gary Hearn is a vampire (clue 6), so the industrial spy going to Pittsburgh, who is also male (clue 2), must be Sean Tallis. Babs Curry isn't going to Atlanta (clue 5), nor, since she's a dentist (clue 5), to St. Louis, the TV critic's destination (clue 4), so she must be going to Memphis. Therefore she's not the alien (clue 1), nor the hired killer, who's traveling as a solicitor (clue 3), so she must be the jewel thief. Terry Wiles isn't the hired killer (clue 3), so must be the alien, and, by elimination, the hired killer traveling as a solicitor must be Jessica Kay. From her stated occupation, her destination isn't St. Louis, so must be Atlanta, and the TV critic going to St. Louis must be Gary Hearn, the vampire. Finally, Sean Tallis isn't the engineer (clue 6), so must be a pilot, and the engineer must be Terry Wiles, going to Minneapolis, who's really an alien.

Babs Curry, dentist, Memphis, jewel thief.
Gary Hearn, TV critic, St. Louis, vampire.
Jessica Kay, solicitor, Atlanta, hired killer.
Sean Tallis, pilot, Pittsburgh, industrial spy.
Terry Wiles, engineer, Minneapolis, alien.

Sporting Gossip, p. 102

Onslow is recovering (clue 7). The darts player who is dieting isn't Duffy or Frost (clue 1), and Costigan plays football (clue 6), so, by elimination, the darts player must be Strong. So he can't be Dean (clue 3), Lloyd, who is Duffy (clue 4) or Anthony, who's retiring (clue 2); nor is he Toby, whose game is golf (clue 5), so he must be Jeff. Toby's forename or sport rule out three surnames, nor is he Frost (clue 5), so he must be Onslow, who's recovering. Lloyd Duffy's sport isn't tennis (clue 4), and his surname rules him out as the football player, so his sport must be boxing. He's not divorcing (clue 4), and we know Anthony's retiring, so Lloyd Duffy must be emigrating. Finally, from clue 5, Costigan the football player can't be Anthony, so he must be Dean, leaving Anthony as the tennis player. By elimina-

tion, his surname must be Frost, and Dean Costigan must be divorcing.

Anthony Frost, tennis, retiring.
Dean Costigan, football, divorcing.
Jeff Strong, darts, dieting.
Lloyd Duffy, boxing, emigrating.
Toby Onslow, golf, recovering.

Codewords, p. 104

Totalized, p. 105

Easy: 7, Medium: 16, Harder: 196

Cell Block, p. 106

Wordwheel, p. 106

The nine-letter word is TARANTULA.

An Eye for a Picture, p. 107

The picture from the garage sale cost $5 (clue 4), so the one that cost $10, which wasn't from a junk shop (clue 3), must have come from the market stall, and was therefore *Autumn Scene* (clue 1). By elimination, the item from the junk shop must have

cost $15, and was thus by Angus McRay (clue 2). Therefore *Still Life* can't have cost $10 (clue 4), so must have been the $5 picture. Therefore *Autumn Scene* must be by Luc Le Beau (clue 4). *Hyacinths* isn't by Enrico Giano (clue 3), so must be the Angus McRay picture from the junk shop, and Enrico Gianoi must have painted *Still Life*.

Autumn Scene, Luc Le Beau, $10, market stall.
Hyacinths, Angus McRay, $15, junk shop.
Still Life, Enrico Giano, $5, garage sale.

Terry Bull Taxis, p. 108

The cab called at 3:15 while its driver was visiting a lady friend is not number 1 (clue 3), nor can the latter cab have been called at 9:50 (clue 1), or 2:55 (clue 4), so Mandy must have tried to contact it at 11:10. So its driver was not answering a call of nature (clue 2), nor can he have been placing a bet (clue 1), and we know he was not visiting a lady friend, so he must have been buying cigarettes. Therefore, from clue 4, cab 2 must have been called at 2:55, and Leroy is the driver of cab 3. We have matched two times with causes for nonresponse, so, from clue 1, the driver placing the bet, who was not called at 9:50, must have been called at 2:55, and was in cab 2, and the 9:50 call must have been to the driver answering a call of nature. Clue 1 now tells us cab 1 is Melvyn's. Adam's is not number 2 (clue 5), so it must be number 4, leaving Vikram's as number 2. Since this is on a side street, from clue 2, the driver answering the call of nature cannot be Leroy, whose cab 3 is also on a side street, so he must be Adam, in cab 4, leaving Leroy as the driver who was visiting a lady friend when called at 3:15.

1, Melvyn, 11:10, buying cigarettes.
2, Vikram, 2:55, placing bet.
3, Leroy, 3:15, visiting lady friend.
4, Adam, 9:50, call of nature.

Guilty!, p. 109

Hood was given 5 years (clue 2). Jesse, sentenced to 8 years (clue 3), can't be James (clue 1) or Turpin (clue 4), so he must be Sikes. So Turpin must have been sentenced to 6 or 7 years, and figure D to 7 years or 8 years (clue 4). Clue 5 rules out 7 years, so figure D was sentenced to 8 years, and is thus Jesse Sikes. Therefore Turpin was sen-

tenced to 7 years (clue 4), and, by elimination, James must have been given 6 years. From clue 5, Turpin, sentenced to 7 years, is either figure B or figure C. Figure A hasn't been sentenced to 6 years (clue 3), so, by elimination, he must be Hood, sentenced to 5 years. Robin isn't figure C (clue 6), and now, from clue 1, he can't be figure A either, so he must be figure B. Figure A isn't Dick (clue 3), so must be Bill, and, by elimination, figure C must be Dick. He can't be Turpin, sentenced to 7 years (clue 1), so he must be James, sentenced to 6 years, and figure B, Robin, must be Turpin.

A, Bill Hood, 5 years.
B, Robin Turpin, 7 years.
C, Dick James, 6 years.
D, Jesse Sikes, 8 years.

A Dearth of Conversation, p. 110

It was one of the women who ate egg and bacon (clue 4), but not Nancy Owen (clue 2), so it must have been Sue Taylor. One person had tea and bacon sandwiches (clue 5), and Kevin Lynn ate a turkey sandwich (clue 1), so Barry Cole, who drank soda and did not eat the egg sandwiches (clue 1), must have eaten cheese and pickle sandwiches, and therefore read the whodunnit (clue 6). Nancy Owen didn't eat bacon sandwiches (clue 2), so must have had egg sandwiches, leaving Gary Hines as the person who drank tea, ate bacon sandwiches, and also read a tabloid newspaper (clue 2). The milk drinker who read the local paper didn't eat egg and bacon or egg sandwiches (clue 3), so must have had a turkey sandwich, and thus was Kevin Lynn. Nancy Owen didn't read a travel book (clue 2), so must have read the magazine, and it must have been Sue Taylor who read the travel book while eating her egg and bacon. Finally, Nancy Owen didn't drink coffee (clue 5), so must have had mineral water, leaving the coffee drinker as Sue Taylor.

Barry Cole, cheese and pickle sandwiches, soda, whodunnit.
Gary Hines, bacon sandwiches, tea, tabloid paper.
Kevin Lynn, turkey sandwich, milk, local paper.
Nancy Owen, egg sandwiches, mineral water, magazine.
Sue Taylor, egg and bacon, coffee, travel book.

Dawn Raid, p. 112

The forger's house was raided at 5:05 a.m. (clue 1), so, from clue 3, the Copse Road address must have been raided at 5:20 and the sneak thief's house at 5:10. So Copse Road is not the home of Wheels Wilf, the getaway driver (clue 5), the safe-cracker, who lives on Crooke Street (clue 4), so it must be the car thief's house. Therefore, Crazy Chris, whose home was raided at 5:07 a.m., must be the safecracker from Crooke Street and, by elimination, getaway driver Wheels Wilf must have been arrested at 5:15 a.m. He doesn't live on Laws Close (clue 5) or Larson Road, where Ronnie the Rabbit lives (clue 6), so it must be Peel Lane. Splinters Dave was not arrested at 5:05 or 5:10 a.m. (clue 1), so he must be the car thief whose Copse Road house was raided at 5:20 a.m. By elimination, the Laws Close address must be that of Smiling Sid. This was not raided at 5:05 a.m. (clue 1), so he must have been the sneak thief arrested at 5:10 a.m., leaving Ronnie the Rabbit at Larson Road as the forger whose home was the first to be raided by the police at 5:05 a.m.

5:05 a.m., Larson Road, Ronnie the Rabbit, forger.
5:07 a.m., Crooke Street, Crazy Chris, safe-cracker.
5:10 a.m., Laws Close, Smiling Sid, sneak thief.
5:15 a.m., Peel Lane, Wheels Wilf, getaway driver.
5:20 a.m., Copse Road, Splinters Dave, car thief.

Battleships, p. 114

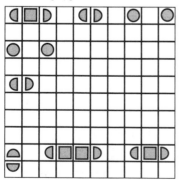

Domino Search, p. 115

4	6	6	5	6	2	0	1
6	0	0	4	2	5	4	2
5	4	5	0	3	5	4	6
2	0	5	6	3	2	6	1
0	1	3	3	3	0	1	2
6	2	3	3	3	1	1	2
0	5	4	1	4	5	1	4

County Girls, p. 116

Samantha is 24 (clue 6) and July's girl is 25 (clue 4), so Lucinda, who appears in August (clue 2) and who isn't 26 (clue 1) or 22 (clue 2), must be 23, and she must be the daughter of Major Weller-Heald (clue 5). The Duke of Richworth's daughter is not featured in either May or June (clue 1). Lucinda Weller-Heald is in the August issue, so the Duke's daughter is also not in September (clue 1), so she must be the 25-year-old in the July issue. Therefore Phyllis must be the June portrait, and the 26-year-old must be in May's *Shire Life* (clue 1). By elimination, June's Phyllis must be 22 and Samantha must be in the September issue. May's 26-year-old is not Annabel (clue 3), so it must be Georgina, who must be the daughter of Lord and Lady Buck (clue 3). This leaves Annabel as the 25-year-old. Finally, Lord Smart's daughter is not Phyllis (clue 2), so it must be Samantha, leaving Phyllis as the daughter of the Hon. Mrs. Broadlands.

May, Georgina, 26, Lord and Lady Buck.
June, Phyllis, 22, Hon. Mrs. Broadlands.
July, Annabel, 25, Duke of Richworth.
August, Lucinda, 23, Major Weller-Heald.
September, Samantha, 24, Lord Smart.

A Week in the Wild, p. 118

The trip to Mount Lunku, where 3 specimens were seen, was earlier than the Thursday trip in search of the spider-lizard (clue 1). However, 2 specimens were seen on Wednesday (clue 6), and the Monday trip was not to a mountain (clue 2), so the trip to Mount Lunku must have been on Tuesday. We know the creature being sought on Tuesday wasn't the spider-lizard, nor was it the copper monkey, which lives on the Sporo Plain (clue 5), or the whistling hog, 9 specimens of which were found (clue 6); the rainbow parrot wasn't sought on a mountain (clue 2), so Tuesday's trip to Mount Lunku must have been to find the ding-bat. The 9 whistling hogs weren't seen on Monday, so must have been seen on Friday. Therefore it must have been in the Gwangi Valley that 2 specimens were seen on Wednesday (clue 4). By elimination, they must have been rainbow parrots, and it must have been Monday when the team went to the Sporo Plain to find the copper monkey. From clue 3, the trip to Mount Borri must have been on Thursday, and the one to the D'Kuna Forest on Friday, when the 9 whistling hogs were seen. There were fewer copper monkeys than there were creatures found on Mount Borri (clue 2), so Monday's trip must have found 6 copper monkeys, and Thursday's must have found 8 spider-lizards on Mount Borri.

Monday, Sporo Plain, copper monkey, 6.
Tuesday, Mount Lunku, ding-bat, 3.
Wednesday, Gwangi Valley, rainbow parrot, 2.
Thursday, Mount Borri, spider-lizard, 8.
Friday, D'Kuna Forest, whistling hogs, 9.

Codewords, p. 120

Totalized, p. 121

Easy: 71, Medium: 43, Harder: 161

Cell Block, p. 122

2			4	
	3			
		2		4
5				2
	6	3		
			5	

Wordwheel, p. 122

The nine-letter word is CHEMISTRY.

Gone Fishin', p. 123

Since Pete Ray has caught 5 fish (clue 1), from clue 3 Don Bass must have caught 4 fish, angler D must have caught 3 fish, and the man in the *Izaak Walton* must have caught 2 fish. Mick Perch's boat has a one-word name (clue 2), so he can't be the man in the *Izaak Walton* who has caught 2 fish, and, by elimination, must be angler D who has caught 3 fish. So, from clue 2, the *Jolly Roger* must be boat C. By elimination, the man in the *Izaak Walton* who has caught 2 fish must be Joe Ling. We now know that the *Izaak Walton* isn't boat C or D, so, as it can't be boat A (clue 4), it must be boat B, and the *Kitty* is therefore boat A (clue 4), which leaves Mick Perch's boat D as the *Lorelei*. Finally, from clue 3, the *Kitty* isn't Don Bass's boat, so must be the one from which Pete Ray has caught 5 fish, leaving Don Bass, who has caught 4 fish, as the man in boat C, the *Jolly Roger*.

A, *Kitty*, Pete Ray, 5 fish.
B, *Izaak Walton*, Joe Ling, 2 fish.
C, *Jolly Roger*, Don Bass, 4 fish.
D, *Lorelei*, Mick Perch, 3 fish.

Five Times Table, p. 124

Cousin Lou is sitting at table 5 (clue 6), so table 3, which isn't Grandad's (clue 2), Uncle Frank's (clue 1), or the one where Auntie Eileen and Ryan are sitting (clue 4), must be where Grandma and Uncle Henry are sitting, and, from clue 1, Uncle Frank must be at table 4. Janet is at table 6 (clue 3), so,

by elimination Auntie Eileen and Ryan must be at table 7 and Grandad must be at table 6. Now, from clue 2, Auntie Brenda and Linda must be at table 5. The groom's Uncle Tommy is not at table 4 or with the bride's Grandad at table 6 (clue 2), so he must be with Auntie Eileen on table 7. From clue 3 Janet is not sitting with the groom's Uncle Henry or Uncle Bob, so it must be Cousin Charles. Therefore Uncle Bob must be at table 4 with Uncle Frank. The friend at their table is not Harriet (clue 5), so it must be Mark, which leaves Harriet at table 3 with Grandma and Uncle Henry.

Table 3, Grandma, Uncle Henry, Harriet.
Table 4, Uncle Frank, Uncle Bob, Mark.
Table 5, Cousin Lou, Auntie Brenda, Linda.
Table 6, Grandad, Cousin Charles, Janet.
Table 7, Auntie Eileen, Uncle Tommy, Ryan.

The Magnificent Six, p. 126

Figure D's cognomen is "the Hawk" (clue 4). Figure F can't be "the Wolf," disguised as a merchant (clue 1), nor "the Colossus" (clue 5), while clue 2 rules out "the Shadow" and clue 7 "the Wanderer," so figure F must be "the Golden," who is Shee-La (intro). Figure A can't be disguised as a shepherd (clue 2), a peddler (clue 5), or a laborer (clue 6), nor can it be Alarkar, who is disguised as a cleric (clue 7); it's figure E who is disguised as a beggar (clue 6), so, by elimination, figure A must be the man disguised as a merchant, whose cognomen is "the Wolf" (clue 1). Thus, from clue 1, figure B is Topal. Clue 3 tells us that figure C is Dionos. We now know that Alarkar, disguised as a cleric, isn't figure A, B, C, E, or F, so he must be figure D, "the Hawk." Therefore, from clue 7, it's Dionos, figure C, whose cognomen is "the Wanderer." Clue 2 rules out figure B's disguise as that of a shepherd, and clue 5 rules it out as the peddler's outfit; we know it's not the merchant's, beggar's, or cleric's outfit, so figure B, Topal, must be disguised as a laborer. Thus, from clue 6, Lyco must be figure A, "the Wolf," which leaves figure E as Promero. His cognomen isn't "the Colossus" (clue 5), so it must be "the Shadow," leaving Topal, figure B, as "the Colossus." Clue 2 now tells us that Shee-La, figure F, is disguised as a shepherd, so figure C, Dionos the Wanderer, must be disguised as a peddler.

A, Lyco the Wolf, merchant.
B, Topal the Colossus, laborer.
C, Dionos the Wanderer, peddler.
D, Alarkar the Hawk, cleric.
E, Promero the Shadow, beggar.
F, Shee-La the Golden, shepherd.

Pilots, p. 128

Hannah's surname is Wright (clue 4), so Bernard, who isn't Cayley (clue 1), must be Maxim, and Ken must be Cayley. Bernard Maxim's work plane is a Tornado (clue 1). The Hercules pilot's hobby plane is a Spitfire (clue 3), so Ken Cayley, whose hobby plane is a Harvard (clue 2), must fly a Boeing 747 for work. By elimination, Bernard Maxim's hobby plane must be a Tiger Moth, and Hannah Wright must be the professional Hercules pilot who flies a Spitfire as a hobby.

Bernard Maxim, Tornado, Tiger Moth.
Hannah Wright, Hercules, Spitfire.
Ken Cayley, Boeing 747, Harvard.

First Night, p. 129

Dirk was in room 103, but not with Marijke (clue 3), or Gretchen, whose room bore an even number (clue 5). Laurens was with Rosa (clue 1), so, by elimination, Dirk's wife must be Magda, and they visited The Deep (clue 2). Neither Rosa (clue 1), nor Gretchen (clue 5), can have been in room 101, so Marijke must have been. We know Gretchen was not with Dirk or Laurens, nor was her partner Peter (clue 5), so she must have been with Jan, leaving Peter with Marijke in room 101. Since the couple in room 103 visited The Deep, clue 1 rules out room 104 for Laurens and Rosa, so the couple there who went over the bridge to Lincoln (clue 4), must have been Jan and Gretchen, leaving Laurens and Rosa in room 102. So, from clue 1, it was Peter and Marijke who went to Wilberforce House, leaving Laurens and Rosa as the pair who visited Beverley Minster.

101, Peter and Marijke, Wilberforce House.
102, Laurens and Rosa, Beverley Minster.
103, Dirk and Magda, The Deep.
104, Jan and Gretchen, Lincoln Cathedral.

Find the Lady, p. 130

Since card 4 is the Diamond (clue 4), clue 2 places Anna's Spade as card 3, and card 1 is a 4. So, from clue 3, card 3, dealt to Anna, must be the 7 of Spades. Of the two remaining cards, one is a Queen (clue 1), and the other is a 10 (clue 5). This cannot be in positions 1 or 2 (clue 5), and we know it is not card 3, so it must be card 4, the Diamond. This leaves the missing lady as card 2. Since Josh was not dealt the 10 of Diamonds (clue 5), Luke must have been (clue 4). Katie was not dealt card 1 (clue 3), so Josh must have been, leaving Katie as the person who was dealt the Queen. This is not a Club (clue 1), so it must be the Queen of Hearts, leaving card 1 as the 4 of Clubs.

1, Josh, 4 of Clubs.
2, Katie, Queen of Hearts.
3, Anna, 7 of Spades.
4, Luke, 10 of Diamonds.

Battleships, p. 131

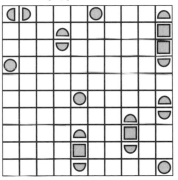

If You Want to Get Ahead, p. 132

She Fell for Him was made in 1934 (clue 1). The top hat was worn in the 1935 film (clue 4), which cannot have been *Coming Home* (clue 2), or *City Life* starring Clark Maybank (clue 6), while it was the derby that was worn in *What's Cooking?* (clue 5), so, by elimination, *Stepping Out* must have been shot in 1935. Therefore, from clue 7, Victor O'Sullivan starred in *She Fell for Him* in 1934. We already know the star of *Stepping Out* was not Clark or Victor, and clue 2 rules out Gene Parker for 1935, and clue 3 tells us Royston Wallace wore a Stetson, so the top hat in *Stepping Out* must have been worn by Jefferson Rodgers. Royston's headgear rules out his film as *What's Cooking?*, so his western must have been called *Coming Home*, and, by elimination, Gene Parker must have starred in *What's Cooking?* Clark Maybank did not wear the fedora (clue 6), so his hat must have been the beret, leaving the fedora for Victor O'Sullivan. From clue 2, the beret, which we now know was not worn in the 1934 or 1935 films, must have been worn by Clark Maybank in 1933, *Coming Home* must have been made in 1932, and *What's Cooking?*, starring Gene Parker, in 1931.

1931, *What's Cooking?*, Gene Parker, derby.
1932, *Coming Home*, Royston Wallace, Stetson.
1933, *City Life*, Clark Maybank, beret.
1934, *She Fell for Him*, Victor O'Sullivan, fedora.
1935, *Stepping Out*, Jefferson Rodgers, top hat.

Boys' Toys, p. 134

Cliff is figure F (clue 4), so clue 3 tells us that figure C is not the electrician; nor can figure C, whose car is the McLaren, be the cab driver or the truck driver (clue 6), while the policeman's car is a Toyota (clue 2) and the bricklayer is figure D (clue 5), so figure C must be the grocer. So, from clue 1, figure D is Jim, the BAR "driver." We know that Ken's car isn't the McLaren or the BAR, and, as he's the cab driver (clue 7), it can't be the Toyota; nor is it the Renault (clue 7), and that clue also rules out the Williams, so Ken's car must be the Ferrari. Clue 2 rules out figures A, B, and C as Phil, and we know that he's not figure D or F, so he must be figure E, and, from clue 2, the policeman with the Toyota must be figure F, Cliff. We know Les isn't figure F, so clue 8 rules out Phil as the truck driver; the truck driver's location rules out three other names, and we know Ken's the cab driver, so Phil must be the electrician. We now know that Ken the cab driver with the model Ferrari is either figure A or B, so, from clue 7, the man with the Williams must be figure B or C. We know he isn't figure C, so he must be figure B and Ken is therefore figure A (clue 7). This leaves the truck driver as figure B, who has the Williams, so, by elimination, Phil, figure E, must have the Renault. Finally, from clue 8, Les must be figure C, the grocer with the McLaren, leaving figure B, the truck driver, as Don.

A, Ken, cab driver, Ferrari.
B, Don, truck driver, Williams.
C, Les, grocer, McLaren.
D, Jim, bricklayer, BAR.
E, Phil, electrician, Renault.
F, Cliff, policeman, Toyota.

Domino Search, p. 136

5	2	0	0	4	6	6	1
1	5	1	2	5	3	1	1
6	6	4	4	3	2	3	3
0	4	3	5	5	5	6	0
0	3	2	3	4	6	2	0
0	5	3	5	4	6	1	0
1	4	6	2	2	1	4	2

Battleships, p. 137

Codewords, p. 138

Y	F	E	K	A	X	W	Q	U	R	S	H	B
O	I	L	T	N	J	C	Z	G	D	P	V	M

Totalized, p. 139
Easy: 11, Medium: 63, Harder: 186

Cell Block, p. 140

Wordwheel, p. 140
The nine-letter word is MAJORETTE.

Battleships, p. 141

Babylon Valley, p. 142

Vineyard 1 produces Old Nick (clue 7), so, from clue 1, Gurrambidgee can't be vineyard 4; nor can it be vineyard 6, which produces the dry white (clue 3), so, from clue 1, it must be vineyard 5, and vineyard 2 must produce Southern Sceptre. So vineyard 1, which produces Old Nick, isn't Cootimumbah (clue 4), nor can it be Forest Hill, which produces the dry red (clue 2); clue 5 rules out King's Rock, Black Dog produces Chateau d'Ilf (clue 6), and we know Gurrambidgee is vineyard 5, so by elimination, vineyard 1 must be Platypus Park. Their product Old Nick isn't the sparkling wine (clue 5), and we know it isn't the dry white or the dry red; nor can it be the sweet red, which is called Eric the Red (clue 4), or the sweet white (clue 8), so, by elimination, Platypus Park's Old Nick must be a medium red. Therefore, from clue 9, Horn of Plenty must come from vineyard 4. So Black Dog, which we know isn't vineyard 5, must be vineyard 6 and produce the dry white (clue 6). Forest Hill, which produces the dry red, can't be vineyard 3 (clue 2), nor can Cootimumbah (clue 4), so it must be King's Rock. So the vineyard producing the sparkling wine, which we know isn't vineyard 1, must be vineyard 2 (clue 5). We now know the name or type of wine produced by five vineyards, so Forest Hill, which produces the dry red, must be vineyard 4, which produces Horn of Plenty. This leaves Cootimumbah as vineyard 2, producing Southern Sceptre, the sparkling wine. Thus, from clue 4, vineyard 3, King's Rock, must produce Eric the Red, the sweet red wine. So, by elimination, the Gurrambidgee vineyard must produce Bandicoot, which must be a sweet white wine.

1, Platypus Park, Old Nick, medium red.

2, Cootimumbah, Southern Sceptre, sparkling.

3, King's Rock, Eric the Red, sweet red.

4, Forest Hill, Horn of Plenty, dry red.

5, Gurrambidgee, Bandicoot, sweet white.

6, Black Dog, Chateau d'Ilf, dry white.

Captain Gore's Last Stand, p. 144

"Dirty Dan" was the southern lookout (clue 3), so, from clue 1, the man who saw the British frigate can't have been looking north; the American ship was to the west (clue 2), and the French one was not to the north (clue 2), so the ship to the north must have flown a Spanish flag. "Mad Malachi" didn't see the brig to the east (clue 5), and we know that "Dirty Dan" wasn't looking east; nor can "Hook-hand Harry" have faced east (clues 1 and 2), so "Scarface Sam" must have done so. Thus, from clue 4, the ship of the line must have been coming from the south, and was thus seen by "Dirty Dan." We know she wasn't flying the American or Spanish flag, and the type of vessel rules out the British, so she must have flown a French flag. Now, by elimination, it must have been "Scarface Sam," looking east, who saw the frigate with the British flag. Therefore, from clue 1, "Hook-hand Harry" must have looked west and seen the American ship, leaving the brig seen by "Mad Malachi" as the one to the north flying a Spanish flag. By final elimination, the American ship "Hook-hand Harry" saw to the west must have been a sloop.

North, "Mad Malachi," brig, Spanish.

East, "Scarface Sam," frigate, British.

South, "Dirty Dan," ship of the line, French.

West, "Hook-hand Harry," sloop, American.

Mix and Match, p. 146

Since Lesley lives at number 7 (clue 2), clue 1 rules out shop D as the grocers, and clue 3 rules it out as the florists, since Tina, who went there, does not live at number 7. Nor can shop D be the hairdressers, patronized by the woman from number 1 (clue 4), so, by elimination, it must be the health food store. Since only Tina lives in the same relative position as the shop she visited (clue 3), we now know Lesley, from number 7, did not visit shop D, the health food store. We already know she did not go to the florists or the hairdresser, so she must have visited the grocers. Therefore, from clue 1, Gill must live at number 5. By elimination, she must have gone to the health food store in position D, the woman from number 1, who went to the hairdressers, must be Eileen, and Tina must live at number 3. So, from clue 3, the florists must be shop B, and, from clue 1, the grocers must be shop A, leaving shop C as the hairdressers.

1, Eileen, hairdresser, shop C.

3, Tina, florist, shop B.

5, Gill, health food store, shop D.

7, Lesley, grocer, shop A.

Bus Stop, p. 147

The woman waiting for the 28 bus to Lovel Park (clue 3) can't be Mrs. Dennis (clue 1) or Mrs. Scammell, whose destination is the City Hospital (clue 4), so must be Mrs. Foden, and Mrs. Dennis's destination must be Victoria Bridge. Neither Carol (clue 1) nor Penny (clue 2) is waiting for the number 14, so that must be Joan's bus. She isn't Mrs. Scammell (clue 4), so she must be Mrs. Dennis who is going to Victoria Bridge, and Mrs. Scammell is waiting for the number 21. Now, from clue 1, Carol must be Mrs. Scammell, leaving Penny as Mrs. Foden, waiting for a number 28 to Lovel Park.

Carol Scammell, City Hospital, 21.
Joan Dennis, Victoria Bridge, 14.
Penny Foden, Lovel Park, 28.

Dick the Driver, p. 148

Mrs. Cook got her delivery at 11:30 a.m. (clue 4), so Mrs. Bruce's delivery, which can't have been at 10:00 a.m. (clue 3), must have been at 1:00 p.m., and was therefore the bed (clue 1). By elimination, Mrs. Adams's wardrobe (clue 2) must have been delivered at 10:00 a.m. Also by elimination, Mrs. Cook must have received a dressing table. Mrs. Bruce can't live in Bollingbrook (clue 1) or Wheaton (clue 3), so must live in Oak Park. Mrs. Adams's home isn't in Wheaton (clue 2), so that must be where Mrs. Cook lives, and Mrs. Adams must live in Bollingbrook.

Mrs. Adams, Bollingbrook, 10:00 a.m., wardrobe.
Mrs. Bruce, Oak Park, 1:00 p.m., bed.
Mrs. Cook, Wheaton, 11:30 a.m., dressing table.

Twitchers, p. 149

Figure D is Jay (clue 3), and figure A is watching a blue swan (clue 4). As figure B is Quail (clue 2), clue 1 rules out Robin, who's watching a mud warbler, as figure C, so he must be figure B, Quail. So, from clue 1, Gull is figure A. She (we've placed both men) isn't Mavis (clue 4), so she must be Mynah, leaving Mavis as figure C. Her surname isn't Finch (clue 4), so it must be Wren. So she's not watching the owl-duck (clue 5) and must be

observing a reedpiper. Finally, by elimination, Jay, figure D, must be Finch and must be watching the owl-duck.

A, Mynah Gull, blue swan.
B, Robin Quail, mud warbler.
C, Mavis Wren, reedpiper.
D, Jay Finch, owl-duck.

Battleships, p. 150

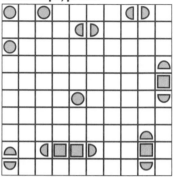

Domino Search, p. 151

1	1	2	2	5	6	6	5
4	0	2	4	2	6	3	6
1	0	5	3	3	3	2	1
5	0	3	6	2	4	4	0
0	0	6	3	6	4	5	4
2	4	3	6	3	0	5	2
1	0	1	5	1	4	5	1

Busy Morning in Black Rock, p. 152

The rustler was arrested in Mason's Barber Shop (clue 2). Jake Morgan, the train robber, wasn't arrested in the blacksmith's forge (clue 4), nor can he have been arrested in the Four Aces Saloon (clue 3), so he must have been arrested in Doolin's Store. It was 9:50 a.m. when "Red" O'Leary was arrested (clue 1). The man arrested at 11:50 a.m. wasn't Jake Morgan (clue 4) or "Dutchy" Kruger (clue 2), so must have been Nat Diamond. He wasn't the bank robber (clue 3), nor was the bank robber "Dutchy" Kruger (clue 2), and we know Jake Morgan was the train robber, so the bank robber must have been "Red" O'Leary, arrested at 9:50 a.m. We know that the arrest of the rustler in Mason's Barber Shop wasn't at 9:50 a.m., nor can it have been at 8:50 a.m. (clue 2) nor, since "Dutchy" Kruger wasn't arrested at 9:50 a.m., can the rustler have been arrested at 10:50 a.m., so he must have been the man arrested at 11:50 a.m., Nat Diamond, and therefore, from clue 2, the 10:50 a.m. arrest was that of "Dutchy" Kruger, and, by elimination, the 8:50 a.m. arrest was that of Jake Morgan the train robber in Doolin's Store. From clue 3, the Four Aces Saloon must have been where the horse thief was arrested, and by elimination, this must have been the 10:50 a.m. arrest of "Dutchy" Kruger. Also by elimination, the man arrested in the blacksmith's forge must have been bank robber "Red" O'Leary, arrested at 9:50 a.m.

8:50 a.m., Jake Morgan, train robber, Doolin's Store.

9:50 a.m., "Red" O'Leary, bank robber, blacksmith's forge.

10:50 a.m., "Dutchy" Kruger, horse thief, Four Aces Saloon.

11:50 a.m., Nat Diamond, rustler, Mason's Barber Shop.

Codewords, p. 154

```
C V S E D W R T X U G L M
J A F I P K O Y N H Z Q B
```

Totalized, p. 155

Easy: 23, Medium: 40, Harder: 376

Cell Block, p. 156

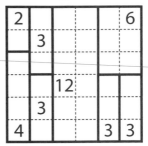

Wordwheel, p. 156

The nine-letter word is REPROBATE.

Curtain Calls, p. 157

Louise was the 10:30 customer (clue 2). The main bedroom curtains were bought at 12:30 (clue 5), but not by Sally (clue 1) or Marie, whose new curtains were for her dining area (clue 4), so Joanne must have been the 12:30 customer. Her curtains were not blue (clue 5), or green (clue 3), and the yellow curtains were for a child's bedroom (clue 1), so, by elimination, the ones for Joanne's main bedroom must have been beige. We have matched colors with two rooms, so the green curtains, which were not for the living room (clue 3), must have been intended for Marie's dining room. We now know the yellow curtains were not bought by Joanne or Marie, and clue 1 rules out Sally, so they must have been bought by Louise at 10:30. By elimination, Sally must have bought the blue material, which must have been for living room curtains. Clue 1 tells us she must have visited the store at 9:30, leaving Marie as the 11:30 customer.

9:30, Sally, living room, blue.

10:30, Louise, child's bedroom, yellow.

11:30, Marie, dining room, green.

12:30, Joanne, main bedroom, beige.

Roadside Census, p. 158

The shortest journey of 25 miles cannot have been that of Susan (clue 2), Ruth (clue 3), or George (clue 4), so it must have been Edward's. He was in car 3 (clue 2), so, from clue 5, Alison must have interviewed the driver of car 1, who must have been

male, and was therefore George. The student questioning the driver of car 4 was not Tom (clue 3). We know she was not Alison, and clue 1 now rules out Bridget, so, by elimination, Daniel must have spoken to driver 4. So this was not Ruth (clue 3), and must have been Susan, leaving Ruth in car 2. She was not interviewed by Tom (clue 3), so her interviewer must have been Bridget, leaving Tom questioning Edward. Now clue 1 tells us George was traveling 150 miles, so, from clue 4, Ruth must have been making the 90 mile journey, leaving 200 miles as the distance being covered by Susan.

1, George, 150 miles, Alison.
2, Ruth, 90 miles, Bridget.
3, Edward, 25 miles, Tom.
4, Susan, 200 miles, Daniel.

Halloween Visitors, p. 159

Farmer is number 3 (clue 2). Since child 1 is the ghost (clue 4), clue 5 rules out positions 1 and 2 for Coles, who therefore must be number 4. From clue 5, Farmer, in position 3, must be the skeleton. We now know Coles is not the ghost or the skeleton, and Walker is the witch (clue 1), so Coles must be dressed up as a demon. By elimination, the child in the sheet, posing as a ghost, must be Drewery, and Walker, the witch, must be number 2. From clue 3, she must be Kirstie. From clue 1, therefore, Lewis must be Farmer or Coles. Clue 5 rules him out as Coles, so he must be Farmer, the skeleton. Drewery is not Jonathan (clue 3), so she must be Miranda, leaving Jonathan as Coles, the demon in position 4.

1, Miranda Drewery, ghost.
2, Kirstie Walker, witch.
3, Lewis Farmer, skeleton.
4, Jonathan Coles, demon.

Metro Musicians, p. 160

Marcel plays the violin (clue 4), and Gautier the guitar (clue 3), so Didier Charpentier, who does not play the harmonica (clue 2), must play the accordion. So he cannot be number 1 or number 2 (clue 1), nor is he number 3 (clue 2), so he must be number 4. Therefore, from clue 1, Alphonse must be number 3, and Lemoine number 2. Marcel's instrument rules him out as Gautier, nor is he

Fourneau (clue 4). We know he is not Charpentier, so he must be Lemoine, number 2. Gautier, who is not Jean (clue 3), must be number 3, Alphonse. By elimination, number 1's full name must be Jean Fourneau, and his instrument must be the harmonica.

1, Jean Fourneau, harmonica.
2, Marcel Lemoine, violin.
3, Alphonse Gautier, guitar.
4, Didier Charpentier, accordion.

Battleships, p. 161

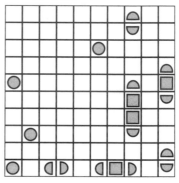

Domino Search, p. 162

3	1	2	3	4	1	1	1
5	1	3	3	5	0	0	4
4	4	5	5	3	2	4	3
0	2	2	2	6	4	6	4
0	1	6	3	2	4	2	5
6	0	0	1	6	0	3	2
6	5	6	1	5	0	5	6

Mixed Doubles, p. 163

Acey, noted for passing shots, must be numbered 1 or 2 (clue 3), but player 1 is best known for forehand shots (clue 4), so Acey must be the surname of player 2, and Letts is therefore number 4 (clue 3). We now know Clive, whose strength is his return of serve (clue 1), is not 1 or 2, nor is he player 3 (clue 1), so he must be number 4, Letts. By elimination, player 3 must be the backhand specialist. Since player 4 is neither Dick nor Miss Deuce, from clue 2 these two must be players 1 and 2, but we know Deuce is not the surname of player 2, so she must be serving in position 1, and Dick must be player 2, whose surname is Acey. By elimination, player 3 must be Lobb. Since Miss Deuce is not Suzanne (clue 4), she must be Melanie, leaving Suzanne as player 3, Miss Lobb.

1, Melanie Deuce, forehand.
2, Dick Acey, passing shot.
3, Suzanne Lobb, backhand.
4, Clive Letts, return of serve.

Battleships, p. 164

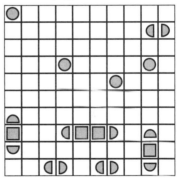

Domino Search, p. 165

0	2	2	5	0	5	2	0
3	5	6	1	1	2	4	5
0	1	3	5	4	3	4	6
0	1	2	2	6	5	5	6
1	2	1	4	3	4	3	3
1	3	4	4	6	0	2	4
0	3	5	6	0	6	1	6

Don't Eat the Bar Snacks!, p. 166

The Skull and Bones is tavern 2 (clue 4), so, from clue 1, the tavern that serves the ale is neither tavern 1 nor number 4; tavern 3 serves the "wine" (clue 5), so, by elimination, the ale must be served at the Skull and Bones, tavern 2, and so, from clue 1, the Blue Ferret must be tavern 3 that serves the "wine." So, from clue 3, the Fox and Werewolf must be tavern 4, and the Dented Drum, owned by Egbert Snakehugger, must be tavern 1. We have now matched three buildings to an owner or a drink, so Hob Stonybroke's tavern, where the rum is served (clue 2), must be the Fox and Werewolf, tavern 4. This leaves the drink at the Dented Drum, tavern 1, as brandy. Finally, from clue 5, tavern 3, the Blue Ferret isn't Mother Hood's tavern, so it must be Clem Grimmett's, and Mother Hood must own the Skull and Bones, tavern 2.

1, Dented Drum, Egbert Snakehugger, brandy.
2, Skull and Bones, Mother Hood, ale.
3, Blue Ferret, Clem Grimmett, wine.
4, Fox and Werewolf, Hob Stonybroke, rum.

Battleships, p. 168

Staff Shortages, p. 169

Nick's surname is Stanier (clue 3), so Brian, who isn't Bulleid (clue 2), must be Gresley, who was late because of a power cut (clue 1). By elimination, Victor must be Bulleid. He wasn't stuck in traffic (clue 2), so his rabbit must have been taken ill, and he therefore got to work at 10:00 a.m. (clue 4). Also by elimination, Nick Stanier must have been stuck in traffic. Finally, from clue 2, Brian Gresley must have got to work at 10:15 a.m., leaving Nick Stanier as the one who arrived at 9:45 a.m.

Brian Gresley, 10:15 a.m., power cut.
Nick Stanier, 9:45 a.m., stuck in traffic.
Victor Bulleid, 10:00 a.m., rabbit taken ill.

Codewords, p. 170

Totalized, p. 171
Easy: 83, Medium: 9, Harder: 625

Cell Block, p. 172

3					3
	8				
			6		5
5					
		3	1	2	

Wordwheel, p. 172
The nine-letter word is DIFFICULT.

Battleships, p. 173

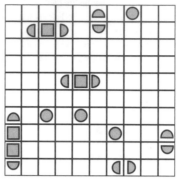

Battleships, p. 174

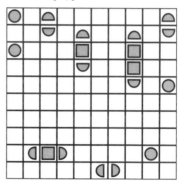

Fathers and Sons, p. 175
Terry Lucas is adult A (clue 4), so Harry's father, who is standing immediately right of Ian Wilsher (clue 3), can't be adult A or B, nor, since he's a fireman (clue 3), can he be adult C, who's a newsreader (clue 1), so he must be adult D and Ian Wilsher must be adult C, the newsreader. We now know the name of the father or son in three pairs, so Ken Spooner and Toby (clue 2) must be pair B, and, by elimination, adult D, Harry's father, must be Eddie Price. Ken Spooner isn't the engineer (clue 2), so he must be a cameraman, and adult A, Terry Lucas, must be the engineer. Finally, from clue 1, Ian Wilsher's son isn't Brendan, so he must be Paul, leaving Brendan as the son of Terry Lucas, and thus child A.

A, Terry Lucas, engineer, Brendan.
B, Ken Spooner, cameraman, Toby.
C, Ian Wilsher, newsreader, Paul.
D, Eddie Price, fireman, Harry.

Police News, p. 176

Gil Fernandez rescued a baby (clue 1) and the Sergeant arrested the burglar (clue 3), so Detective Harvey McCuen, who hasn't had a heart attack (clue 1), must be on corruption charges. Bernie Carlson from the 24th Precinct, isn't the Patrolman (clue 2) and can't be the Sergeant, who doesn't have a six-letter first name (clue 3), so must be the Lieutenant, and, by elimination, must have had a heart attack. Gil Fernandez is not the Sergeant (clues 1 and 3), so must be the Patrolman, leaving Ollie Stein as the Sergeant. Neither he nor Harvey McCuen comes from the 10th Precinct (clue 4), so that must be Gil Fernandez's precinct, and, from clue 4, Ollie Stein must be attached to the 14th and Harvey McCuen to the 27th.

Bernie Carlson, Lieutenant, 24th Precinct, heart attack.
Gil Fernandez, Patrolman, 10th Precinct, rescued baby.
Harvey McCuen, Detective, 27th Precinct, corruption charges.
Ollie Stein, Sergeant, 14th Precinct, arrested burglar.

My Guests This Evening, p. 178

One guest was Dominic Hepburn (clue 6) and the third guest was surnamed Karrol (clue 2), so the fourth guest, Lauren, whose surname wasn't Bergin (clue 2) or, from clue 3, Chang, must be Finley, and is thus the impressionist (clue 5). The illusionist wasn't the first or second guest (clue 3), and, since Lauren was fourth, the illusionist can't have been fifth (clue 3) and must be the third, surnamed Karrol. Thus, from clue 3, Matt was second and Chang was the first guest, who was a juggler (clue 1). By elimination, the second guest, Matt, must be Bergin, and Dominic Hepburn must have been fifth. The first guest, Chang the juggler, wasn't Tristan (clue 1), so must have been Cheryl, leaving Tristan as the third guest, Karrol the illusionist.

Finally, the pianist wasn't Matt Bergin (clue 4), so must have been Dominic Hepburn, the fifth guest, leaving guest 2, Matt Bergin, as a tap dancer.

First, Cheryl Chang, juggler.
Second, Matt Bergin, tap dancer.
Third, Tristan Karrol, illusionist.
Fourth, Lauren Finley, impressionist.
Fifth, Dominic Hepburn, pianist.

Relics of the Railroad, p. 180

Loco 8 was built in 1893 (clue 6), and *Stampede*, in position 2, was not built in the 1870s (clue 4), so clue 8 rules out positions 1, 2, and 4 for *Goliath*, which must therefore, from that clue, be number 3. So, from clue 8, loco 6 must have been built in 1878. Therefore, from clue 2, *Cowpuncher* must be the one built in 1874. We know *Apache*'s position on the turntable is not 2 or 3, and clue 3 also rules out 4, 6, 7, or 8. Nor can it be loco 1 (clue 7), so, by elimination, it must be number 5, and, from clue 3, loco 7 dates from 1861. We now know *Little Lucy*, built in 1869 (clue 5), is none of locos 2, 3, 5, 6, 7, or 8, and we know it was *Cowpuncher*, not *Iron Maiden*, which was built in 1874, so clue 7 rules out position 1 for *Little Lucy*, which must therefore be loco 4. We have now matched seven positions with a name or a year, so, by elimination, *Cowpuncher*, built in 1874, must be loco 1. Therefore, from clue 7, *Iron Maiden* must be loco 6, built in 1878. This leaves positions 7 or 8 for *Prairie King*. Since loco 4 dates from 1869, clue 1 rules out position 8 for *Prairie King*, so it must be loco 7, and, from clue 1, *Goliath*, in position 3, was built in 1857. Clue 7 rules out loco 5, *Apache*, for 1886, so it must have been built in 1890, leaving 1886 as the year *Stampede*, loco 2, was built. By elimination, loco 8, built in 1893, must be called *Leviathan*.

1, *Cowpuncher*, 1874.
2, *Stampede*, 1886.
3, *Goliath*, 1857.
4, *Little Lucy*, 1869.
5, *Apache*, 1890.
6, *Iron Maiden*, 1878.
7, *Prairie King*, 1861.
8, *Leviathan*, 1893.

Poker Faces, p. 182

Since player A has a full house (clue 5) and player B is Ernie Lambros (clue 4), neither of these can be Stu Fontana, who is holding fours (clue 6); so, from that clue, both he and the player from London must be either player D or player E. Therefore the player from Singapore who has threes can't be player D or player E, nor player F (clue 2); we know he isn't player A, and player C lives in Las Vegas (clue 7), so, from clue 2, the Singapore-based player with threes must be player B, Ernie Lambros, and Sam Cleary is therefore player D. We know that Stu Fontana is either player D or player E, so now we see he must be player E and player D, Sam Cleary, must live in London (clue 6). We now know either the name or the hometown of four players, so Tony Morgan from Manchester, who isn't player F (clue 1), must be player A. Now, from clue 3, the player from Atlantic City must be Stu Fontana, player E, and player F must hold the straight. By elimination, player F must live in Vancouver. Leo Kang isn't player C (clue 7), so he must be player F, and player C must be "Dandy" Penn. He isn't holding two pairs (clue 7), so must have a royal flush, leaving the player with two pairs as Sam Cleary, player D.

A, Tony Morgan, Manchester, full house.
B, Ernie Lambros, Singapore, threes.
C, "Dandy" Penn, Las Vegas, royal flush.
D, Sam Cleary, London, two pairs.
E, Stu Fontana, Atlantic City, fours.
F, Leo Kang, Vancouver, straight.

Battleships, p. 184

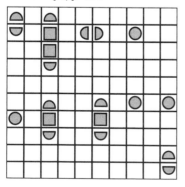

Domino Search, p. 185

0	4	0	4	4	2	1	3
0	2	5	2	3	2	2	1
2	0	3	6	3	5	5	1
4	1	6	6	5	0	0	1
4	5	1	3	1	4	5	5
2	2	0	1	4	3	3	0
6	6	4	6	5	6	3	6

Romantic Writers, p. 186

One of the novelists aims to write 6,000 words each day in her summerhouse (clue 5). The one who writes only 2,000 words does not work in her library or her conservatory (clue 2), nor is it her study (clue 4), so she must have converted the room over her garage, and therefore must be Maria Darcy (clue 6). Therefore, *A Summer Affair* must be by the author producing 3,000 or 4,000 words a day (clue 4), but as 6,000 are written in the summerhouse, the writer using her study must aim for 5,000 words (also clue 4), and the author of *A Summer Affair* must produce 3,000 words. She does not write in her library (clue 3), so it must be her conservatory. By elimination, Betty Sansom, who produces 4,000 words daily, must work in her library. She is not working on *Change of Heart* (clue 3) or Virginia Champion's *Hearts Are Trumps* (clue 1), so it must be *The House on the Green*. As Amanda Fancy does not write in her conservatory (clue 2), her output is not 3,000 words, and as she writes less than Virginia Champion (clue 1), it cannot be 6,000 words, so must be 5,000 words, and she must write in her study. Therefore Miss Champion must produce 6,000 words a day, must currently be writing *Hearts Are Trumps* (clue 1), and must write in her summerhouse. By elimination, the writer who uses her conservatory must be Candida Moore, and Amanda Fancy must be the author of *Change of Heart*, producing 5,000 words per day.

Virginia Champion, summerhouse, 6,000 words, *Hearts Are Trumps*.
Maria Darcy, room over garage, 2,000 words, *For Love or Money*.
Amanda Fancy, study, 5,000 words, *Change of Heart*.
Candida Moore, conservatory, 3,000 words, *A Summer Affair*.
Betty Sansom, library, 4,000 words, *The House on the Green*.

Codewords, p. 188

G		F		I		O		J		A		E
E	X	I	T	S		B	R	U	I	S	E	S
N		D		O		J		M		H		P
I	N	D	U	L	G	E		P	H	O	T	O
E		L		A		C				R		U
	V	E	N	T		T	U	N	N	E	L	S
F				E				I				E
A	C	C	U	S	E	D		C	O	O	S	
B		O				R		E		D		W
R	I	P	E	N		O	U	T	S	I	Z	E
I			I		O		W		I		O	L
C	A	N	Y	O	N	S		E	Q	U	A	L
S		G		K		Y		S		S		S

D	O	X	P	I	T	Z	A	Y	M	L	F	C
G	N	V	U	J	S	Q	K	H	W	B	R	E

Totalized, p. 189

Easy: 55, Medium: 333, Harder. 76

Cell Block, p. 190

	2		4		
3				2	2
	2	1		2	
	2				3
3			1	2	
		4		3	

Wordwheel, p. 190

The nine-letter word is TECHNICAL.

Sea View, p. 191

The youngest woman, aged 77, is not Nora (clue 1), Doris (clue 2), or Madge (clue 3), so she must be Lottie. So, from clue 4, Mrs. Stout is 79. Number 1 on the bench is not Doris (clue 2), Madge (clue 3), or Lottie (clue 4), so she must be Nora. Therefore neither she nor Doris is 85 (clue 2), and we know Lottie is 77, so, by elimination, it must be Madge who is 85. Nor, from clue 2, can Nora be 83, so she must be 79, and is Mrs. Stout. This leaves Doris's age as 83. So, from clue 2, Madge, aged 85, must be Mrs. Viggar. Clue 1 now places Lottie, Nora's immediate junior, in position 2, so, from clue 4, Doris, aged 83, must be number 3, leaving Madge Viggar in position 4. Therefore, from clue 3, Doris, number 3, must be Mrs. Allweather, leaving Lottie's surname as Hardy.

1, Nora Stout, 79.
2, Lottie Hardy, 77.
3, Doris Allweather, 83.
4, Madge Viggar, 85.

On Patrol, p. 192

Elmett's partner is Wayne, and Kevin's is Alan (clue 2), so Lewis Cuff, who is not with Joe (clue 4), must be partnered by Daniel. Elmett is not Bradley (clue 2), and we know he is not Kevin or Lewis, whose partners are respectively Alan and Daniel, so he must be Colin, and he and Wayne are heading south (clue 3). By elimination, the fourth pair must be Bradley and Joe. We know neither Lewis Cuff or Joe is heading south, so neither can be going north either (clue 4), leaving Kevin and Alan in the car heading north. We now know Elmett is driving south, and Pincham is going east (clue 5), so Sargent, whose car is not going west (clue 1), must be heading north, so he is Kevin. This leaves Cuff and Daniel in the westbound car. So, from clue 4, Joe is heading east with Bradley, whose surname is therefore Pincham.

North, Kevin Sargent and Alan.
South, Colin Elmett and Wayne.
East, Bradley Pincham and Joe.
West, Lewis Cuff and Daniel.

Battleships, p. 193

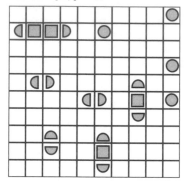

Showing This Week, p. 194

Ben Tyrrell's male star of *Assassin* (clue 1). The male star of *Star Ranger* is not Steve Jay (clue 2), so must be Nic Decker, and, by elimination, Steve Jay is the male star of *14th Street*; his female co-star is Marion Du Nord (clue 2). *Star Ranger* is on Screen 2 (clue 2), so *Assassin*, which is not on Screen 1 (clue 1), must be on Screen 3, leaving *14th Street* on Screen 1. Finally, from clue 3, Candy Kaine isn't the female star of *Assassin* on Screen 3, so she must be in *Star Ranger* on Screen 2, leaving the female star of *Assassin* as Tina St. John.

Screen 1, *14th Street*, Steve Jay, Marion Du Nord.
Screen 2, *Star Ranger*, Nic Decker, Candy Kaine.
Screen 3, *Assassin*, Ben Tyrrell, Tina St. John.

Couples, p. 195

Mrs. Smith is Susan (clue 2), and the Masons are going as Romeo and Juliet (clue 1), so Judy and her husband, who are going as Sonny and Cher (clue 4), must be the Greens. So, by elimination, the Smiths must be going as Caesar and Cleopatra, and Mr. Smith is thus Mark (clue 3). Also, by elimination, Mrs. Mason must be Linda. Her husband isn't Howard (clue 1), so he must be Patrick, leaving Howard as Mr. Green, Judy's husband.

Howard and Judy Green, Sonny and Cher.
Mark and Susan Smith, Caesar and Cleopatra.
Patrick and Linda Mason, Romeo and Juliet.

Superheroes, p. 196

Patsy Ryan is Powerwoman (clue 1), and Ray Salvio is based in Las Piedras (clue 5), so Blue Flash, based in Ocean City, who isn't Bill Colman (clue 3), must be Jack Kreski. The Champion is a songwriter (clue 4); his base city isn't San Marco, where the film critic is based (clue 2), nor Las Piedras (clue 5), so must be Crescent Falls, and, by elimination, he must be Bill Colman and Ray Salvio must be Shadowman. We now know the base cities of three heroes, so the film critic based in San Marco must be Patsy Ryan, alias Powerwoman. Finally, from clue 4, the librarian isn't Ray Salvio, alias Shadowman, so must have been Jack Kreski, alias Blue Flash, from Ocean City, and Ray Salvio must have been a gem cutter in everyday life.

Bill Colman, songwriter, The Champion, Crescent Falls.
Jack Kreski, librarian, Blue Flash, Ocean City.
Patsy Ryan, film critic, Powerwoman, San Marco.
Ray Salvio, gem cutter, Shadowman, Las Piedras.

The Arena of Death, p. 198

Orklaga, armed with a net and trident, isn't gladiator A (clue 2), gladiator C, who has a sword and shield (clue 3), or gladiator D, who is called Garogh (clue 4), so he must be gladiator B. The man from Pellia who has a spear (clue 1) is not Sebru, who is from Dagonia (clue 2), or Garogh (clue 4), so must be Thespius. By elimination, Thespius must be gladiator A. Also by elimination, Garogh, gladiator D, must be armed with a battle-axe. We have now identified the men in three positions, so Sebru from Dagonia must be gladiator C. Finally, from clue 1, the man from Auzakia can't be Garogh, so must be Orklaga, leaving Garogh's homeland as Sogdia.

A, Thespius, Pellia, spear.
B, Orklaga, Auzakia, net and trident.
C, Sebru, Dagonia, sword and shield.
D, Garogh, Sogdia, battle-axe.

Battleships, p. 199

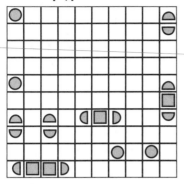

Wanted Men, p. 200

Picture 3 shows Lubbock (clue 6), and picture 4 shows Cheyenne, whose first name has more than six letters (clue 3), so clue 1 rules out pictures 1, 2, 3, 4, and 6 for Samuel Mitchell, who must therefore be shown in picture 5. So, from clue 1, Lubbock in picture 3 is Windy. Now, from clue 2, Clayton, whose picture is also in the left-hand column, must be in picture 1 and picture 2 must show Tiger. We now know that Nathaniel, whose nickname is Ace (clue 8), isn't shown in picture 2, 3, 4, or 5, and clue 8 rules out photo 6, so he must be the man in picture 1, Clayton, and Lester is therefore Tiger in picture 2 (clue 8). We know David isn't in picture 1 or 5, so, from clue 8, he must be in picture 3, and is therefore Windy Lubbock. Gato can't be in picture 5 (clue 5), so must be in picture 6, which, by elimination, leaves the nickname of Samuel Mitchell in picture 5 as Snake. Gato in picture 6 can't be Crooley (clue 5), or Dickinson (clue 7), so must be Rawlins. Therefore he isn't Jonathan (clue 4), so he must be Bartholomew, leaving Jonathan as Cheyenne in picture 4. From clue 7, his surname must be Dickinson, so, by elimination, Lester must be Tiger Greeley in picture 2.

1, Nathaniel Ace Clayton.
2, Lester Tiger Greeley.
3, David Windy Lubbock.
4, Jonathan Cheyenne Dickinson.
5, Samuel Snake Mitchell.
6, Bartholomew Gato Rawlins.

Codewords, p. 202

Totalized, p. 203

Easy: 16, Medium: 169, Harder: 198

Cell Block, p. 204

				5
	3		4	
6				2
		4		
	6			3
			3	

Wordwheel, p. 204

The nine-letter word is ALLIGATOR.

Walking the Dog, p. 205

Sam's dog can't be called Sally (clue 1), nor is this dog, which is a dalmatian, called Muffin (clue 3), so it must be named Bingo. Mick's dog can't be Muffin (clue 1), so must be Sally, and, by elimination, Muffin must be Bill's dog. Mr. Pye's corgi isn't Sally (clue 2), and we know it isn't Bingo, Sam's dalmatian, so it must be Muffin, and Mr. Pye is therefore Bill. By elimination, Mick's dog Sally is a boxer. From clue 4, Sam, the owner of Bingo the dalmatian, isn't Mr. Gunn, so he must be Mr. Toye, and Mr. Gunn must be Mick, owner of the boxer named Sally.

Bill Pye, corgi, Muffin.
Mick Gunn, boxer, Sally.
Sam Toye, dalmatian, Bingo.

The Location Man, p. 206

Oblivion is a horror film (clue 4). *Wild Honey*, which Miles was scouting for in March (clue 2), can't have been the crime drama with locations in Moscow (clue 1), nor can the crime drama be *Starlight*, which had its locations in Sydney (clue 6), while, from clue 1, the crime drama can't be *Nameless*, so it must be *Brotherhood*. We now know that the city in which locations for *Wild Honey* were scouted in March wasn't Moscow or Sydney, nor was it Rio de Janeiro (clue 2); Dublin was scouted in May (clue 4), so *Wild Honey*'s locations must have been in Bangkok. We know that *Wild Honey* isn't a crime drama or a horror film; nor is it the comedy (clue 3) or the science-fiction film, for which Miles scouted in September (clue 5), so it must be the romance. We have now matched three cities with the movies that had locations there, so the Dublin locations, which weren't for *Oblivion* (clue 4), must have been for *Nameless*, leaving *Oblivion*'s locations in Rio de Janeiro. Now, from clue 1, it was in July that Miles went to Moscow to scout locations for *Brotherhood*, the crime drama. Since *Oblivion*'s the horror film, Miles can't have scouted its Rio locations in September, when he was working on the science-fiction film's locations, so must have done so in November, and the science-fiction film for which Miles scouted in September must have been *Starlight*, with its locations in Sydney. Finally, by elimination, in May Miles must have gone to Dublin, to scout locations for *Nameless*, a comedy.
March, Bangkok, *Wild Honey*, romance.
May, Dublin, *Nameless*, comedy.
July, Moscow, *Brotherhood*, crime drama.
September, Sydney, *Starlight*, science fiction.
November, Rio de Janeiro, *Oblivion*, horror.

San Guinari Nights, p. 208

On Tuesday, Cindy was taken to a night club (clue 5), but not by Ricardo Ortiz, the politician (clue 1), Tomas Bartolo, her Monday date (clue 2), Luis Vargas (clue 3), or Angel Salinas, who took her to dinner on his yacht (clue 4), so her escort to the night club must have been Julio Diaz. Since he took her to the night club, he can't have been the movie star, who took her to a film premiere (clue 2), the arms dealer (clue 3), or the army officer (clue 5), and we know he wasn't the politician, so he must be a judge. From clue 3, the arms dealer didn't take Cindy out on Monday or Tuesday, so he must have taken her out on Wednesday, she must have gone to the carnival on Thursday, and Luis Vargas must have taken her out on Friday. We now know the name or occupation of Cindy's escorts on four evenings, so Ricardo Ortiz, the politician, must have taken her out on Thursday, to the carnival, and, by elimination, Angel Salinas, who took her to dinner on his yacht, must have been the arms dealer who dated her on Wednesday. Finally, the movie star who took her to the movie premiere wasn't Tomas Bartolo, who took her out on Monday (clue 2), so must have been Luis Vargas, her Friday escort, and, by elimination, her Monday escort, Tomas Bartolo, must have been an army officer, and he must have taken her to a party at his home.
Monday, Tomas Bartolo, army officer, party at home.
Tuesday, Julio Diaz, judge, night club.
Wednesday, Angel Salinas, arms dealer, dinner on yacht.
Thursday, Ricardo Ortiz, politician, carnival.
Friday, Luis Vargas, movie star, movie premiere.

Domino Search, p. 210

5	5	6	3	6	0	0	6
4	4	6	5	6	6	5	0
5	4	3	3	5	5	0	5
2	2	6	4	4	4	4	1
1	6	3	3	3	0	1	4
2	2	1	2	0	1	3	2
1	1	0	0	1	2	2	3

Snow Fun, p. 211

Oliver lives at number 3 (clue 2). Jayne's snowman with the brown headgear is not at number 5 (clue 4), and, since the bobble-hat is on view at number 7 (clue 3), clue 1 rules out number 5 as Kelly's house, so it must be Andrew who lives there. Therefore, clue 5 places the green item with Oliver's snowman at number 3, and the cloth cap at number 1. We now know the black top hat (clue 1) is not at any of numbers 1, 3, or 7, so it must adorn Andrew's snowman at number 5, and Kelly therefore lives at number 7 (clue 1), and used the bobble-hat for her snowman. Oliver's address rules him out for the snowman with the cloth cap, so his creation must be wearing a green beret, leaving the cloth cap as Jayne's brown item, so she lives at number 1. By elimination, the bobble-hat on Kelly's snowman at number 7 must be blue.

Number 1, Jayne, brown cloth cap.
Number 3, Oliver, green beret.
Number 5, Andrew, black top hat.
Number 7, Kelly, blue bobble-hat.

Battleships, p. 212

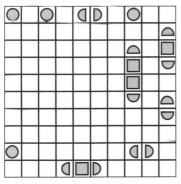

Dropping In, p. 213

Two climbers were rescued from Mount Dastardly (clue 4). The four climbers in difficulties were not on the Devil's Pitchfork, peak A (clue 1), nor can they have been on Peak Perilous (clue 2), so they must have been rescued from Heartbreak Crags. This was not on Monday (clue 3), nor was Peak Perilous the Monday location (clue 2). Clue 1 rules out the Devil's Pitchfork, so, by elimination, the

Monday rescue was from Mount Dastardly, and involved two climbers. So, from clue 2, a single climber must have been winched off Peak Perilous, which leaves three as the number on the Devil's Pitchfork. Since that is peak A, peak B cannot be Peak Perilous (clue 2), nor is it Heartbreak Crags (clue 3), so it must be Mount Dastardly. So clue 2 places Peak Perilous as C, leaving D as Heartbreak Crags. Clue 3 now tells us the latter was the scene of the Tuesday rescue, so, from clue 1, the Wednesday call-out was to the Devil's Pitchfork, leaving the single climber on Peak Perilous as the one rescued on Thursday.

A, Devil's Pitchfork, Wednesday, 3 climbers.
B, Mount Dastardly, Monday, 2 climbers.
C, Peak Perilous, Thursday, 1 climber.
D, Heartbreak Crags, Tuesday, 4 climbers.

Men and Mounts, p. 214

Horse C is Jesse's (clue 5). He cannot be in seat 3 (clue 1), and clue 3 also now rules out horse A or horse D for the man in that seat, so he must own horse B. Therefore horse A must be Hank's (clue 3). Horse D cannot belong to cowboy 4 (clue 1), nor is its owner in seat 2 (clue 5), so he must be in seat 1. We now know neither Jesse nor Hank is in seats 1 or 3, so each must be in 2 or 4. Therefore, from clue 2, Lou and Herd must each occupy seat 1 or seat 3. Stockman is not in seat 2 (clue 5), and Lariatt is in position 4 (clue 4), so, by elimination, seat 2 must be Roper's. So, from clue 4, Frank must be in seat 1, and owns horse D. By elimination, Lou must be in seat 3, and owns horse B, and, from clue 2, Herd must be Frank, in seat 1. By elimination, Lou's surname must be Stockman. Clue 4 now tells us Roper cannot ride horse C, so he is not Jesse, and must be Hank, in seat 2. This leaves Jesse in seat 4, and his surname as Lariatt.

1, Frank Herd, horse D.
2, Hank Roper, horse A.
3, Lou Stockman, horse B.
4, Jesse Lariatt, horse C.

Sunk!, p. 215

The *White Knight* wasn't a tanker (clue 2), and can't have been the freighter, sunk in 1940 (clues 2 and 3), so must have been the collier, which was

sunk by being shelled (clue 1). It wasn't sunk in 1942 (clue 2), so must have been sunk in 1944, and the tanker must have been sunk in 1942. The *Alston Castle* wasn't torpedoed (clue 4), so must have been bombed, and the *North Cape* must have been torpedoed. From clue 4, it was the freighter sunk in 1940, and the *Alston Castle* must have been the tanker, which was sunk in 1942.

***Alston Castle*, tanker, bombed, 1942.**
***North Cape*, freighter, torpedoed, 1940.**
***White Knight*, collier, shelled, 1944.**

Codewords, p. 216

Totalized, p. 217

Easy: 63, Medium: 43, Harder: 300

Cell Block, p. 218

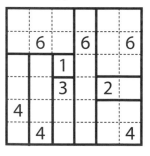

Wordwheel, p. 218

The nine-letter word is YOUNGSTER.

Battleships, p. 219

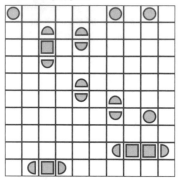

Domino Search, p. 220

6	3	5	2	6	1	0	1
4	2	4	4	6	6	2	2
1	6	4	1	1	5	3	5
2	6	6	0	0	0	1	0
0	5	5	3	3	3	1	2
4	4	3	1	5	0	3	4
2	5	0	5	6	2	3	4

Learn the Lingo, p. 221

Book 3 was used in 2004 (clue 2), so the one used in 2000, which cannot be 1 or 2 (clue 1), must be number 4. The subject of book 3, used in 2004, cannot be Greek (clue 1), nor is it Spanish (clue 2), and clue 3 rules out that year for Swedish, so it must be Russian. Clue 4 now rules out 1998 and 2004 as the year Polly used the green book, and, since we know book 4 was used in 2000, clue 4 also rules out 2002 for the green book, so it must have been used in 2000, and is book 4. So book 1 was used in 1998 (clue 4), and, by elimination, Polly must have used book 2 in 2002. So, from clue 5, the blue book, which we know was not used in 2000, must have been used in 1998, and is book 1. Its subject cannot be Swedish (clue 3), nor is it Spanish (clue 2), so it must be Greek. The book on Spanish cannot be number 4 (clue 2), so

the latter must be on Swedish, leaving book 2 as the one on Spanish. Now, from clue 3, the yellow book must have been used in 2002, so it is book 2, which leaves the red book as the one on Russian, used in 2004.
1, Greek, blue, 1998.
2, Spanish, yellow, 2002.
3, Russian, red, 2004.
4, Swedish, green, 2000.

Windows of the Devil's Castle, p. 222

Anibal del Campo was an army general (clue 1), so can't be the man who has spent 22 years in jail, who was a police general (clue 2), nor has he served 10 years in jail (clue 1). From clue 1, he must be in cell B or C, since he has two neighbors, but the man who has been in jail for 18 years is in an end cell (clue 3), so Anibal del Campo must have been in jail for 13 years. Therefore he's not in cell C (clue 5) and must be in cell B. So, from clue 3, the man in jail for 18 years can't be in cell A and must be in cell D, and the former Minister of Finance must be in cell C. Therefore the former police general who has been in jail for 22 years must be in cell A. So, from clue 2, Cesar Flores must be the ex-Minister of Finance in cell C, and by elimination must have been in jail for 10 years. Also by elimination, the former Prime Minister must be in cell D, so the prisoner in that cell isn't Diego Mendez (clue 5), and must be Jorge Rubio, leaving Diego Mendez as the former police general in cell A.
Cell A, Diego Mendez, police general, 22 years.
Cell B, Anibal del Campo, army general, 13 years.
Cell C, Cesar Flores, Minister of Finance, 10 years.
Cell D, Jorge Rubio, Prime Minister, 18 years.

Family on the Phone, p. 224

Sylvia is Nigel's sister (clue 2), so Dorothy, who isn't his cousin (clue 4), must be his mother, and therefore called at 11:45 a.m. (clue 3). By elimination, Joanne is his cousin. She can't have called at 9:00 a.m. (clue 1), so must have called at 10:15 a.m., and Sylvia, the sister, must have called at 9:00 a.m. Dorothy didn't call about car trouble

(clue 4), nor can she have phoned about a lottery win (clue 1), so her topic must have been a family reunion. Clue 1 tells us that Joanne didn't phone about a lottery win either, so she must have phoned about car trouble, and Sylvia must have called about her lottery win.
9:00 a.m., Sylvia, sister, lottery win.
10:15 a.m., Joanne, cousin, car trouble.
11:45 a.m., Dorothy, mother, family reunion.

Battleships, p. 225

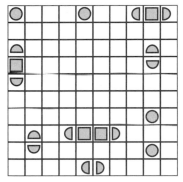

Domino Search, p. 226

2	1	1	5	5	6	6	6
1	1	1	0	6	5	5	4
6	4	6	0	1	2	5	4
1	5	4	0	0	0	6	4
3	2	5	0	3	0	3	4
1	2	4	2	6	0	4	5
2	2	2	3	3	3	3	3

Musical Lives, p. 227

Angela is married to Ray Sacbut (clue 2), so Daphne, who plays the violin and isn't married to Paul Rebec (clue 1), must be married to David Fife, and it must be Gloria who is married to Paul Rebec. Gloria doesn't play the piano (clue 3), so she must play the flute, and Angela must play the piano. Gloria's husband, Paul Rebec, is a music

publisher (clue 3), so Angela's husband, Paul Sacbut, who isn't a composer (clue 2), must be an orchestra leader, leaving the composer as Daphne's husband, David Fife.

Angela, piano, Ray Sacbut, orchestra leader.
Daphne, violin, David Fife, composer.
Gloria, flute, Paul Rebec, music publisher.

Battleships, p. 228

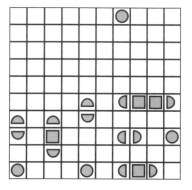

Changing Times, p. 229

The first conversion, in 1978, cannot have been the mosque (clue 1), the auction rooms (clue 3), or the sports center (clue 4), so it must have been the bingo hall. The 1990 venture cannot have been at site 1 (clue 3), or location 2 (clue 4), and clue 5 rules out location 3, so it must have taken place in location 4. We know this was not the bingo hall, nor can it have been the mosque (clue 1), and clue 3 rules out the auction rooms, so the sports center must be in location 4. Cinema 1 cannot have been the Plaza (cue 1), nor was it the Carlton (clue 3), and clue 5 rules out the Roxy, so it must have been the Palace. Therefore, from clue 2, building 2 changed its use in 1986. We have now matched years with two locations. Clue 5 tells us site 3 did not reopen in 1978, so the bingo hall must be in location 1, the former Palace cinema, leaving 1982 as the year of the change of use at site 3. This cannot have been the Carlton (clue 3), nor was it the Roxy (clue 5), so it must have been the

Plaza. So the mosque opened in 1986 at site 2 (clue 1), leaving 1982 as the year the new auction rooms began operating. Clue 3 tells us the Carlton was reopened in 1982 as a mosque in location 2, leaving the Roxy as the former cinema on the site of the sports center.

1, Palace, bingo hall, 1978.
2, Carlton, mosque, 1986.
3, Plaza, auction rooms, 1982.
4, Roxy, sports center, 1990.

Lots of Pictures, p. 230

Since lot 53 is the hunting scene (clue 2), Brusch cannot have painted lot 53 or lot 54 (clue 1), and Hoyle's work is lot 55, so, Brusch's picture must be lot 56. So, from clue 1, Hoyles painted the seascape. Pallet did not paint lot 53, the hunting scene (clue 2), so Frame must have done, leaving Pallet as the painter of lot 54. The 1775 picture was not by Brusch (clue 1), Frame (clue 2), or Hoyles (clue 4), so it must have been painted by Pallet. Therefore, from clue 2, lot 53 dates from 1835. Lot 54 is not the Parisian street scene (clue 3), so it must be the landscape, leaving the street scene as lot 56, by Brusch. Clue 1 now tells us lot 55 was painted in 1870, and lot 56 in 1900.

Lot 53, hunting scene, Frame, 1835.
Lot 54, landscape, Pallet, 1775.
Lot 55, seascape, Hoyles, 1870.
Lot 56, Parisian street scene, Brusch, 1900.

Enjoying the Open Air, p. 231

Figure 2 works in the factory (clue 4). Figure 1 can't work in advertising (clue 2) or the stores, where Nina Price works (clue 3), so she must work in R&D, and therefore had a black eye (clue 1). Figure 4 can't have had a wasp sting (clue 2) or a blistered heel (clue 3), so must have had net-tle stings, and therefore figure 3 is Joan Lacey (clue 5). We know that she doesn't work in R&D or the factory, and that it's Nina Price who works in the stores, so Joan Lacey must work in advertis-ing, and therefore figure 2 must have had a wasp sting (clue 2). By elimination, Nina Price from the stores must be figure 4, who was stung by nettles, and figure 3, Joan Lacey from advertising, must have had a blistered heel. Figure 2, the factory worker, isn't Terri Vyne (clue 4), so must be Carol Ellis, leaving Terri Vyne as the black-eyed figure 1.

1, Terri Vyne, R&D, black eye.
2, Carol Ellis, factory, wasp sting.
3, Joan Lacey, advertising, blistered heel.
4, Nina Price, stores, nettle stings.

Domino Search, p. 232

4	1	2	3	3	5	5	2
0	1	4	6	4	5	3	5
2	4	2	2	0	4	2	6
2	3	2	1	5	0	0	6
6	0	3	5	3	5	1	6
6	0	3	0	5	4	4	6
1	1	0	1	6	4	1	3

Desperados, p. 233

Figure 1 is "Laredo" (clue 2). Figure 4 isn't "Bull" (clue 1), nor can he be "Preacher" (clue 4), so he must be "Rocky." So figure 3 is the brother born in 1854 (clue 3). He's not "Preacher" (clue 4), so, by elimination, he must be "Bull." Therefore, from clue 1, Enoch Elijah was born in 1856. By elimination, "Preacher" must be figure 2, so Reuben Raphael is figure 3, "Bull" (clue 4). So, from clue 4, Enoch Elijah, born in 1856, must be figure 2, "Preacher." Clue 2 now tells us Nathaniel Noah must be figure 4, "Rocky," and must have been born in 1858, and Jeremiah Jude must have been born in 1860, and be figure 1, "Laredo."

1, Jeremiah Jude, "Laredo," 1860.
2, Enoch Elijah, "Preacher," 1856.
3, Reuben Raphael, "Bull," 1854.
4, Nathaniel Noah, "Rocky," 1858.

Can't get enough of USA TODAY puzzles?

You can play more USA TODAY puzzles:

- In your daily *USA TODAY* newspaper

- On USATODAY.com at puzzles.usatoday.com

- On mobile phones (certain puzzles only—check with your individual carrier)